Jack C. Richards & Chuck Sandy

Passages

Third Edition

Student's Book **2**

CAMBRIDGE
UNIVERSITY PRESS

CAMBRIDGE
UNIVERSITY PRESS

University Printing House, Cambridge CB2 8BS, United Kingdom

One Liberty Plaza, 20th Floor, New York, NY 10006, USA

477 Williamstown Road, Port Melbourne, VIC 3207, Australia

314–321, 3rd Floor, Plot 3, Splendor Forum, Jasola District Centre, New Delhi – 110025, India

79 Anson Road, #06–04/06, Singapore 079906

Cambridge University Press is part of the University of Cambridge.

It furthers the University's mission by disseminating knowledge in the pursuit of education, learning and research at the highest international levels of excellence.

www.cambridge.org
Information on this title: www.cambridge.org/9781107627734

First published 1998
Second edition 2008

20 19 18 17 16 15 14 13 12 11 10 9 8 7 6

Printed in Great Britain by CPI Group (UK) Ltd, Croydon CR0 4YY

A catalog record for this publication is available from the British Library.

ISBN 978-1-107-62707-9 Student's Book 2
ISBN 978-1-107-62714-7 Student's Book 2A
ISBN 978-1-107-62715-4 Student's Book 2B
ISBN 978-1-107-62726-0 Workbook 2
ISBN 978-1-107-62734-5 Workbook 2A
ISBN 978-1-107-62780-2 Workbook 2B
ISBN 978-1-107-62766-6 Teacher's Edition 2 with Assessment Audio CD/CD-ROM
ISBN 978-1-107-62749-9 Class Audio 2 CDs
ISBN 978-1-107-62773-4 Full Contact 2
ISBN 978-1-107-62774-1 Full Contact 2A
ISBN 978-1-107-62777-2 Full Contact 2B
ISBN 978-1-107-62764-2 DVD 2
ISBN 978-1-107-68650-2 Presentation Plus 2

Additional resources for this publication at www.cambridge.org/passages

Cambridge University Press has no responsibility for the persistence or accuracy of URLs for external or third-party Internet Web sites referred to in this publication and does not guarantee that any content on such Web sites is, or will remain, accurate or appropriate. Information regarding prices, travel timetables, and other factual information given in this work is correct at the time of first printing but Cambridge University Press does not guarantee the accuracy of such information thereafter.

Art direction, book design, layout services, and photo research: Q2A / Bill Smith
Audio production: John Marshall Media
Video production: Steadman Productions

Authors' Acknowledgments

A great number of people contributed to the development of *Passages Third Edition*. Particular thanks are owed to the following reviewers and institutions, as their insights and suggestions have helped define the content and format of the third edition:

Paulo A. Machado, Rio de Janeiro, Brazil; Simone C. Wanguestel, Niterói, Brazil; Athiná Arcadinos Leite, **ACBEU**, Salvador, Brazil; Lauren Osowski, **Adult Learning Center**, Nashua, NH, USA; Brenda Victoria, **AIF System**, Santiago, Dominican Republic; Alicia Mitchell-Boncquet, **ALPS Language School**, Seattle, WA, USA; Scott C. Welsh, **Arizona State University**, Tempe, AZ, USA; Silvia Corrêa, **Associação Alumni**, São Paulo, Brazil; Henrick Oprea, **Atlantic Idiomas**, Brasília, Brazil; Márcia Lima, **B.A. English School**, Goiânia, Brazil; Carlos Andrés Mejía Gómez, **BNC Centro Colombo Americano Pereira**, Pereira, Colombia; Tanja Jakimoska, **Brava Training**, Rio de Janeiro, Brazil; Paulo Henrique Gomes de Abreu, **Britannia International English**, Rio de Janeiro, Brazil; Gema Kuri Rodríguez, **Business & English**, Puebla, Mexico; Isabela Villas Boas, **Casa Thomas Jefferson**, Brasília, Brazil; Inara Lúcia Castillo Couto, **CEL-LEP**, São Paulo, Brazil; Ana Cristina Hebling Meira, **Centro Cultural Brasil-Estados Unidos**, Campinas, Brazil; Juliana Costa da Silva, **Centro de Cultura Anglo Americana**, Rio de Janeiro, Brazil; Heriberto Díaz Vázquez, **Centro de Investigación y Docencia Económicas**, Mexico City, Mexico; D. L. Dorantes-Salas, **Centro de Investigaciones Biológicas del Noroeste**, La Paz, Mexico; Elizabeth Carolina Llatas Castillo, **Centro Peruano Americano El Cultural**, Trujillo-La Libertad, Peru; Márcia M. A. de Brito, **Chance Language Center**, Rio de Janeiro, Brazil; Rosalinda Heredia, **Colegio Motolinia**, San Juan del Río, Mexico; Maria Regina Pereira Filgueiras, **College Language Center**, Londrina, Brazil; Lino Mendoza Rodriguez, **Compummunicate**, Izúcar de Matamoros, Mexico; Maria Lucia Sciamarelli, **Cultura Inglesa**, Campinas, Brazil; Elisabete Thess, **Cultura Inglesa**, Petrópolis, Brazil; Catarina M. B. Pontes Kruppa, **Cultura Inglesa**, São Paulo, Brazil; Sheila Lima, **Curso Oxford**, Rio de Janeiro, Brazil; Elaine Florencio, Beth Vasconcelos, **English House Corporate**, Rio de Janeiro, Brazil; Vasti Rodrigues e Silva, **Fox Idiomas**, Rio de Janeiro, Brazil; Ricardo Ramos Miguel Cézar, Walter Júnior Ribeiro Silva, **Friends Language Center**, Itapaci, Brazil; Márcia Maria Pedrosa Sá Freire de Souza, **IBEU**, Rio de Janeiro, Brazil; Jerusa Rafael, **IBEUV**, Vitória, Brazil; Lilianne de Souza Oliveira, **ICBEU**, Manaus, Brazil; Liviane Santana Paulino de Carvalho, **ICBEU**, São Luís, Brazil; Manuel Marrufo Vásquez, **iempac Instituto de Enseñanza del Idioma Ingles**, Tequila, Mexico; Nora Aquino, **Instituto de Ciencias y Humanidades Tabasco**, Villahermosa, Mexico; Andrea Grimaldo, **Instituto Laurens**, Monterrey, Mexico; Cenk Aykut, Staci Jenkins, Kristen Okada, **Interactive College of Technology**, Chamblee, GA, USA; Imeen Manahan-Vasquez, Zuania Serrano, **Interactive Learning Systems**, Pasadena, TX, USA; Nicholas J. Jackson, **Jackson English School**, Uruapan, Mexico; Marc L. Cummings, **Jefferson Community and Technical College**, Louisville, KY, USA; Solange Nery Veloso, **Nery e Filho Idiomas**, Rio de Janeiro, Brazil; Tomas Sparano Martins, **Phil Young's English School**, Curitiba, Brazil; Paulo Cezar Lira Torres, **PRIME Language Center**, Vitória, Brazil; Angie Vasconcellos, **Robin English School**, Petrópolis, Brazil; Barbara Raifsnider, **San Diego Community College District**, San Diego, CA, USA; James Drury de Matos Fonseca, **SENAC**, Fortaleza, Brazil; Manoel Fialho da Silva Neto, **SENAC**, Recife, Brazil; Marilyn Ponder, **Tecnológico de Monterrey**, Irapuato, Mexico; Linda M. Holden, **The College of Lake County**, Grayslake, IL, USA; Janaína da Silva Cardoso, **UERJ**, Rio de Janeiro, Brazil; Gustavo Reges Ferreira, Sandlei Moraes de Oliveira, **UFES**, Vitória, Brazil; Nancy Alarcón Mendoza, **UNAM, Facultad de Estudios Superiores Zaragoza**, Mexico City, Mexico; Rosa Awilda López Fernández, **UNAPEC**, Santo Domingo, Dominican Republic; Vera Lúcia Ratide, **Unilínguas**, São Leopoldo, Brazil; Elsa Yolanda Cruz Maldonado, **Universidad Autónoma de Chiapas**, Tapachula, Mexico; Deida Perea, **Universidad Autónoma de Ciudad Juárez**, Ciudad Juárez, Mexico; Gabriela Ladrón de Guevara de León, **Universidad Autónoma de la Ciudad de México**, Mexico City, Mexico; Juan Manuel Ardila Prada, **Universidad Autónoma de Occidente**, Cali, Colombia; Lizzete G. Acosta Cruz, **Universidad Autónoma de Zacatecas**, Fresnillo, Mexico; Ary Guel, Fausto Noriega, Areli Martínez Suaste, **Universidad Autónoma de Zacatecas**, Zacatecas, Mexico; Gabriela Cortés Sánchez, **Universidad Autónoma Metropolitana Azcapotzalco**, Mexico City, Mexico; Secundino Isabeles Flores, Guillermo Guadalupe Duran Garcia, Maria Magdalena Cass Zubiria, **Universidad de Colima**, Colima, Mexico; Alejandro Rodríguez Sánchez, **Universidad del Golfo de México Norte**, Orizaba, Mexico; Fabiola Meneses Argüello, **Universidad La Salle Cancún**, Cancún, Mexico; Claudia Isabel Fierro Castillo, **Universidad Politécnica de Chiapas**, Tuxtla Gutierrez, Mexico; Eduardo Aguirre Rodríguez, M.A. Carolina Labastida Villa, **Universidad Politécnica de Quintana Roo**, Cancún, Mexico; Gabriela de Jesús Aubry González, **Universidad TecMilenio Campus Veracruz**, Boca del Rio, Mexico; Frank Ramírez Marín, **Universidad Veracruzana**, Boca del Río, Mexico.

Additional thanks are owed to Alex Tilbury for revising the Self-assessment charts, Paul MacIntyre for revising the Grammar Plus section, and Karen Kawaguchi for writing the Vocabulary Plus section.

Welcome to **Passages!**

Congratulations! You have learned the basics; now it's time to raise your English to a whole new level.

Your journey through each unit of *Passages Third Edition* will include a range of activities that will **progressively expand your language ability** in a variety of contexts, including formal and informal communication.

Along the way, you will encounter frequent communication reviews and progress checks that will **systematically consolidate your learning**, while **additional grammar and vocabulary practice** is available whenever you need it in the Grammar Plus and Vocabulary Plus sections in the back of this book.

RAISING YOUR ENGLISH TO A WHOLE NEW LEVEL
Unique features to boost your English proficiency!

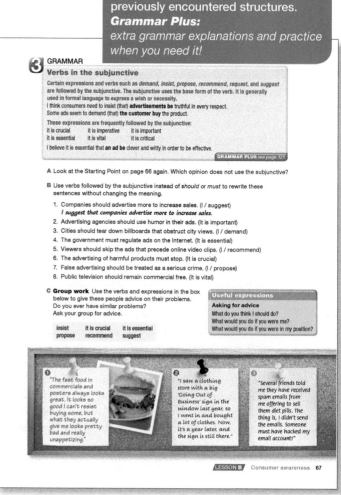

STARTING POINT
presents new grammar in a variety of real-world contexts.

LISTENING
activities sharpen essential listening comprehension skills.

GRAMMAR
is explored in context and builds on previously encountered structures.
Grammar Plus:
extra grammar explanations and practice when you need it!

Different attitudes

A Look at these expressions. Which ones express a positive attit
attitude, or a neutral attitude? Write +, –, or ~.

_____ 1. aware of _____ 5. familiar with
_____ 2. curious about _____ 6. suspicious of
_____ 3. sick of _____ 7. intimidated by
_____ 4. fed up with _____ 8. knowledgeable abou

B **Group work** Look at the list of inventions and technologies. O
What are your feelings about them? Discuss with your group.

1. spacecraft for private flights 5. wearable electronics
2. touch-screen technology 6. mobile apps
3. speech-translation technology 7. laser surgery
4. video surveillance 8. robots

"So, what do you think about spacecraft for private flights?"
*"I'm a little intimidated by the idea of being in space. I'm curious
about it, but I wouldn't try it."*

VOCABULARY PLUS *see page 132*

VOCABULARY
expands upon prior knowledge
and improves vocabulary
building skills.
NEW *Vocabulary Plus:*
*extra vocabulary practice when
you need it!*

Passages Third Edition is a two-level course
that will open the door to communicating with
greater fluency and proficiency, with:

- **more sophisticated** real-world grammar
  and vocabulary,
- **thought-provoking** discussions and
  academic writing activities,
- **more challenging** listening and reading
  comprehension topics.

Tech savvy?

A Are you a technophile or a technophobe? Complete the survey to find out.

TECHNOPHILE or TECHNOPHOBE?

	Agree (2 pts.)	Not Sure (1 pt.)	Disagree (0 pts.)
1. If technology permits it, I would favor the development of machines that surpass humans in intelligence.			
2. Governments need to generously fund research and development in technology.			
3. Everyone should try to stay informed about the latest innovations in technology.			
4. Genetic technologies should be used to gradually improv the human body over the course of generations.			
5. Science and technology will someday solve the world's problems of famine, war, disease, and overcrowding.			
6. It's important to adopt new technological devices short after they come out.			
7. Social media has a positive effect on people's social live			
8. Being connected to the Internet is a human right.			

SCORE
0–4 You are a technophobe, a person who has a strong
mistrust of technology.
5–8 While not in love with technology, you see the need
for it in our world.

B **Group work** Discuss your answers to the survey. Ta
your choices and whether or not you agree with your

24

SPEAKING
activities spark lively
discussions focusing
on interesting and
relevant situations.

Compare-and-contrast essays

A compare-and-contrast essay presents the similarities and differences of two or
more things. The thesis statement expresses your position on the subject, and it is
followed by supporting paragraphs that discuss similarities and differences.

A Read the essay and circle the thesis statement. Then match each paragraph to
the headings below. Underline the words that show

_____ introduction _____ differences _____ con

THE BEATLES V

1 Although the Beatles and the Rolling Stones
have both been called the "greatest rock 'n'
roll band of all time," the prize should go to the
Rolling Stones. While both bands have had a
huge influence on popular music, the Beatles
broke up in 1970, and the Rolling Stones went
on recording and performing for over 50 years.

2 Both the Beatles and the Rolling Stones began
as four-member British bands that first became
popular in the 1960s. The two bands released
their first records within a year of each other,
and both featured a pair of talented songwriters:
Paul McCartney and John Lennon for the
Beatles, and Mick Jagger and Keith Richards for
the Rolling Stones. Like the Rolling Stones, the
Beatles were famous for their cutting-edge style
at the time of their debut, and both bands were
known for their energetic stage performances.

B Choose two bands, singers, or musical styles to c
make a list of similarities and differences. Then cor
that expresses your view.

C Write a four-paragraph essay. Make sure it has an
thesis statement, two paragraphs describing simila
an effective conclusion.

D **Pair work** Take turns reading your essays. Do no
Can your partner guess your point of view?

READING
passages drawn from
authentic sources
promote critical thinking
and analysis.

WRITING
tasks build academic
writing skills through
step-by-step activities.

Technology and friendship

A **Pair work** Discuss these questions. Then read the article to compare your
ideas with the author's.

1. What are some ways that interacting online might encourage people to
   connect in real life?
2. How could social media help shy students participate more in class?

HOW SOCIAL MEDIA "FRIENDS" TRANSLATE INTO REAL-LIFE FRIENDSHIPS

When social media first gained attention, I heard
many people say online connections couldn't
possibly be real friends. Some even feared people
might trade face-to-face interaction for a virtual life
online. But now the majority of the people I know
consider at least some of their online friends to be
like extended family. Which made me wonder – does
social media actually encourage people to connect
"in real life"?

One example of online life translating into real-life
interaction happens on *Mashable*'s Social Media
Day, when thousands of people attend in-person
meet-ups to celebrate the power of online
connections. Another example is location-based
apps that help users connect face-to-face by
allowing them to see who else has checked in at
the same store, restaurant, or party – or even who
is living in a city they plan to visit. They might then
decide to seek each other out "in real life."

A Pew Internet and American Life Project report
found that people using social networking sites have
more close relationships and receive more support
than others. They are also more likely to reconnect
with old friends and use social networking to keep
up with those they are already close to.

Other research shows that social media may
also deepen what could otherwise be passing
relationships. A study by Dr. Rey Junco found that
college students who interacted with each other
and their professors on Twitter were more likely to
meet outside class to study. They also developed

unexpected real-life connections and were also
more likely to ask questions in class.

"What I find most fascinating is that I've
consistently seen that students who start a course
being more introverted and not speaking up during
class discussions become more extroverted and
participate more when encouraged to communicate
through social media with their professors and their
classmates," Junco said.

However, if social media does increase the likelihood
of real-life interaction, it can also sometimes
complicate it. When fans of social media meet
face-to-face, their computers and mobile devices
may actually make the meeting less productive.
Instead of looking at each other, they may be glued
to their screens!

Source: "How Social Media 'Friends' Translate Into Real-Life Friendships," by Terri Thornton, Mediashift

B **Group work** Discuss these questions. Then share your answers with the class.

1. In what ways are virtual friendships similar to and different from real-life friendships?
2. Would you be more or less willing to share ideas on social media than you would
   in class? Why?
3. What other issues and complications might come up when online friends meet
   face-to-face?

KEEP MOVING UP!
More support is always available – when and where you need it!

The **WORKBOOK** provides
extensive practice of grammar and
vocabulary as well as additional
reading and writing activities.

The **ONLINE WORKBOOK** –
a digital version of the Workbook –
enables your teacher to provide
instant feedback on your work.

The *PASSAGES* **ONLINE VOCABULARY
ACCELERATOR** increases the speed and
ease of learning new vocabulary through powerful
and innovative digital learning techniques.

Plan of **BOOK 2**

	FUNCTIONS	GRAMMAR	VOCABULARY
UNIT 1 Relationships pages 2–9			
A The best of friends **B** Make new friends, but keep the old . . .	■ Defining and describing friendship ■ Expressing opinions ■ Disagreeing politely ■ Stating preferences ■ Sharing advice about friendship	■ Phrasal verbs ■ Gerund and infinitive constructions	■ Adjectives and verbs to describe friendship ■ *re-* verbs
UNIT 2 Clothes and appearance pages 10–17			
A The way we dress **B** How we appear to others	■ Discussing approaches to fashion ■ Describing style and trends ■ Expressing opinions about clothing ■ Talking about first impressions ■ Describing outward appearance	■ Review of verb patterns ■ Cleft sentences with *what*	■ Adjectives to describe style ■ Adjectives to describe outward appearance
UNIT 3 Science and technology pages 18–25			
A Good science, bad science **B** Technology and you	■ Talking about scientific advances ■ Analyzing the effects of science and technology ■ Expressing caution and confidence ■ Describing technology troubles	■ Indefinite and definite articles ■ *-ing* clauses	■ Adjectives to discuss technology-related issues ■ Collocations to express different attitudes
UNITS 1–3 Communication review pages 26–27			
UNIT 4 Superstitions and beliefs pages 28–35			
A Superstitions **B** Believe it or not	■ Talking about personal beliefs ■ Comparing beliefs ■ Reporting what other people believe ■ Expressing opinions	■ Reporting clauses ■ Reporting clauses in the passive	■ Expressions with *luck* ■ Adjectives to describe truth and fabrication
UNIT 5 Movies and television pages 36–43			
A Movies **B** Television	■ Discussing movie trends ■ Expressing your attitude about trends ■ Discussing movie genre aspects and preferences ■ Discussing TV show preferences ■ Explaining the popularity of TV shows	■ Sentence adverbs ■ *Such . . . that* and *so . . . that*	■ Adjectives to describe movies ■ Types of TV programs
UNIT 6 Musicians and music pages 44–51			
A A world of music **B** Getting your big break	■ Sharing views on music ■ Expressing preferences ■ Comparing and contrasting ■ Defining success	■ Double comparatives ■ *Will* and *would* for habits and general truths	■ Collocations to describe music ■ Idioms used in the entertainment industry
UNITS 4–6 Communication review pages 52–53			

SPEAKING	LISTENING	WRITING	READING
■ Talking about what friends should have in common ■ Talking about the best way to meet people ■ Discussing ways to maintain friendships	■ A talk about differences between friendships among men and friendships among women ■ A young woman describes a chance encounter	■ Developing a thesis statement ■ Writing a composition with paragraphs supporting a thesis statement	■ "How Social Media 'Friends' Translate into Real-life Friendships": Does social media encourage people to connect in real life?
■ Discussing different opinions on fashion ■ Discussing how first impressions are formed ■ Discussing tips for making a good first impression ■ Discussing how people respond to appearance	■ Three people describe their taste in fashion ■ Three people explain what is important for them when forming an impression	■ Writing a composition about a personal belief ■ Giving examples to support a thesis statement	■ "Overcoming a Bad First Impression": How to change a bad first impression
■ Discussing the positive effects and negative consequences of technology and science ■ Discussing your feelings about new technology ■ Taking a survey about your relationship with technology	■ A reporter and technology editor talk about the impact of driverless car technology ■ A comedian talks about difficulties he has had with technology	■ Identifying essential information for a summary of a text ■ Writing a summary of an article	■ "I Took My Kids Offline": A mother bans all technology at home for six months
■ Describing superstitions from your country or culture ■ Discussing superstitions ■ Taking a survey about luck ■ Telling stories ■ Discussing hoaxes and why people create them	■ Three people give explanations for some superstitions ■ Two people discuss a journalistic hoax	■ Restating the thesis in the last paragraph ■ Writing a composition about superstitions	■ "Do Good Luck Charms Really Work in Competitions?": The effectiveness of superstitious rituals in sports
■ Talking about movie trends ■ Talking about the results of a survey on movie genre preferences ■ Discussing aspects of different movie genres ■ Discussing what makes a TV show popular ■ Discussing and presenting an idea for a new TV show	■ Four people describe what makes some movie genres effective ■ TV network employees brainstorm and present ideas for new TV shows	■ Identifying essential information for a movie review ■ Writing a movie review	■ "*One Day on Earth*: A Time Capsule of Our Lives": A movie shot in every country of the world on the same day
■ Talking about personal tastes in music ■ Talking about styles of music ■ Discussing the role of music in different contexts ■ Discussing advice for success	■ Two people share their opinions on different types of music ■ A young woman gives her friend advice on his music career	■ Writing a compare-and-contrast essay ■ Describing similarities and differences	■ "On the Trail of Sixto Rodriguez": Searching for a musician who was famous and didn't know it

SPEAKING	LISTENING	WRITING	READING
■ Discussing trends ■ Talking about personal changes ■ Talking about the results of a survey on coping with change	■ A corporate executive speaks about the attitudes of different generations in the workplace ■ Two people talk about a volunteer program	■ Writing about a personal experience ■ Providing background information and giving details	■ "Leaving the Rat Race for the Simple Life": Reflections on a major change in lifestyle
■ Talking about the best ways to shop for different items ■ Discussing compulsive shopping ■ Discussing the ethics of undercover marketing strategies	■ Two people talk about their shopping preferences ■ Three radio advertisements	■ Supporting an opinion ■ Writing a composition using details and examples to support an opinion about shopping	■ "Word-of-Mouth Marketing": Testing the power of word-of-mouth as a marketing strategy
■ Discussing the ethics of using animals in different fields ■ Discussing a survey on ethics associated with animals ■ Discussing ways of being in touch with nature	■ News reports on animals that help people ■ The manager of an eco-resort describes its features to a reporter	■ Organizing information into clear categories ■ Writing a classification essay	■ "A Summer Job that's a Walk in the Park": The daily tasks of a park ranger fellow in New York City
■ Discussing the qualities of effective communicators ■ Discussing a survey on public speaking ■ Discussing opinions about language issues ■ Talking about "text speak" and its appropriateness ■ Role-playing different ways of speaking	■ An expert gives advice on how to make effective presentations ■ Three one-sided conversations	■ Persuasive writing ■ Supporting a position ■ Arguing against the opposing position	■ "Slang Abroad": Different varieties of English
■ Discussing people who have had an impact on the world ■ Discussing the qualities and values of exceptional people ■ Discussing quotations from high achievers ■ Talking about heroic behavior in everyday life	■ A motivational speaker talks about the qualities of high achievers ■ Two people talk about others who have made a difference in their lives	■ Organizing information in chronological order ■ Writing a biographical profile	■ "Ann Cotton, Social Entrepreneur": Advice from a successful NGO executive
■ Discussing successful companies ■ Discussing job advertisements ■ Discussing a survey on ideal working conditions ■ Analyzing the qualities of the ideal job ■ Discussing the qualities of a successful worker	■ Two people discuss unsuccessful business ventures ■ Three people talk about workshops they attended	■ Understanding the parts of a formal letter ■ Writing a formal letter	■ "The Value of Difference": Individual differences in the workplace

RELATIONSHIPS

LESSON A ▶ *The best of friends*

1 STARTING POINT
The nature of friendship

A Read these statements about friendship. Can you explain what they mean?
What other statements would you add to the list?

WHAT IS A **Friend?**

1. A friend is someone who brings out the best in you.
2. Good friends are always happy to help when you run into a problem.
3. A friend is someone who cheers you up when you're feeling bad.
4. True friends don't drift apart even after many years of separation.
5. A real friend will always stand up for you when others are putting you down.
6. Never be afraid to open up and ask a friend for advice. A true friend will never turn you down.
7. Make new friends, but hang on to the old ones.
8. Good friends are hard to come by, harder to leave, and impossible to do without.

"The first statement means a friend inspires you to show all your positive qualities."

B Group work Consider the statements in part A. What makes a good friend? Discuss with your group.

"In my opinion, a good friend is someone who makes you a better person. It's someone who brings out the best in you."

> **Useful expressions**
>
> **Expressing opinions**
> In my opinion, . . .
> I have to say that . . .
> The way I see it, . . .
> Personally, I (don't) think . . .

2 LISTENING & SPEAKING
Friendship among women and men

 A Listen to a professor talk about author Deborah Tannen's ideas. In Tannen's opinion, what is the main difference between friendship among men and friendship among women?

B Listen again. According to Tannen, which of these things do male friends often do (*M*) and which do female friends often do (*F*)? Write the correct letter.

M 1. are direct and to the point   *M* 4. prefer to share factual information
F 2. discuss daily life at length   *M* 5. value activities over talk
F 3. reveal private thoughts   *M* 6. talk as a way to better understand their lives

C Group work Do you agree or disagree with Tannen's ideas about friendship? Why or why not?

"I have to say that I think some of her ideas seem to be accurate . . ."

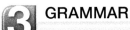

3 GRAMMAR

Phrasal verbs

A phrasal verb is a verb plus a particle, such as *down*, *into*, *out*, or *up*.
The meaning of a phrasal verb is usually different from the meaning of its parts.

Separable phrasal verbs can take objects before or after the particle.
If the object is a pronoun, it always appears before the particle.
A friend is someone who **brings out** the best in you.
A friend is someone who **brings** the best **out** in you.
A friend is someone who **cheers** you **up** when you're feeling bad.

With inseparable phrasal verbs, the object cannot go between the verb and the particle.
Good friends are always happy to help when you **run into** a problem.

Three-word phrasal verbs have a particle and a preposition.
Make new friends, but **hang on to** the old ones.

Intransitive phrasal verbs don't take objects.
True friends don't **drift apart**.

GRAMMAR PLUS *see page 106*

A Look at the Starting Point on page 2 again. Can you find the phrasal verbs?
Which are separable, inseparable, and/or three-word verbs? Which are also
intransitive? Write them in the chart.

Separable	Inseparable	Three-word verbs	Intransitive

B Complete the questions with the phrasal verbs and objects in parentheses.
Sometimes more than one answer is possible.

1. Have you ever had a friend who ___*brought out the worst /*___
   ___*brought the worst out*___ (bring out / the worst) in you?

2. Have you ever _____ (run into / a friend)
   that you hadn't seen in a long time?

3. Do you usually _____ (stand up for /
   your friends) when other people criticize them?

4. Can you _____ (do without / a cell phone)
   and still keep in touch with friends?

5. When friends ask you for a favor, do you usually say yes, or do
   you _____ (turn down / them)?

6. Do you _____ (hang on to / your old friends)
   or do you drift apart as time goes by?

7. Some people like to _____ (put down /
   their friends) by insulting them. How would you feel if a friend
   did that to you?

C **Pair work** Discuss the questions in part B.

"Have you ever had a friend who brought out the worst in you?"

"Yeah, I once had a really messy roommate. She made me so angry."

VOCABULARY
Describing friendship

A **Pair work** Complete the chart with the correct parts of speech.

	Verb	Adjective		Verb	Adjective
1.	admire		4.	empathize	
2.		beneficial	5.	endure	
3.	clash		6.		harmonious

B Choose the word from the chart in part A that best replaces the boldfaced words. Compare answers with a partner.

1. Ryan and Tina work to keep their friendship **free of conflict**. _harmonious_
2. Sometimes their opinions **are very different**, but they still get along.
3. They work to make their friendship **valuable and constructive**.
4. Having the same background helps them **understand and identify** with each other.
5. Ryan and Tina **think very highly of** each other's accomplishments.
6. Their friendship will certainly **last a long time**.

VOCABULARY PLUS see page 130

DISCUSSION
What should friends have in common?

A Look at the statements about friendship below. Do you agree with the statements? Add a statement of your own.

> **»PEOPLE ...**
>
> | | Agree | Disagree |
> |---|---|---|
> | **1.** who are close in age empathize with each other better. | ☐ | ☐ |
> | **2.** with similar social backgrounds have more harmonious friendships. | ☐ | ☐ |
> | **3.** who have similar values and beliefs have stronger connections. | ☐ | ☐ |
> | **4.** with similar personalities have the most enduring friendships. | ☐ | ☐ |
> | **5.** benefit from having friends with the same educational background. | ☐ | ☐ |
> | **6.** should only mingle with friends who have the same interests. | ☐ | ☐ |
> | **7.** from different cultures often clash with each other. | ☐ | ☐ |
> | **8.**_____. | ☐ | ☐ |

B **Group work** Share your opinions and explain your reasons.

"The way I see it, people who are close in age can empathize better with each other. They share many of the same experiences and understand each other."

"I see your point, but I don't think age is that important. If people like doing similar things, they can be good friends."

C **Group work** How many people agreed or disagreed with each statement? Report your findings to the class.

"Three of us agreed that friends who are close in age empathize with each other better . . ."

> **Useful expressions**
>
> **Disagreeing politely**
> I see your point, but . . .
> I see what you mean, but . . .
> I'm not sure I agree.
> Do you think so?

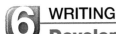

6 WRITING
Developing a thesis statement

> The first paragraph of a composition contains a thesis statement, which presents the main idea. The remaining paragraphs each have a single focus expressed in a topic sentence that develops the thesis statement.

A Read the composition. Underline the thesis statement in the first paragraph.

B Match each of the other paragraphs with the phrase below that best summarizes its focus.

__4__ why we have a close friendship   __3__ what we have in common   __2__ how we are different

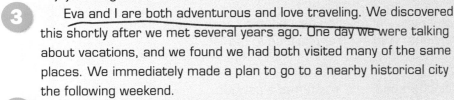

1 My best friend, Eva, and I are different in many ways, but we have one important thing in common – we love to travel. Whenever I have the urge to explore a new place, I can always count on Eva to go with me. Our friendship shows that people who are very different can still have similar interests.

2 The differences between Eva and me are significant. Eva is an artist who loves to take photographs and draw pictures of the interesting things she sees. I am a marketing representative for a pharmaceutical company and spend a lot of my time estimating sales figures. Eva is a very impulsive person, and I'm very organized. She's very quiet, but I'm a very talkative person who enjoys telling stories.

3 Eva and I are both adventurous and love traveling. We discovered this shortly after we met several years ago. One day we were talking about vacations, and we found we had both visited many of the same places. We immediately made a plan to go to a nearby historical city the following weekend.

4 Although we are quite different in many ways, Eva and I have become close over the years, and we now have a very special and enduring friendship. Every time we get together, we always have so much to talk about and have the best time. One reason for this is that we share a love of travel and adventure. The other reason is that our differences complement each other, so we always get along well whenever we travel together.

C Write a composition about a close friend. Then exchange your composition with a partner, and answer these questions.

1. What is the thesis statement? Underline it.
2. Does each paragraph have a single focus? Write the focus for each in the margin of the text.
3. What else would you like to know about your partner's friend? Ask at least two questions.

LESSON B ▶ *Make new friends, but keep the old . . .*

1 STARTING POINT
Meeting new people

A Read about how Yuan Lin, Brandon, and Jacob met new people. Which way of meeting people do you think is best?

Yuan Lin

"I decided to move to England last year. I felt really lonely at first. In fact, I regretted moving here. But I never gave up trying new things. Then, I saw an ad for a Chinese-English language exchange. It was a great way to meet cool people!"

Brandon

"I'd been planning to take a class, but was putting off enrolling. Well, last month I started taking a cooking class. I never expected to meet so many nice people! Some of us get together at each other's homes and practice what we learn. We've become really good friends!"

Jacob

"I didn't know many people at my new job, but I kept being invited by my co-workers to a lunchtime yoga class. I'm so glad I finally said yes! A couple of my colleagues play soccer, too, and they're considering starting a company team!"

"A language exchange is a great idea. You can meet people who are interested in languages and culture, so everyone already has something in common."

B **Group work** What other ways of meeting new people can you suggest to someone in these situations? Add another situation to the list.

Someone who . . .

- moved to a new neighborhood
- has little free time
- started a new job
- is very shy
- is over 65 years old
- _____

2 LISTENING
A chance meeting

A **Pair work** When was the last time you unexpectedly ran into someone you know? Tell your partner about your experience.

B Listen to Dena talk about how she met her friend Kate. Where were they when they first met? Where did they meet again?

C Listen again. Then answer the following questions.

1. Why were Dena and Kate going to Los Angeles?
2. What did Dena regret after she said good-bye to Kate?
3. How much time passed between their first and second meetings?
4. How did Samantha, the guest at the party, know Kate?

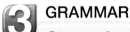

GRAMMAR

Gerund and infinitive constructions

These verbs are normally followed by a gerund: *appreciate, consider, enjoy, give up, keep, put off, suggest.*
They're **considering starting** a company team!

These verbs are normally followed by an infinitive: *ask, decide, expect, intend, need, refuse, seem, tend.*
I never **expected to meet** so many nice people!

These verbs are followed by either a gerund or an infinitive: *begin, bother, continue, hate, prefer, start.*
Last month I **started taking / to take** a cooking class.

Infinitives and gerunds can also occur in the passive voice. They follow the pattern
subject + verb + *being / to be* + past participle.
I **kept being invited** by my co-workers to a lunchtime yoga class.
She **asked to be chosen** for the job.

GRAMMAR PLUS *see page 107*

A Look at the Starting Point on page 6 again. Can you find another verb followed by a gerund and another verb followed by an infinitive?

B Choose the correct form of the verbs. Sometimes both answers are possible.

Monday, March 18

I've never been a really popular guy. I'm the type of person who tends **1** *to have / having* one or two good friends rather than lots of acquaintances. Well, when I moved away from my hometown after getting a job in Denver, I really needed **2** *to make / making* some new friends. Because I'm shy, I considered **3** *to change / changing* my personality to become more outgoing. But that was very difficult for me. Just the same, I didn't give up **4** *to try / trying*. I decided **5** *to create / creating* a new image for myself. I bought myself some new shoes, new clothes, and I even got a new haircut and started **6** *to wear / wearing* contact lenses. However, it didn't seem **7** *to change / changing* anything. I was beginning to regret **8** *to leave / leaving* my hometown when, all of a sudden, I got a call from my old friend Jim. He was planning **9** *to move / moving* here pretty soon. He wanted some advice about finding an apartment in the city, and I suggested **10** *to share / sharing* an apartment with me. Well, he agreed! I really enjoy **11** *to have / having* someone to spend time with, and together we've made a lot of new friends.

Posted by DenverDan 2 COMMENTS

C **Pair work** Complete these sentences with your own information, and add details. Then compare with a partner.

1. I don't like it when friends refuse . . . to return my phone call
   to do small favors for me, like lending me a book. It's so rude.

2. It can be annoying when friends expect . . .

3. I couldn't say no if a friend suggested . . .

4. When I'm with my good friends, I don't bother . . .

4 VOCABULARY
re- verbs

A Which word best completes these sentences? Write the correct letter.

a. rebuild   c. reconnect   e. rehash   g. replace

b. recall   d. redefine   f. rekindle   h. resurface

1. You can __f__ old friendships by sharing memories.

2. Don't __e__ old arguments over and over.

3. People often __d__ themselves, but they're essentially the same.

4. A close friend is impossible to __g__.

5. Can you __b__ the first time you met your best friend?

6. Friends you think are gone forever sometimes __h__ unexpectedly.

7. Visit your hometown and __c__ with your roots.

8. It takes time to __a__ a damaged friendship.

B Pair work What other *re-* verbs do you know? How would you define them? Compare your list with a partner.

Recapture, reconsider, . . .

VOCABULARY PLUS *see page 130*

5 DISCUSSION
Friendship maintenance

A Look at these ideas for maintaining friendships. Choose three that you think are the most important.

Advice for Maintaining *FRIENDSHIPS*

▶ Praise your friends often and keep a positive, optimistic attitude when you're around them.

▶ Never betray a friend's trust – it can cause real resentment.

▶ Try to be completely honest with your friends at all times.

▶ Don't hold unkind words against a friend. Consider any problems he or she has that might be the cause of the hurtful words.

▶ Use social media to help you feel connected to friends but not to replace face time.

▶ Be a good listener and try to empathize with your friends.

▶ Respect your friends' point of view even when you disagree. Don't rehash old arguments.

▶ Watch out for "unhealthy" friendships. Sometimes it's better to end a friendship and move on with your life.

B Group work Tell your group which three pieces of advice you chose, and explain why. Then share any other ideas you have about maintaining friendships.

"Well, I think it's important to always be completely honest with your friends. If you aren't honest with your friends, they might not be honest with you."

Useful expressions
Agreeing on importance
Well, I think it's important . . .
Yeah, that's true, but even more important is . . .
And let's not forget . . .
You're right . . . is also quite important.

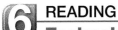

Technology and friendship

A **Pair work** Discuss these questions. Then read the article to compare your ideas with the author's.

1. What are some ways that interacting online might encourage people to connect in real life?

2. How could social media help shy students participate more in class?

HOW SOCIAL MEDIA "FRIENDS" TRANSLATE INTO REAL-LIFE FRIENDSHIPS

When social media first gained attention, I heard many people say online connections couldn't possibly be real friends. Some even feared people might trade face-to-face interaction for a virtual life online. But now the majority of the people I know consider at least some of their online friends to be like extended family. Which made me wonder – does social media actually encourage people to connect "in real life"?

One example of online life translating into real-life interaction happens on *Mashable*'s Social Media Day, when thousands of people attend in-person meet-ups to celebrate the power of online connections. Another example is location-based apps that help users connect face-to-face by allowing them to see who else has checked in at the same store, restaurant, or party – or even who is living in a city they plan to visit. They might then decide to seek each other out "in real life."

A Pew Internet and American Life Project report found that people using social networking sites have more close relationships and receive more support than others. They are also more likely to reconnect with old friends and use social networking to keep up with those they are already close to.

Other research shows that social media may also deepen what could otherwise be passing relationships. A study by Dr. Rey Junco found that college students who interacted with each other and their professors on Twitter were more likely to meet outside class to study. They also developed

unexpected real-life connections and were also more likely to ask questions in class.

"What I find most fascinating is that I've consistently seen that students who start a course being more introverted and not speaking up during class discussions become more extroverted and participate more when encouraged to communicate through social media with their professors and their classmates," Junco said.

However, if social media does increase the likelihood of real-life interaction, it can also sometimes complicate it. When fans of social media meet face-to-face, their computers and mobile devices may actually make the meeting less productive. Instead of looking at each other, they may be glued to their screens!

Source: "How Social Media 'Friends' Translate Into Real-Life Friendships," by Terri Thornton, Mediashift

B **Group work** Discuss these questions. Then share your answers with the class.

1. In what ways are virtual friendships similar to and different from real-life friendships?

2. Would you be more or less willing to share ideas on social media than you would in class? Why?

3. What other issues and complications might come up when online friends meet face-to-face?

2 CLOTHES AND APPEARANCE

LESSON A ▶ *The way we dress*

1 STARTING POINT
Fashion sense

A What's your approach to fashion? Complete this survey.

Clothing Survey

	Agree	Disagree
1 When I choose clothes, I tend to think of comfort first and appearance second.	☐	☐
2 I hate choosing my outfits in the morning. I just put on anything I can find.	☐	☐
3 Celebrities sometimes inspire me to change the way I look.	☐	☐
4 Companies should discourage employees from wearing casual clothes to work.	☐	☐
5 I don't like to draw attention to myself, so I wear pretty conventional clothes.	☐	☐
6 I enjoy shopping for clothes. I don't mind spending hours in clothing stores.	☐	☐
7 High prices rarely prevent me from buying quality clothing.	☐	☐
8 Peer pressure sometimes compels me to wear brand-name clothing.	☐	☐

B **Group work** Discuss your answers to the survey.

"I tend to think of comfort first when I choose clothes. When I'm comfortable, I feel good, and that's more important to me than looking good."

2 DISCUSSION
Judging by appearances

A **Pair work** Read these famous quotations. In your own words, explain to a partner what they mean. Do you agree with the quotations?

It's always the badly dressed people who are the most interesting.
– Jean Paul Gaultier

You're never fully dressed without a smile.
– Martin Charnin

Three-tenths of good looks are due to nature; seven-tenths to dress.
– Chinese proverb

"I think the first one means interesting people focus on more meaningful things than clothes. I think it's often true. For example, scientists and inventors don't always dress very well."

B **Group work** Discuss these questions. Explain your answers.

1. Do you think it's fair for people to judge you by the way you dress?
2. If you had an unlimited clothing budget, would you change your style?
3. Would you change the way you dress to please someone else?

GRAMMAR

Review of verb patterns

Study the following common verb patterns.

a. verb + infinitive
When I choose clothes, I **tend to think** of comfort first and appearance second.

b. verb + object + infinitive
Celebrities sometimes **inspire me to change** the way I look.

c. verb + gerund
I **hate choosing** my outfits in the morning.

d. verb + object + preposition + gerund
High prices rarely **prevent me from buying** quality clothing.

GRAMMAR PLUS *see page 108*

A Look at the Starting Point on page 10 again. Can you find another example of each verb pattern above?

B Pair work Which verb patterns from the box do these sentences follow? Write *a*, *b*, *c*, or *d*.

_____ 1. I enjoy making a statement with my clothes.

_____ 2. I like to wear unusual color combinations.

_____ 3. I refuse to shop with my friends.

_____ 4. I can't help being critical of what others wear.

_____ 5. Parents should allow their children to wear whatever they want.

_____ 6. My friends usually advise me against spending too much on clothes.

_____ 7. My parents have always discouraged me from wearing sloppy clothes.

_____ 8. Advertising definitely convinces me to buy certain articles of clothing.

C Pair work Which statements above are true for you? Explain and give examples.

D Pair work Complete each sentence with a verb from the box and your own ideas. Then add a follow-up comment, and compare with a partner.

advise	discourage	encourage	require	tend
allow	don't mind	permit	seem	try

1. Some schools _____*require*_____ students to wear _____*school uniforms*_____.
   They think that students will spend more time studying and less time thinking about clothes.

2. Parents often _____ their children from _____.

3. Some restaurants don't _____ customers to _____.

4. I _____ to wear clothes that _____.

5. Experts _____ people against wearing _____.

6. My clothes always _____ to make me look _____.

7. I _____ buying expensive _____.

8. Young people _____ to be concerned about _____.

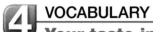

VOCABULARY
Your taste in clothes

A Look at the words below. Do some have similar meanings? Which ones would you use to describe your own style?

chic	conservative	fashionable	formal	functional	quirky	sloppy	stylish
classic	elegant	flashy	frumpy	funky	retro	stuffy	trendy

B Pair work What do you think of these styles? Describe the people in the picture.

Holly

Hugo

Heather

Bruce

Ryan

Erica

"Erica's outfit is pretty functional. She's probably going to the gym."

"Yes, but I'd say it's fashionable, too. The colors and design are stylish, and it fits her well."

VOCABULARY PLUS *see page 131*

LISTENING
Fashion developments

A Pair work Was your style the same five years ago? In what ways has your style changed? In what ways has it remained the same?

 B Listen to Mark, Shelby, and Carlos describe how their tastes in fashion have changed. What was their style, and what is their style now?

	Then	Now
1. Mark		
2. Shelby		
3. Carlos		

C Listen again. Write the items of clothing or accessories you hear for each of the looks below.

grunge _____   bohemian _____

urban _____   sporty _____

goth _____   preppy _____

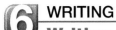

WRITING
Writing about personal beliefs

In a composition about a personal belief, clearly state that belief in a thesis statement in the first paragraph. In the following paragraphs, give examples to support your thesis.

A Look at these fashion mottos. Which motto best reflects your opinion about fashion? Why? Share your ideas with a partner.

> Don't just get dressed.
> Make a statement.

> **Why look like everyone else?**

> Feel comfortable.
> That's all that matters.

> Don't live in the past.
> Wear today's styles!

B Use the motto you chose as the basis for a thesis statement about your personal belief about fashion. Compare your ideas with a partner.

> Your clothes should make a statement about who you are.

C Use your thesis statement to develop a composition of about 200 words in three paragraphs that describes your approach to clothes.

> I believe that clothes should be more than functional. They should make a statement about who you are. Before you get dressed or go shopping for clothing, it's important to think about what kind of message your clothes will send to others.
>
> I think of my clothes as a reflection of my personality. When people look at me and my clothes, they can get an idea of the kind of person I am. I'm interested in the arts, and I'm concerned about environmental issues. Therefore, I not only wear colorful clothes that are a bit unusual, but I also wear natural fabrics that are made locally. This is important to me.
>
> I don't follow trends because I don't like to look like everyone else. I'm unique, and I want my clothes to show it.

D Pair work Exchange compositions and answer these questions.

1. Does the thesis statement in the first paragraph clearly state the writer's point of view?
2. Do the examples given in the other paragraphs support the thesis statement and clarify the writer's point of view?
3. What else do you want to know about your partner's attitude toward clothes?

1 STARTING POINT
Forming an impression

A Look at the statements about how people form a first impression of someone. Choose the statements that are true for you.

First Impressions
What People Notice First When They Meet Someone New

- ☐ What I notice is the other person's eyes.
- ☐ What's really important to me is a person's smile.
- ☐ What I always notice is a person's hands.
- ☐ I look at people's clothes first.
- ☐ What I notice is a person's figure (or physique).
- ☐ What strikes me first is the way people wear their hair.
- ☐ I always appreciate a nice pair of shoes.
- ☐ I have no idea what I notice first.

B Group work What other traits help you form an impression of a person? What are the three most important traits for the people in your group? Are they the same for men and women?

2 LISTENING
Important traits

A Listen to Gabriela, Joon, and Alice talk about what is important to them when forming an impression. Complete the chart.

	What is important
1. Gabriela	
2. Joon	
3. Alice	

B Listen again. Which speakers mention what is *not* very important to them? What do they mention? Complete the chart.

	What is not very important
1. Gabriela	
2. Joon	
3. Alice	

C Pair work Which speaker thinks the most like you? Share your reasons with a partner.

GRAMMAR

Cleft sentences with *what*

You can add *what* and a form of *be* to a sentence when you want to emphasize information. The resulting sentence is called a *cleft* sentence.

A person's smile **is really important to me**.   **What's really important to me is** a person's smile.

For sentences with verbs other than *be*, insert *what* at the beginning of the sentence and a form of *be* after the main verb.

I always notice a person's hands.   **What I always notice is** a person's hands.

GRAMMAR PLUS *see page 109*

A Look at the Starting Point on page 14 again. Can you find more cleft sentences? Try to change them into declarative sentences.

B Rewrite these sentences to add emphasis by beginning them with *what*. Which statements are true for you? Compare answers with a partner.

1. I appreciate a person with a good sense of humor.
   What I appreciate is a person with a good sense of humor.
2. I always notice the way people look at me.
3. A person's fashion sense is important to me.
4. I pay attention to people's manners.
5. I really dislike sarcasm.
6. I'm interested in the subjects people talk about.
7. A kind face is appealing to me.

DISCUSSION

Good first impressions

A **Pair work** Read these tips on making a good first impression. Choose the tip you think is the most useful. Then explain your choice to a partner.

QUICK TIPS for Making a Lasting Impression

1. Appearance matters. Dress a little nicer than you need to when meeting new people.

2. Occasionally, use the names of the people you are talking to, for example: *Amy, have you seen that movie yet?*

3. Break the silence with small talk about a topic that you think will interest others.

4. When it's in good taste, use humor. A joke can be a nice way to break the ice, but what you should avoid is sarcasm.

5. Everyone likes compliments, so give plenty of them. Just make sure you are sincere.

6. Be yourself, and be sure to smile. A friendly smile can make other people feel at ease.

B **Group work** What's the best way to make a good first impression in these situations? Discuss and add some tips of your own.

- a dinner party at a new friend's home
- an initial interview for a job you want
- the first day in a fitness class
- the first time you meet new neighbors

"At a dinner party with new friends, what's really important is good table manners."
"That's true. Also, what I always do is compliment my hosts on the food."

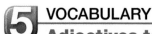

5 VOCABULARY
Adjectives to describe outward appearance

A Which adjectives seem to have a positive meaning, a negative meaning, or both? Write +, −, or +/−.

____ a. arrogant ____ d. innocent ____ g. sinister ____ i. sympathetic

____ b. dignified ____ e. intense ____ h. smug ____ j. trustworthy

____ c. eccentric ____ f. intellectual

B Now match the words with their definitions. Write the correct letter.

1. rational and studious ____

2. kind and understanding ____

3. worthy of respect or honor ____

4. reliable ____

5. forceful; with strong opinions ____

6. proud in an unpleasant way ____

7. self-satisfied; pleased with oneself ____

8. without blame; childlike and pure ____

9. strange or unusual in an amusing way ____

10. evil or ominous ____

C **Pair work** What famous people do you think the adjectives describe?

"To me, Johnny Depp looks intellectual."

"Oh, I don't know. He looks eccentric, in my opinion."

VOCABULARY PLUS *see page 131*

6 DISCUSSION
Faces matter

Gisele Bündchen

John Cho

Psychologist Leslie Zebrowitz found that people are usually categorized by their faces. She gave résumés of equally qualified people to groups of business students, with photos attached. It was discovered that the students recommended baby-faced people for jobs that required more sympathetic and submissive people, while people with mature faces were seen as more dignified or intense and were recommended for high-powered jobs, like lawyers. "We found that the more baby-faced people had baby-faced jobs," Zebrowitz said. "People seemed to be chosen for jobs, or to select themselves into jobs, to match their appearance."

Source: "Judging Faces Comes Naturally," by Jules Crittenden, *Boston Herald*

Zooey Deschanel

Elijah Wood

Group work Answer these questions.

1. Which of the people above do you think have "baby faces"? What makes a baby face different from a mature face?

2. In what ways can having a baby face be useful? In what situations is it better to have a mature face?

3. In some countries, job applications sometimes require a recent photo of the candidate. Do you agree with this practice? Why or why not?

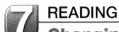

7 READING

Changing a negative perception

A **Pair work** In what ways could someone make a bad first impression? Once a bad impression is made, what can be done to change the negative perception? Discuss with a partner. Then read the article.

OVERCOMING A BAD FIRST IMPRESSION

Have any of these situations happened to you? Forgetting someone's name after you've just met, spilling coffee on your potential boss during an interview, or unintentionally insulting a co-worker on your first day? Ouch! You never have a second chance to make a first impression, so what happens when that first impression is a negative one? Here is how you can recover.

Apologize immediately. As soon as you realize that you may have offended someone, address it. The more time that passes, the more the story can become blown out of proportion. While first impressions stick, so do last impressions. Take control of the situation by making your last impression a positive one.

Avoid over-apologizing. Saying you're sorry is important, but overdoing it can create another uncomfortable situation. Your goal is to acknowledge your mistake and re-position yourself as being responsible and sensitive. If you repeatedly bring up the past, groveling and begging for forgiveness, you're defeating your purpose. It puts the other person in the uncomfortable position of having to constantly reassure you.

Make no assumptions. It's easy to assume that others think the worst of you, but usually what we imagine is far worse than reality. So, don't start out with, "You must think I'm a total idiot." Say something like, "I'm uncomfortable with how I behaved yesterday

because I realized I might have offended you. Did you feel the same way?" The other person may think it was no big deal.

Be sincere. A sincere apology requires three steps. First, don't blame what happened on other people or circumstances. Second, acknowledge how your actions affected the other person – which means listening without defending yourself. Third, explain what you will do differently in the future to avoid making the same mistake. Such an apology might sound like, "I want to apologize for what I said yesterday. After speaking with you, I can hear how much my comments offended you and caused embarrassment. I want you to know that in the future I will be more sensitive."

Humor works. A little self-deprecating humor can save you, but make sure it is really only directed at yourself and does not increase anybody else's level of discomfort. Sometimes humor breaks the tension and provides an opening for you to recover.

Monitor future behavior. Communication has a cumulative effect. Every impression you make builds on the previous one. Overcoming a bad impression requires that all future behavior be consistent with how you want to be perceived. It will take time and trust to change perceptions, but it can be done!

Source: "Overcoming a Bad First Impression," by Susan Fee, www.susanfee.com

B **Pair work** Read the article again. Then take turns summarizing the advice in your own words.

C **Group work** Discuss these questions. Then share your answers with the class.

1. How effective do you think the advice in the article would be in changing a bad first impression?

2. How could an incident get blown out of proportion if someone doesn't apologize right away?

3. Do you believe that time and trust can change a negative perception? Explain.

LESSON A ▶ *Good science, bad science*

1 STARTING POINT
What's new?

A Read about these advances in science. What are the possible benefits and dangers?

DNA for Information Storage
Incredibly, scientists can now synthesize DNA to hold digital information, such as a video or text. The information can later be read by machines called DNA sequencers. DNA offers the longest duration for digital storage, keeping data safe for tens of thousands of years.

Thought Identification
Technology can already identify thoughts from scans of activity patterns in the human brain. The first attempts identified simple thoughts, but researchers are finding ways to reveal more complex thoughts and intentions.

Animal Cloning
With just one cell from a live or dead animal, an exact copy of the animal can be created with a technique known as cloning. The technique has been used to clone various pets, and cloned horses can even take part in the Olympics now.

B Pair work Read more about the scientific advances in part A. Do you think each statement is a good idea (*G*) or a bad idea (*B*)? Discuss each statement with a partner.

_B_ 1. DNA storage could one day provide so much storage space that no data would ever need to be erased again.

_B_ 2. Instead of questionnaires, marketers have used brain scans to check customer responses to products.

_B_ 3. Scientists have successfully stored a song in the DNA of living bacteria.

_B_ 4. An application of thought-identification technology allows a person to type on a computer just by thinking.

_B/G_ 5. To avoid taking any more animals from the wild, some scientists hope to clone endangered animals for use in zoos.

_B_ 6. Scientists want to create a clone from the frozen remains of an extinct mammoth.

2 LISTENING & SPEAKING
The effects of technology

🔊 **A** Listen to a show about driverless car technology. Choose the areas in which the impact of the technology would be mostly positive according to the speakers.

☐ accidents   ☐ fuel consumption   ☐ car repair
☐ road construction   ☒ parking   ☐ traffic

🔊 **B** Listen again and take notes about the impact of driverless car technology on the areas in part A. Then take turns describing the impact with a partner.

C Pair work Give an example of a new technology that has reshaped your daily life. What are the positive effects? What are the negative consequences?

GRAMMAR

Indefinite and definite articles

Review these rules for the indefinite articles *a* and *an* and the definite article *the*.

Use an indefinite article (*a* or *an*) when you mention a singular countable noun for the first time, or no article for plural countable and uncountable nouns. When you refer to the same item again, use *the*.
With just one cell from **a** live or dead **animal**, an exact copy of **the animal** can be created.

If you use a plural noun to make a general statement, do not use an article. However, if you make the same statement using a singular noun, use *the* or *a / an*.
Technology can already identify thoughts from scans of activity patterns in **human brains**.
Technology can already identify thoughts from scans of activity patterns in **the / a human brain**.

When making a general statement, do not use an article with uncountable nouns (*technology, education, shopping, love*, etc.).
DNA offers the longest duration for digital **storage**.

Use *the* with superlatives and with sequence markers such as *first, last, next*, etc., but don't use *the* with time expressions such as *last night* or *next month*.
The first attempts identified simple thoughts.

GRAMMAR PLUS see page 110

A Look at the Starting Point on page 18 again. Can you find other examples of article usage for each rule in the grammar box?

B Complete these sentences with the correct article. Write *X* where none is needed.

1. Nowadays, __X__ tracking technologies enable __X__ websites to trace what online shoppers buy.

2. In some countries, __X__ brain-scan evidence has been used in court to help convict killers.

3. __A__ robot at Stanford University has used tools to successfully assemble __a__ bookcase.

4. __The__ first microbes able to consume oil were created to help clean up __the__ oil spills.

5. Cloning could bring __an__ animal back from extinction provided that DNA of __the__ animal is still available.

6. I'm sure that a new computer will be even less expensive __X__ next year.

7. It's a fact that __X__ wireless technology makes the Internet available on a much wider scale.

8. For me, __the__ most interesting new transportation technology is __the__ driverless car.

C **Pair work** Write statements about the items below. Then discuss your ideas with a partner.

1. the most interesting electronic device in stores
2. the most exciting app or software on the market
3. the greatest advance in medicine
4. the most amazing invention of the twentieth century

"For me, the most interesting electronic device is the personal 3-D viewer."
"Oh, yeah. I tried one in a store. It feels just like you're in a movie theater."

4 VOCABULARY
A brave new world

A Match the words on the left with their definitions on the right.

1. audacious _C_   a. silly and wasteful; carelessly self-indulgent
2. confidential _d_   b. avoiding unnecessary risks
3. frivolous _a_   c. having a willingness to take risks
4. hazardous _f_   d. private or secret
5. problematic _g_   e. against accepted beliefs about good behavior
6. prudent _b_   f. dangerous
7. unethical _e_   g. full of difficulties that are hard to solve

B Complete the sentences with the words in part A. Then compare your answers with a partner. Sometimes more than one answer is possible.

1. Sadly, much of our _confidential_ personal information is now on the Internet.

2. While switching to driverless cars would have benefits, the possible disruption to the economy makes the switch _problematic_.

3. Some _prudent_ scientists think it would be wise to do more research before using genetically modified plants in food.

4. Some people feel that denying any patient access to medical technology due to cost is _unethical_

5. Due to its potential for serious accidents, many believe nuclear power is too _hazardous_ to use safely.

6. One bold and _audacious_ dream of thought-identification researchers is to create a machine that can read all human thought.

7. With thousands of dogs and cats looking for homes, cloning additional ones for pets seems _frivolous_.

> **VOCABULARY PLUS** see page 132

5 DISCUSSION
Pros and cons

Group work Look at these news headlines. Discuss the positive effects and negative consequences of the events in the headlines.

Cosmetic Surgery Better and Cheaper Than Ever
Many men and women today are considering

Use of Personal Data by Social Media Sites Raises Privacy Concerns
Concerns rise as more social media sites use

More Farmers Plant Genetically Engineered Crops to Save Money

Microchip Implant Allows Criminals to Be Followed 24 Hours a Day
There is a debate over whether or not microchip

"Too many people are having cosmetic surgery for frivolous reasons these days. They should think twice about all the potential risks."
"Well, I'm all for it as long as people are prudent."

> **Useful expressions**
>
> **Expressing caution and confidence**
> I'm a bit leery of . . .
> You should think twice about . . .
> I'm all for . . .
> I have every confidence that . . .

When you write a summary, state in your own words the main points of a text, leaving out most of the supporting details. The summary must accurately reflect the ideas of the original text.

A Read the article and underline the main points.

ANIMAL CLONING
BENEFITS AND CONCERNS

Animal cloning is the technique of creating an exact genetic copy of an animal from a single cell. It has previously been used to create copies of, for example, sheep, cows, and cats. While animal cloning is an amazing and powerful technology with possible benefits to science and humanity, many people are voicing concerns about the ethics and wisdom of this scientific innovation.

On the surface, animal cloning simply seems to be the "copying" of an animal, and it is difficult to see the benefits. However, the potential benefits of animal cloning are many. Cloned animals can be useful in the production of certain drugs to treat human illnesses. Through cloning, scientists can modify animal organs, such as heart valves, so that they can be safely transplanted into the human body. Cloning could also be very useful in saving endangered species. Two types of Asian cattle, the gaur and the banteng, have been helped in this way. Furthermore, cloning can be used to produce animals that are unable to reproduce naturally, such as mules.

Those who argue against cloning warn of its dangers. Organs transplanted from animals to humans might not always be safe, and there is a risk of disease. Additionally, for every animal that is successfully cloned, there are frequently a number of others that are not healthy enough to live. Cloned animals can also be weaker than those born by normal reproduction. When it comes to saving endangered animals, critics argue that cloning is too expensive and takes the attention and resources away from the real problem – the destruction of animal habitat.

In conclusion, it is unlikely that people on the two sides of the animal cloning issue will arrive at an agreement any time soon. But, as scientific progress presents us with new technologies such as animal cloning, it is important to discuss their benefits and voice our concerns about their use.

B Read the summary. Some main points from the article are not included. What are they?

Summary

Animal cloning is a technique for creating a copy of an animal from a single cell. People who support animal cloning argue that it can be useful in the production of drugs and transplant organs for humans. They also point out its value in preserving endangered species. Those who are against animal cloning argue that its medical uses are actually unsafe, that it produces unhealthy animals, and that it distracts us from the real problems that endangered animals face.

C **Pair work** Find an article on technology or a related topic. Then choose an important paragraph, and write the main idea. Compare with your partner.

D Write a summary of all or part of the article in one or more paragraphs.

LESSON B ▶ *Technology and you*

1 STARTING POINT
Technology troubles

A Read about three people who had trouble with technology. How would you have felt in their situation? What would you have done?

Stan, 36

"Working from home one Friday, I opened my company network login page. Unfortunately, I'd forgotten the password my boss had given me, and he had taken the day off. Being too embarrassed to call him at home, I had to go to work after all to access the network."

Peter, 18

"I had dinner plans with my parents, but I was still out hiking when I was supposed to meet them at the restaurant. I kept trying to call them, but the calls were dropped before I could even say hello. Having gotten several calls from me, my parents became really worried. They were relieved when I finally got through an hour later."

Vera, 24

"I had a great presentation ready for the business class I'm taking. Being a perfectionist, I had prepared it in detail on my laptop. The next day in class, my laptop crashed opening the file. Trying to stay calm, I gave the presentation as best I could from memory."

B Pair work What technology gives you the most trouble? Tell your partner a story of a time you had trouble with technology.

"Sometimes my Wi-Fi stops working. It's really frustrating. I remember one day . . ."

2 LISTENING
The convenience of technology?

◀») **A** Listen to a comedian talk about problems he had with technology. Write the types of technology and the problems he mentions in the chart.

	Technology	Problem	Example
1.			
2.			
3.			

◀») **B** Listen again. What examples does he give of how the problems affected him? Complete the chart.

C Pair work Have you had similar problems with technology? How could the comedian have avoided them?

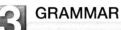

GRAMMAR

-ing clauses

To express two actions performed by the same person or thing in a single sentence, we can include an *-ing* clause. An *-ing* clause contains an *-ing* participle.

The two actions happen at the same time or one action happens during another action.
The next day in class, my laptop crashed **opening** the file.
(My laptop crashed while / when it was opening the file.)

Trying to stay calm, I gave the presentation as best I could from memory.
(I was trying to stay calm while I gave the presentation.)

She is at her desk **typing** a paper.
(She is at her desk, and she is typing a paper.)

When one action happens before another action, use *having* + past participle.
Having gotten several calls from me, my parents became really worried.
(My parents got several calls from me, and then they became really worried.)

Reasons and explanations for actions can also be expressed with *-ing* clauses.
Being too embarrassed to call him at home, I had to go to work after all to access the network.
(Because I was too embarrassed to call him at home, I had to go to work.)

GRAMMAR PLUS *see page 111*

A Look at the Starting Point on page 22 again. Can you find more examples of *-ing* clauses in the stories?

B Combine the sentences using an *-ing* clause. Then compare answers with a partner.

1. I was unable to remember my password. I clicked the link to have it sent to my email.
   Being unable to remember my password, I clicked the link to have it sent to my email.

2. My computer froze up. It was streaming a movie I'd already paid for.

3. I am very clumsy. I tripped and broke my brand-new tablet.

4. Zoe smiled from ear to ear. Zoe took a picture of herself to post on her website.

5. Harry invited some friends to join a club. Harry used a social networking site to do this.

6. The police implanted the criminal with a microchip. The police easily tracked him to his hideout.

7. Wen learned a lot about cloud computing. Wen was reading *TechToday* magazine.

8. Mari just got her first smartphone. Mari now spends all of her extra money on apps.

C Pair work Complete the sentences with your own ideas. Compare answers with a partner.

1. Having broken my . . .
   cell phone, I finally had a good reason to upgrade to a better one.

2. Being a creative person, . . .

3. Trying to keep up with new technologies, . . .

4. Having purchased a new . . .

4 VOCABULARY & SPEAKING
Different attitudes

A Look at these expressions. Which ones express a positive attitude, a negative attitude, or a neutral attitude? Write +, −, or ~.

_____ 1. aware of

_____ 2. curious about

_____ 3. sick of

_____ 4. fed up with

_____ 5. familiar with

_____ 6. suspicious of

_____ 7. intimidated by

_____ 8. knowledgeable about

_____ 9. crazy about

_____ 10. reliant on

_____ 11. grateful for

_____ 12. leery of

B Group work Look at the list of inventions and technologies. Can you think of more? What are your feelings about them? Discuss with your group.

1. spacecraft for private flights

2. touch-screen technology

3. speech-translation technology

4. video surveillance

5. wearable electronics

6. mobile apps

7. laser surgery

8. robots

"So, what do you think about spacecraft for private flights?"

"I'm a little intimidated by the idea of being in space. I'm curious about it, but I wouldn't try it."

VOCABULARY PLUS *see page 132*

5 DISCUSSION
Tech savvy?

A Are you a technophile or a technophobe? Complete the survey to find out.

TECHNOPHILE *or* TECHNOPHOBE?	Agree (2 pts.)	Not Sure (1 pt.)	Disagree (0 pts.)
1. If technology permits it, I would favor the development of machines that surpass humans in intelligence.	☐	☐	☐
2. Governments need to generously fund research and development in technology.	☐	☐	☐
3. Everyone should try to stay informed about the latest innovations in technology.	☐	☐	☐
4. Genetic technologies should be used to gradually improve the human body over the course of generations.	☐	☐	☐
5. Science and technology will someday solve the world's problems of famine, war, disease, and overcrowding.	☐	☐	☐
6. It's important to acquire new technological devices shortly after they come out.	☐	☐	☐
7. Social media has a positive effect on people's social lives.	☐	☐	☐
8. Being connected to the Internet is a human right.	☐	☐	☐

SCORE

0–4 You are a technophobe, a person who has a strong mistrust of technology.

5–8 While not in love with technology, you see the need for it in our world.

9–12 You're a fan of technology and may be showing some signs of being a geek.

13–16 You're a technophile, a person who is crazy about technology.

B Group work Discuss your answers to the survey. Talk about the reasons for your choices and whether or not you agree with your score.

6 READING
A holiday from technology

A Pair work Scan the article. Which of the technologies mentioned do you use? How would your life change if you stopped using them for six months? Discuss with a partner. Then read the article.

I Took My Kids Offline

Susan Maushart was fed up. All she usually saw of her 15-year-old son, Bill, was the back of his head as he played video games. Her elder daughter, Anni, 18, had become overly reliant on social networking sites, and 14-year-old Sussy seemed physically attached to her laptop, often staying logged on to the Internet through the night.

"My concern," she says, "was that we had ceased to function as a family. We were just a collection of individuals who were very connected outwards – to friends, business, school, and sources of entertainment and information. But we simply weren't connecting with one another in real space and time in any sort of authentic way."

Having decided to take action, Maushart came up with a plan. She initiated an "experiment in living" and banned all technology at home for six months. Her kids really didn't believe her at first, but once they realized their mother was serious, they adapted well to an offline world.

Anni, Bill, and Sussy confronted boredom – something that they were previously unfamiliar with because of their endless access to online entertainment. They found out that it made them resourceful. Indeed, their mother thinks boredom is fundamentally important in terms of creativity: "If nothing's wrong, you're never motivated to change, to move out of that comfort zone."

Maushart had high expectations for her experiment: "I hoped that it would transform our lives – that we would become a closer family, read more, sit around the table to eat and play more music . . . that we would feel closer to one another." To her delight, many of these expectations were met.

During their half-year of technological deprivation, the family did eat together more regularly. They talked more. They played board games. They went on outings to the cinema and restaurants. Anni started studying in the university library. Bill rediscovered his saxophone and got into reading novels. Sussy, as the youngest and most technologically literate, struggled more, but eventually succumbed.

The family hasn't remained app-free, but there have been permanent changes. Because they'd come to understand how it was interfering with their social life, her older two teenagers have both taken holidays from Facebook. Bill sold his game console to buy a new saxophone, and Anni still prefers to study in the library, in a social-networking-free zone.

Maushart's children have all expressed a willingness to go offline again. It is something she too would love to do. "I'd look forward to a technology vacation," she says, "just like I look forward to going on a yoga retreat. I see it as an intermittent thing that straightens your head out, not a way of life."

Source: "Family: I Unplugged My Kids," by Melissa McClements, *The Guardian*

B Group work Discuss these questions. Then share your answers with the class.

1. What effects did Maushart's experiment have on her family? Was it a success?
2. How did being bored increase Anni, Bill, and Sussy's resourcefulness? Would it increase yours?
3. Would taking a "holiday from technology" be beneficial to most people? Why or why not?

COMMUNICATION REVIEW

UNITS 1–3

✓ SELF-ASSESSMENT

How well can you do these things? Choose the best answer.

I can . . .	Very well	OK	A little
▶ Understand a conversation about people's appearance and personality (Ex. 1)	☐	☐	☐
▶ Take part in a discussion about attitudes toward clothes and fashion (Ex. 2)	☐	☐	☐
▶ Take part in a discussion about the impact of technology on people's lives (Ex. 3)	☐	☐	☐
▶ Take part in a discussion about issues associated with technology (Ex. 4)	☐	☐	☐

Now do the corresponding exercises. Was your assessment correct?

1 LISTENING
Class reunion

🔊 **A** Listen to a conversation between two friends. What is Karla trying to do? Choose the correct answer.

☐ a. She's trying to set up her personal profile on a social networking site.

☐ b. She's using a website to organize a class reunion.

☐ c. She's replying to messages she got from ex-classmates.

🔊 **B** Listen again. Are these statements true or false? Choose the correct answer.

	True	False
1. Karla is intimidated by the website technology.	☐	☐
2. Lucy isn't sure that the reunion will be completely harmonious.	☐	☐
3. Neither woman liked Andrew very much.	☐	☐
4. Renée's fashion taste has changed since she was in high school.	☐	☐
5. Mike's style has changed since he was in high school.	☐	☐

2 SPEAKING
Fashion statements

A Which of these statements about clothing do you agree with most?

- What you wear is who you are.
- People often discriminate against others because of the way they dress.
- Buying new clothes all the time is unethical.
- Clothes are like art that you wear.
- People who are interested in fashion are shallow and superficial.

B Group work Compare and explain your answers to part A. Try to find two statements that you all agree with.

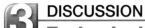

DISCUSSION
Technological advances

A Which of these advances in technology has had the most positive or negative impact on our lives?

social media

internal combustion engine

genetically modified food

large-scale farming

medical technology

renewable energy technology

B Pair work Compare your answers with a partner.

"I think social media has had the most positive impact on our lives. We are so much more connected than we were a few years ago."

"Well, that's true, but medical technology has had more of a positive influence on people around the world."

DISCUSSION
Is technology good or bad?

A Read these opinions about technology. What are the main issues they raise? What's your own point of view on these issues?

When you are ready to invest in a new technology, there are a few questions you should ask yourself. First, is the new item cheaper than what it replaces? Does it save space? Will it make your life easier? Is it energy efficient? Will you be able to recycle it or at least dispose of it properly? If not, don't buy it.

— Kwang-hyun Lee, Busan, Korea

How we think about technology is flawed. We are overeager to have the newest gadget. We are too impressed by speed, noise, compactness, and general flashiness. We need a more mature and cautious way of thinking about technology. New is not always better.

— Inés Candia, Asunción, Paraguay

B Group work Compare your ideas. Are your points of view similar? How?

4 SUPERSTITIONS AND BELIEFS

LESSON A ▶ *Superstitions*

1 STARTING POINT
The things people believe!

A Read the list of superstitions. Do you believe in any of them?

Beliefs Across Cultures

In Turkey, many people agree that when someone goes on a journey, you should pour water on the ground behind him or her to bring the person back safely.

In Brazil, people claim you should enter a place using your right foot to have good fortune.

In Russia, looking into a broken mirror will bring bad luck.

In Italy, many people believe that if visitors toss a coin into the Trevi Fountain in Rome, they will return to that city in the future.

In Japan, it is very bad luck to give a present that consists of four pieces.

In Venezuela, some people say that if someone passes a broom over your feet, you will never get married.

In Greece, you should place your shoes with the soles on the floor when you take them off because overturned shoes are considered unlucky.

B Pair work Which superstitions do some people in your culture believe?

2 VOCABULARY
Expressions with *luck*

A Match the statements with the replies containing *luck*.

1. "I've got to go. I have a big test tomorrow." ____
2. "I'm out of cash. Is there an ATM nearby?" ____
3. "He won the first game of chess he ever played!" ____
4. "He lost his job and house, and now he's sick." ____
5. "Are you going to Europe this summer?" ____
6. "How did you win those soccer tickets?" ____
7. "Thanks for the $20. Can I have $40 more?" ____

a. "That was beginner's luck."
b. "No such luck. I'm staying home."
c. "I'm afraid you're out of luck."
d. "Wow! He's got bad luck."
e. "Well, best of luck!"
f. "Don't push your luck."
g. "It was the luck of the draw."

B Pair work Use the expressions with *luck* to write short conversations. Act them out with your partner.

"I really want tickets to the Jay Z concert."
"I'm afraid you're out of luck. They sold out in 10 minutes!"

VOCABULARY PLUS *see page 133*

3 GRAMMAR

Reporting clauses

To report what someone says, thinks, believes, etc., you can use a sentence that includes a reporting clause. The use of the word *that* is optional.

In Turkey, **many people agree (that)** when someone goes on a journey, you should pour water on the ground behind him or her to bring the person back safely.

In Venezuela, **some people say (that)** if someone passes a broom over your feet, you will never get married.

The following verbs are often used in reporting clauses.
More formal: argue assert claim report
More conversational: admit agree assume believe doubt explain feel say

GRAMMAR PLUS *see page 112*

A Look at the Starting Point on page 28 again. Can you find two other sentences that contain reporting clauses? For the sentences that don't, add a reporting clause and rewrite the sentence.

B Rewrite each sentence with a reporting clause. Use a different reporting verb to introduce each one.

1. Everyone is superstitious about a few things.
   Many people agree that almost everyone is superstitious about a few things.

2. It's fine to follow superstitions for fun, but not to really believe in them. *Some people think it's fine to follow*

3. Superstitions are an important part of our cultural heritage.
   Some people think that superstitions are

4. Superstitions are dangerous because they prevent people from thinking scientifically.

5. Many holiday rituals are based on ancient beliefs and superstitions.

6. Superstitions sometimes contain truths handed down from the past.

I think, I believe
Some ppl think

C Pair work Share your answers with your partner. Then give your opinions about the statements.

"Many people agree that almost everyone is superstitious about a few things. It's true! When I spill some salt, I always throw a little over my left shoulder so I don't have bad luck."

4 DISCUSSION

Everyday superstitions

A Pair work Do you know any superstitions connected with these things? Describe them to your partner.

- animals and plants
- days, dates, or months
- household objects
- clothing
- food
- colors
- money
- numbers
- weddings

B Group work Join another pair and compare your answers. Ask follow-up questions.

"In parts of Great Britain, people who aren't feeling well sometimes stick coins into the trunk of a tree that has fallen down."

"Why is that?"

"Well, some people believe that if you put a coin in wood, it can make illnesses go away. They call these trees 'wishing trees.'"

5 LISTENING
Common explanations

🔊 **A** Listen to people talk about superstitions. What superstitions are they talking about? How is each superstition explained?

🔊 **B** Listen again. Answer these questions.

1. How did the woman with allergies react to the man's explanation?
2. Why did the son feel it was necessary to say that he was only kidding?
3. Why does the man suggest not telling Mr. Wilson that being left-handed was once thought to be suspicious?

6 DISCUSSION
Are you superstitious?

A **Pair work** Take turns interviewing each other, and complete the questionnaire. Then calculate your scores.

Lucky or Unlucky?

FRI 13

	YES (1 pt.)	NO (0 pt.)
1. Is it unlucky not to say something like "Bless you!" when someone sneezes?	☒	☐
2. Are there any particular days that you consider unlucky?	☒	☐
3. Do you have any lucky numbers?	☒	☐
4. Do you think some colors bring good luck?	☐	☐
5. Do you avoid walking under a ladder because it might bring you bad luck?	☒	☐
6. Are there any animals you consider unlucky?	☒	☐
7. Do you believe that certain actions before a wedding bring good or bad luck?	☒	☐
8. Do you carry any good luck charms or have any in your house?	☒	☐
9. Do you have a piece of clothing that brings you good luck?	☐	☒
10. Do you avoid having specific items in your house because they might bring bad luck?	☒	☐

SCORE

0–1 Life is not a matter of luck to you!	**5–7** You're fairly superstitious, aren't you?
2–4 You're not very superstitious, but . . .	**8–10** Wow! You're really superstitious!

B **Group work** Compare your scores. Then explain some of the things you're superstitious about. Is there anything else that you think brings good or bad luck?

"Well, when I talk about something that's going well, I say 'knock on wood.'"
"Really? Why do you do that?"
"Well, they say that if you knock on something made of wood, your luck will continue."

> The first paragraph of a composition provides the thesis statement and sometimes gives general examples. The last paragraph restates the thesis statement.

A Read this composition. Find the thesis statement and a supporting example in the first paragraph. Then look at the last paragraph. Which sentence restates the thesis statement?

SUPERSTITIONS: HARD TO IGNORE

Some people think that certain objects bring them good luck; others avoid certain things or situations that they believe might bring them bad luck. Even people who claim not to believe in superstitions sometimes use phrases such as "knock on wood" when they speak. Superstitions concerning both good and bad luck are part of everyone's life in the United States – even if you don't believe in them, they are difficult to ignore.

It's easy to find superstitions relating to good luck. For example, my friend Irene carries a fake rabbit's foot in her pocket to bring her good luck. Another friend, who plays baseball, panics whenever his mother washes his "lucky" baseball socks. My mother believes that nine is her lucky number, and even my level-headed father has hung a horseshoe over the entrance of our home to bring us good luck and good fortune.

Superstitions concerning bad luck are just as common. My mother believes that certain days are bad for events like marriages and ceremonies, while my uncle always says "knock on wood" and then looks for something made of wood to knock on with his hand. Then there's my friend who goes out of his way to avoid black cats. My sister never puts her bag on the floor because she thinks doing so will bring her bad luck.

Personally, I am not very superstitious. I don't have any lucky socks, and I don't have any lucky or unlucky numbers. Still, I find myself avoiding black cats, and I knock on wood every now and then. Superstitions are just a part of life, whether you believe them or not.

B Write a composition about superstitions and good and bad luck in your culture. Do your first and last paragraphs follow the guidelines stated in the box above?

C Pair work Exchange your composition with a partner, and answer these questions.

1. Does the first paragraph contain a thesis statement and give general examples?
2. How well do the examples in the middle paragraphs support the thesis? Are there enough examples?
3. Does the last paragraph restate the thesis?

LESSON B ▶ *Believe it or not*

1 STARTING POINT
Fact or fiction?

A Three of these news stories are true and one is false. Decide which one is false.

1 A company has produced a device designed to chase away loitering children and teenagers. It was explained that the device emits a sound that irritates young people.

2 It's been confirmed that if an egg is placed directly between two cell phones that are in "talk mode," the egg will be cooked in about an hour.

3 A candy company is selling lollipops with a variety of insects inside, including crickets, ants, and scorpions. It is claimed that the lollipops are actually quite tasty.

4 It was reported that a website broadcast live video of a wheel of cheddar cheese as it ripened. It is said that the video ran for over nine months.

B **Pair work** Tell your partner your choice and explain why you think it is false. (For the answer, see page 142.)

2 VOCABULARY & SPEAKING
That sounds fishy!

A Which of these words describe something likely to be true? Which describe something likely to be fabricated? Divide them into two groups. Then add two more items to each group.

believable	convincing	dubious	fishy	misleading	plausible
conceivable	credible	far-fetched	iffy	phony	well-founded

B Use the words in part A to write about each story in the Starting Point.

The article about the candy company sounds completely phony to me. It's just not a plausible story.

C **Group work** Take turns making statements, some true and some false, about yourself to your group. Respond using the words describing truth and fabrication.

"I have a very good singing voice, and I sing with a band on the weekend."
"Well, your speaking voice is very nice, so that seems pretty believable to me."

VOCABULARY PLUS *see page 133*

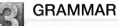

GRAMMAR

Reporting clauses in the passive

To report a general claim or opinion, you can use a passive form of a reporting verb and *it*.
Notice that the agent is often omitted and understood to be "some people" or "many people."
It was explained (that) the device emits a sound that irritates young people.
It is said (that) the video ran for over nine months.

GRAMMAR PLUS *see page 113*

A Look at the Starting Point on page 32 again. Can you find other examples of reporting clauses in the passive?

B Rewrite these statements with a reporting clause in the passive with *it*.

1. People estimate that 50 percent of the population believes in ghosts.
   It is estimated that 50 percent of the population believes in ghosts.

2. Some sources say that the idea of horseshoes being lucky dates back to the ancient Greeks.

3. Many claim that some people can communicate with plants.

4. People once thought the sun moved around the earth.

5. Some sources have reported that practical jokes on April 1 are becoming less common.

6. Experts argue that people create Internet hoaxes for a wide variety of reasons.

7. Sociologists think that people developed the first superstitions in an attempt to gain control over things they didn't understand.

8. People too easily assume that just because something is in print, it's true.

C Pair work Use reporting clauses in the passive to talk about these interesting facts.

1. A company makes a bicycle that seats seven people.
2. A 33-year-old man married a 104-year-old woman.
3. On April 1, 2006, a flight was denied permission to land because the air traffic controller was on a tea break.
4. Butterflies can taste with their feet.
5. You can send a coconut through the mail in the United States without any wrapping.
6. A crocodile measuring over six meters long was found in the Philippines.
7. The world's first webcam was used to let staff in a university computer department see the office coffee pot.

"Get this – it's been reported that a company makes a bicycle that seats seven people."

Useful expressions

Reporting something surprising
Get this – . . .
Believe it or not, . . .
Did you hear what happened?

D Pair work Complete these statements about beliefs using your own information. Compare your statements with a partner.

1. People don't believe this anymore, but it used to be said that . . .
2. Recently, it has been reported in the news that . . .

4 LISTENING
Shocking news

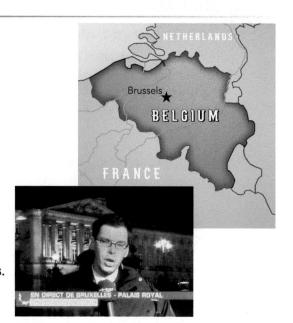

A Look at the map of Belgium. What do you know about this country?

 B Listen to a conversation about a journalistic hoax that affected many people in Belgium. What was the hoax?

C Listen again. Which events actually happened? Choose the correct answers.

- ☐ 1. The king and queen left the country.
- ☐ 2. People panicked.
- ☐ 3. A television station website crashed.
- ☐ 4. Foreign ambassadors called the Belgian authorities.

5 DISCUSSION
Internet hoaxes

A Pair work Have you ever read or heard about something on the Internet that was a hoax? Tell your partner about it.

B Pair work Read these claims found on the Internet. Choose the ones you think are hoaxes. Then discuss with a partner. (For the answers, see page 142.)

Website Claims   HOAX?

1. A man offers $10,000 to anyone who can find him a wife.	☐
2. There is a group dedicated to preventing cruelty to insects throughout the world.	☐
3. Each year, the Internet must be shut down for 24 hours to allow authorities to clean it.	☐
4. There is a new chewing gum that you can recharge with flavor when the taste fades.	☐
5. An 85-year-old woman is training to climb Mount Everest with her little dog.	☐
6. An adventure company is now reserving seats for a trip to the center of the earth.	☐
7. A new technology allows you to get a suntan from your computer screen.	☐
8. A company can deliver tacos to homes using delivery robots.	☐

C Group work Discuss these questions with your group.

1. Which of the website claims seems the most plausible to you? Which seems the most iffy? Why?
2. Why do you think people create hoax websites and hoax emails?
3. Do you think people who create Internet hoaxes should be punished?

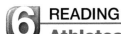

Athletes and their superstitions

A Pair work Research suggests that good luck charms and lucky rituals can actually have an effect on an athlete's performance. Why might this be so? Discuss with a partner. Then read the article.

DO GOOD LUCK CHARMS REALLY WORK IN COMPETITIONS?

To avoid jinxing herself, Canadian hurdler Angela Whyte never carries her podium clothes with her to the track at international competitions. But before the 100-meter hurdle final at the Commonwealth Games in New Delhi, Ms. Whyte faced a dilemma, because her roommate – whom she would usually ask to bring them – was gone for the day.

"I packed the podium clothes in a separate backpack, so they wouldn't touch the competition gear," she laughed, after winning a silver medal. "It's a little psycho, but it worked!"

Ms. Whyte isn't alone in her faith in the power of superstition. Numerous studies have examined the prevalence of "magical thinking" among athletes, finding that the greater the interest in sports, the more superstitious a person is likely to be.

Intrigued by stories about athletes such as Michael Jordan, who wore his old college shorts under his uniform throughout his professional career, Dr. Lysann Damisch led a study in which

she found that following a lucky ritual enhances self-confidence. This leads one to set higher goals and be more persistent, ultimately achieving greater success.

Not all athletic rituals work this way, though. Dr. Damisch claims that routines such as bouncing a basketball exactly three times immediately before shooting a foul shot does more than simply boost confidence. This routine actually serves to focus attention and also triggers well-learned motor sequences. Other apparent superstitions may have more to do with creating a relaxed and positive mindset. Ms. Whyte, for example, always travels to competitions with a teddy bear named O.T. – but not because she believes O.T. brings her luck. "I've had him since I was two years old," she explains, "so he reminds me of my home and family when I'm traveling. He's my security blanket."

The effectiveness of superstitious rituals may explain why they have persisted across cultures and eras, Dr. Damisch points out. But there are limits to their power. Following such rituals "doesn't mean you win, because of course winning and losing is something else."

Source: "Do Good Luck Charms Really Work In Competitions?" by Alex Hutchinson, The Globe and Mail

B Read the article again. Are the statements true (*T*), false (*F*), or is the information not given (*NG*) in the article? Write the correct letters and correct the false statements.

_____ 1. Angela Whyte considers her ritual of not carrying her podium clothes to the track completely rational.

_____ 2. Those with an avid interest in sports are not likely to be influenced by superstitions.

_____ 3. Dr. Damisch was fascinated by Michael Jordan's professional career.

_____ 4. An increase in self-confidence can make people set and reach more challenging goals.

_____ 5. Some lucky rituals actually help the brain and body prepare for performance.

C Group work Discuss these questions. Then share your answers with the class.

1. What other good luck charms and lucky rituals used in sports do you know about? How do they relate to the findings of the research mentioned in the text?

2. What things do you do to increase confidence and keep a positive mindset? Which is most effective?

5 MOVIES AND TELEVISION

LESSON A ▶ *Movies*

1 STARTING POINT
Movies today

A Read the statements about some movie trends. Which of these trends have you noticed?

Movie Trends

Unquestionably, studios are interested in producing a lot more movies about superheroes, because these are so popular with audiences! That's good news if you love superhero movies as much as I do! **—Maura B., Ireland**

For a long time, box office hits were predictably followed by sequels. But nowadays, the production of prequels has become a pretty exciting trend. **—Alejandro H., Mexico**

Box office profits will possibly continue to fall in the United States. Fortunately, for the movie studios, revenues continue to increase in several overseas markets. **—Naomi S., the United States**

Independent filmmakers often go into debt producing their movies, so many now turn to crowdsourcing websites for funding. Many fans like me make donations to film projects they support. **—Masako N., Japan**

Seemingly, there have been more women cast in leading roles in successful movies. Honestly, I hope that having more courageous heroines will be a trend that lasts and not just a passing fad. **—Leonard W., Canada**

Overall, the animated movies I take my children to see these days are visually spectacular and have sophisticated humor and storylines. Not surprisingly, the other adults I see at the theater also enjoy these movies as much as the kids do. **—Lucas M., Brazil**

B Pair work What other movie trends have you noticed? Discuss them with your partner.

"It seems to me that quite a few plays and musicals are being made into movies lately."

2 VOCABULARY
Reacting to movies

A Do these adjectives have a positive or a negative meaning? Mark them + or –.

____ a. clichéd   ____ d. inspiring   ____ g. predictable

____ b. engrossing   ____ e. mediocre   ____ h. riveting

____ c. formulaic   ____ f. moving   ____ i. touching

B Complete the sentences with the adjectives from part A. Sometimes more than one answer is possible.

1. _____ movies affect your emotions or bring tears to your eyes.

2. A/An _____ movie completely captures your attention.

3. A/An _____ movie isn't very good, and probably not worth watching.

4. A movie is _____ if its plot is obvious and you can guess the ending.

VOCABULARY PLUS *see page 134*

GRAMMAR

Sentence adverbs

Sentence adverbs modify a whole sentence, not just part of it. Many adverbs can be used in this way. Sentence adverbs express the speaker's attitude, opinion, or reason for speaking.

Certainty: *clearly, definitely, obviously, unquestionably*
Unquestionably, studios are interested in producing a lot more movies about superheroes.

Less certainty: *apparently, seemingly, supposedly*
Seemingly, there have been more women cast in leading roles in successful movies.

Possibility and probability: *possibly, potentially, probably*
Box office profits will **possibly** continue to fall in the United States.

Talking honestly and directly: *frankly, honestly, seriously*
Honestly, I hope that having more courageous heroines will be a trend that lasts and not just a passing fad.

Summarizing: *basically, essentially, fundamentally, mainly, overall*
Overall, the animated movies I take my children to see these days are visually spectacular.

Other attitudes: *amazingly, surprisingly, not surprisingly, predictably, fortunately, unfortunately*
Not surprisingly, the other adults I see at the theater also enjoy these movies as much as the kids do.

GRAMMAR PLUS see page 114

A Look at the Starting Point on page 36 again. Can you find other sentences with adverbs from the grammar box? What attitude or opinion do they convey?

B **Pair work** Rewrite each sentence using one of the adverbs from the grammar box. Compare with a partner.

1. No one is surprised that movie attendance is declining in the United States due to the many forms of home entertainment available.
   Not surprisingly, movie attendance is declining in the United States due to the many forms of home entertainment available.

2. It's been said that men prefer action movies while women favor romantic ones.

3. It's likely that more and more independent films will win awards in the future.

4. In truth, many people enjoy engrossing movies full of action and special effects.

5. It's clear that in the future nearly all movies will be shot and projected using digital technology instead of film.

6. A potential result is that young filmmakers may never use film.

7. It's amazing that studios routinely spend hundreds of millions of dollars to make a movie.

8. It's possible that watching violent movies can make some children more aggressive.

C **Group work** Use sentence adverbs to express your attitude about trends in the areas below, or use your own ideas. Listen to your classmates' reactions.

- shopping
- television
- music
- smartphones
- transportation
- computers
- magazines
- video games
- language learning

"You can supposedly get discounts from stores by indicating you like them on social media sites."

"Really? I'll have to give that a try. Frankly, I hate paying full price for anything."

4 LISTENING
Behind all good movies . . .

A **Pair work** Look at the movie genres. What elements do you consider
essential for each genre? Discuss with a partner.

animated movies   musicals   romantic comedies   sci-fi movies

 B Listen to four people talk about key elements of the movie genres in part A.
Complete the chart with the genre each speaker is talking about.

	Movie genre	Key elements
1. Heather		
2. Josh		
3. Felipe		
4. Dana		

C Listen again. What three elements does each person consider essential for
each movie genre? Complete the chart. Are their opinions similar to yours?

5 DISCUSSION
Movie genre preferences

A **Pair work** Discuss the results of this survey on movie genre preferences.
Do you think the preferences are the same where you live?

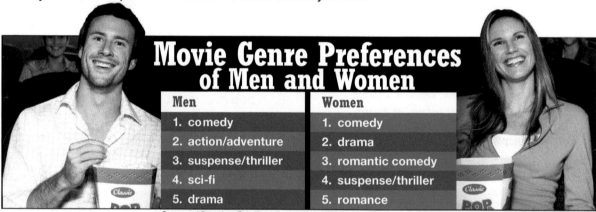

Movie Genre Preferences of Men and Women

Men	Women
1. comedy	1. comedy
2. action/adventure	2. drama
3. suspense/thriller	3. romantic comedy
4. sci-fi	4. suspense/thriller
5. drama	5. romance

Source: "Opening Our Eyes," a study by Northern Alliance and Ipsos MediaCT for the British Film Institute

B **Group work** Discuss different aspects of each movie genre in the survey.
What is it about them that men, women, or both might like?

"Thriller movies often have riveting action scenes. I think that's more of a guy thing."

*"I don't agree. I think both genders enjoy thriller movies because of the element of surprise
that many of them have."*

C **Group work** Name actors and actresses who have starred in the various
movie genres. Discuss their performances and whether the genre suits them.

*"I think Will Smith is perfect in sci-fi movies. He can be serious and funny, which makes the
movies riveting and entertaining."*

"That's true. But I think he's better suited for comedies – when he's not serious at all!"

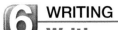

Writing a movie review

> An effective movie review generally provides information about the movie, summarizes the plot, and offers a recommendation based on the writer's opinion.

A Read the questions and the movie review. Underline the answers to the questions in the review and write the number of the question.

1. What is the title of the movie, and what genre is it?
2. What made you decide to watch the movie? What is your general impression?
3. What is the movie about?
4. Who are the main characters and actors? Who is the director?
5. Would you recommend this movie to others? Why or why not?

MOVIE REVIEW:
Safety Not Guaranteed

1 I'm a huge fan of both indie films and movies about time travel, so choosing to watch *Safety Not Guaranteed* was an easy decision to make and a very good one. *Safety Not Guaranteed* is an offbeat romantic comedy with an original storyline, an excellent cast, and an unexpected ending. It's about time travel, but it's also about why people long to revisit the past and about why some people are willing to believe in the impossible.

Three magazine reporters from Seattle head out on an assignment to interview a guy who placed a classified ad looking for a partner to travel back in time with him. They think it's a joke, but as the movie progresses, they gradually discover that Kenneth (played by Mark Duplass), the would-be time-traveler, actually believes he's built a working time machine. Along the way, Darius (Aubrey Plaza), one of the reporters, falls in love with Kenneth. Meanwhile, Jeff (Jake Johnson), another one of the reporters, does some time-traveling of his own as he takes time off to look up an old girlfriend and teach Arnou (Karan Soni), the third reporter, a little bit about love. In the end, it all comes together in a marvelous way.

Directed by Colin Trevorrow, the movie is charming, likable, and funny. Every line of its clever script either makes you laugh or moves the story in a new direction. Best of all, it's a movie so magical that it might make you want to believe in time travel yourself. Highly recommended.

B Think of a movie you've seen recently, and make notes to answer the questions in part A. Then use your notes to write a movie review.

C **Pair work** Exchange your movie review with a partner, and answer these questions.

1. Does your partner's review answer all of the questions in part A? Find the answers.
2. Is the information in the review organized effectively? How could it be improved?
3. What else would you like to know about the movie reviewed? Ask at least two questions.
4. Would you follow the recommendation in your partner's review after reading it? Why or why not?

> **Useful expressions**
>
> **Suggesting improvements**
> It might be better if you . . .
> I think what it needs is . . .
> You might want to . . .
> It'd be even better if . . .

1 STARTING POINT
TV time

A Read these posts about TV programs. Which program would you most like to watch? Which one would least interest you? Why?

What's On? *A Blog for TV Lovers*

Today's Question: What TV shows could you watch over and over again?

Posted at 9:24 by Donna
House is such a riveting show that I could watch it again and again. Frankly, Dr. Gregory House (played by Hugh Laurie) is so foul-tempered that I hated him when I first started watching the show. But the amazing plots combining medical mysteries and detective work really drew me in. It's such a great show that I bought all eight seasons and have watched many episodes more than once.

Posted at 9:03 by Justin
I could watch many sitcoms forever, but my busy schedule leaves me so little TV time that I don't want to waste it watching mediocre sitcoms. So, I watch only the best ones, like *The Big Bang Theory*. It centers on the hilarious lives of four geeky scientists. The show's intelligent, witty dialogue is packed with so many great jokes that it's nonstop laughs from beginning to end.

Posted at 8:46 by Franco
I never get tired of watching *CSI*. The unique murder investigations are always thrilling! They include so many scientific details that I always learn something. Plus, I love the humor, and the chemistry between the characters is great! Some of my favorite actors are on *CSI New York*, so those are the episodes I stream the most.

B Pair work What are your favorite TV shows of all time? Why do you like them?

"One of my favorite shows is Law and Order, *a crime drama series. The plots are always engrossing with lots of surprising twists."*

2 VOCABULARY
Types of TV programs

A Pair work Look at the different types of TV programs. Select the ones that you know. Then ask a partner about the ones you don't know.

☐ 1. game show
☐ 2. soap opera
☐ 3. sitcom
☐ 4. cartoon
☐ 5. documentary
☐ 6. drama series
☐ 7. sports program
☐ 8. talk show
☐ 9. sketch comedy show
☐ 10. cooking show
☐ 11. reality TV show
☐ 12. news program

B Group work Which types of TV shows do you watch? Give an example of each.

VOCABULARY PLUS *see page 134*

Such . . . that and so . . . that

So and *such*, *such . . . that*, *so . . . that*, *so much / little . . . that*, and *so many / few . . . that*
are commonly used to express extremes in exclamatory sentences.

a. *Such* is followed by a noun (usually
modified by an adjective).

It's **such** a great show **that** I bought all
eight seasons.

b. *So* is followed by an adjective
or adverb.

Dr. House is **so** foul-tempered **that** I hated
him when I first started watching the show.

c. *So many* and *so few* are followed by
countable nouns.

The dialogue is packed with **so many** jokes **that** it's
nonstop laughs from beginning to end.

d. *So much* and *so little* are followed by
uncountable nouns.

My busy schedule leaves me **so little** TV time **that**
I don't want to waste it watching mediocre sitcoms.

GRAMMAR PLUS *see page 115*

A Look at the Starting Point on page 40 again. Can you find more sentences with
so and *such*? Which patterns do the sentences follow?

B Complete these sentences with *so many*, *so few*, *so much*, or *so little*.

1. My brother watches _____**so much**_____ reality TV that he hardly does anything else.

2. There are __So many__ fans of that drama series that it's consistently the
highest rated show on TV.

3. There was __So little__ interest in the cartoon that the network canceled it.

4. Bob knows __So many__ useless facts that he should go on a trivia
game show.

5. Ads for that new talk show generated __So much__ hype that most viewers
were disappointed once it came out.

6. There are _____ trustworthy news programs that I've started going to
reliable websites instead.

C Rewrite these sentences using *such . . . that* or *so . . . that*. Then compare with
a partner.

1. The referee did a terrible job during the soccer
game. My father was yelling at the TV set.
*The referee did such a terrible job during the
soccer game that my father was yelling at
the TV set.*

2. There are many TV programs available on the
Internet. I'm using my TV set less and less.
(*There are so many* ... *that*)

3. That new sitcom was well reviewed. I wouldn't be
surprised if it won an award. (*so*)

4. Certain singers attract huge audiences. They
charge ridiculously high prices for concert tickets. (*such a*)

5. Some documentaries today deal with critical social
issues. They can have a political effect.

4 LISTENING
New TV shows

🔊 **A** Listen to some TV network employees discuss ideas for new shows with their boss, Rick. Write the type and the basic idea of each show in the chart.

	Café People	*Serve Yourself!*	*New Borders*
Type of show			
Basic idea			
Accepted?			
Reasons			

🔊 **B** Listen again. Were the show ideas accepted? Write *Yes* or *No* and Rick's reasons for the decisions in the chart.

C Pair work Make a list of three TV shows that are popular in your community. Then discuss the reasons why these programs are so popular.

"Modern Family is a really popular comedy show. I think that's because it lets people laugh at problems all families have, and it's presented in an interesting fake documentary style."

5 DISCUSSION
Your own TV show

A Pair work Work with your partner to develop a new TV show. Choose one of the genres in the form below or add one. Brainstorm ideas for the show. Then complete the form with your best ideas.

New TV Show Proposal Form

Title: _____

Genre: ☐ drama series ☐ game show ☐ reality TV show ☐ Other:
☐ cooking show ☐ soap opera ☐ sitcom _____

Target audience (age, gender, etc.):

Basic idea of the show:

Casting ideas (Who will be on the show?):

Reasons people will want to watch it:

B Group work Role-play a meeting at a TV network. Present your show idea to the group and try to convince them to produce it. Then decide whose idea was the best.

A movie starring everyone

A **Pair work** How could someone make a movie showing what life is like on a single day in every country on earth? What would a project like that involve? Discuss with a partner. Then read the article.

One Day on Earth: *A Time Capsule of Our Lives*

It is considered one of the most audacious documentary film projects ever made: a film shot in every country of the world on the same day, involving 3,000 hours of footage in 70 languages from 19,000 volunteer filmmakers around the world. The 104-minute film, *One Day on Earth*, is a visual poem starring everyone on the planet. It's about you and me, the times we live in, and our place in the puzzle of humanity.

Director Kyle Ruddick and executive producer Brandon Litman are the two young forces behind *One Day on Earth*. They met at the University of Southern California, where Ruddick studied film and Litman majored in business. Although both had worked on short-length commercial and broadcast projects, they had never attempted anything like *One Day on Earth* – their first feature-length film – and neither had anyone else.

Ruddick and Litman came up with the idea for the film in 2008 at a world music festival, where they heard musicians who had never met before play together for the first time. After a few awkward attempts, the musicians soon discovered a way to create a beautiful fusion of music. In a similar way, "the editorial process was a process of discovery," said Ruddick. "You couldn't make this sort of film without being completely open to what you receive."

Common themes arose organically, and the filmmakers structured the documentary around film clips that underscore larger global issues. A sense of communal experience further grounded the wide-ranging film as the grassroots filmmakers worked to painstakingly capture the beauty and tragedy of the human experience.

In one of the more touching moments of *One Day on Earth*, a man looks into the camera and says, "I want to thank you for recording this story of my life and replaying it for others." He says he hopes the viewer may find a lesson in it. His words tap into greater truths about this time-capsule art – about how the drive to understand others often derives from a more personal need to understand ourselves.

The film is also about a need to reaffirm just how alike we are despite our outward differences. "The world is a vast spectacle that we indulge and love and also struggle through," said Ruddick. "We're born, we're young, we dance, we sing, and despite all of that, we have incredible challenges." Yet, "cinema is this universal language that anyone can understand and relate to," Ruddick said. "It goes beyond borders."

Source: "'One Day on Earth' Debuts Worldwide, Offers Time Capsule of Our Lives," by Mark Johanson, *International Business Times*

B **Group work** Discuss these questions. Then share your answers with the class.

1. What factors do you think had to come together to make *One Day on Earth* possible?

2. Do you agree with Ruddick that film is a universally understood language? Why or why not?

3. In your opinion, is it true that people all over the world are alike despite our outward differences? Explain.

6 MUSICIANS AND MUSIC

LESSON A ▶ *A world of music*

1 STARTING POINT
Taste in music

A Read the statements expressing different views on music. Which ones do you agree with?

Overheard on the Streets

1 "I think the more you like to dance, the more you appreciate music with a Latin beat."

2 "At first, I didn't like rap music. But the more I listened to the lyrics, the more I understood its powerful social message."

3 "Some of the greatest music is in movie soundtracks. The more exciting the soundtrack, the better the movie seems."

4 "Radio stations kill music sales by overplaying songs. The more I hear a pop song on the radio, the less I feel like buying it."

5 "I'm interested in how a band plays, not how it looks. The more a band focuses on its appearance, the less interesting the music is."

6 "Classical music has many layers of complexity. The more knowledgeable you are about it, the more you'll be able to enjoy it."

7 "TV commercials often feature a catchy tune – and the catchier the tune, the more likely you are to remember the name of the product."

8 "A lot of my friends like to go to clubs with really loud music, but not me. The louder the music gets, the sooner I feel like leaving."

B Pair work What kinds of things do you look for in new songs or artists? What makes certain songs more successful than others?

"I love sampling. You know, when artists mix older songs with new music and lyrics."

"Me, too. I like recognizable tunes, but with a new twist."

> **Useful expressions**
>
> **Asking about opinions**
> What do you think of/about . . . ?
> How do you feel about . . . ?
> Are you into . . . ?

2 LISTENING
Awesome tunes

🔊 **A** Listen to Adam and Lisa talk about music. What are they doing?

🔊 **B** Listen again. What are the three types of music Adam and Lisa listen to? What do they think about the types of music they hear? Complete the chart.

	Type of music	Lisa's opinion	Adam's opinion
1.			
2.			
3.			

3 GRAMMAR

Double comparatives

You can use two comparatives, each preceded by *the*, in order to show how one quality or amount is linked to another. The first comparative expresses a condition for the second comparative.

The more you like to dance, **the more** you appreciate music with a Latin beat.
The more I hear a pop song on the radio, **the less** I feel like buying it.
The more exciting the soundtrack, **the better** the movie seems.
The louder the music gets, **the sooner** I feel like leaving.
The less 80s pop music I hear, **the better**.

GRAMMAR PLUS *see page 116*

A Look at the Starting Point on page 44 again. How many double comparatives can you find?

B **Pair work** Match the clauses to make logical statements. Then compare answers with a partner. Which statements do you agree with?

1. The more types of music you try to listen to, __c__
2. The more often you go to dance clubs, ____
3. The more companies a new artist sends a demo recording to, ____
4. The more you study the history of American popular music, ____
5. The less emphasis schools place on music, ____

a. the fewer new musicians will be developed.
b. the more you realize how much influence African music has had on it.
c. the more likely you are to enjoy a wide variety of genres.
d. the greater your chance of suffering some hearing loss.
e. the better his or her chances are of getting a recording contract.

"I agree with the first statement. Listening to lots of different genres naturally leads you to appreciate more of them."

C Complete these sentences with your own ideas. Can you add further information to clarify or support the statements you wrote?

1. The earlier children start playing music, . . .
2. The more famous a recording artist becomes, . . .
3. The catchier the melody of a pop song, . . .
4. The more expensive a musical performance is, . . .
5. The more thoughtful the song's lyrics are, . . .
6. The older I get and the more I listen to music, . . .

D **Pair work** Compare and discuss the sentences you wrote above. Share your opinions with the class.

"The earlier children start playing music, the better. Research suggests that music improves memory and increases attention."

"I agree. I think that sometimes we just think of math or language classes as being beneficial, but in fact, . . ."

VOCABULARY
Describing music

A Look at the collocations below. Match the adjectives used to describe music with their definitions.

(handwritten margin notes: "cellento" "feljeben" örületes, érett, fülbemászó)

1. a **soothing** rhythm ___e___
2. a **monotonous** beat ___g___
3. an **exhilarating** tempo ___h___
4. **evocative** music ___c___
5. a **frenetic** pace ___a___
6. a **haunting** melody ___b___
7. **mellow** sounds ___f___
8. a **catchy** tune ___d___

a. fast and energetic, and rather uncontrolled
b. sadly beautiful and difficult to forget
c. bringing to mind a strong emotion or image
d. pleasing and easy to remember
e. relaxing, calming, and comforting
f. cool, laid-back, and smooth
g. following the same pattern; unchanging
h. making you feel very excited and happy

B Pair work Which of the adjectives from part A could you use to describe these types of sounds, music, and performances?

- a live performance by a punk rock band
- the sound of rain and howling wind
- the soundtrack to an action movie
- the sound of ocean waves
- fast-paced techno music
- classical music played by an orchestra
- soft jazz with a slow beat
- a children's nursery rhyme

VOCABULARY PLUS see page 135

DISCUSSION
Music everywhere

A Pair work What kind of music would you expect to hear in these places or at these events? What purpose does music serve in each situation?

- the street
- a wedding
- a clothing store
- a café
- a supermarket
- a gym
- a sports event
- a birthday party

"On the street, I would expect to hear musicians playing catchy or evocative tunes in order to convince passersby to donate some money."

B Group work What are some of the ways that music is or could be used in these fields? Discuss the benefits and drawbacks.

- education
- health care
- advertising
- entertainment

"I think music, especially if it's mellow, can be used in the classroom to focus students' attention."

"Yes, but I think people are different, and some require silence to concentrate."

6 WRITING
Compare-and-contrast essays

A compare-and-contrast essay presents the similarities and differences of two or more things. The thesis statement expresses your position on the subject, and it is followed by supporting paragraphs that discuss similarities and differences.

A Read the essay and circle the thesis statement. Then match each paragraph to the headings below. Underline the words that show comparison or contrast.

____ introduction   ____ differences   ____ conclusion   ____ similarities

THE BEATLES VS. THE ROLLING STONES

1 <u>Although</u> the Beatles and the Rolling Stones have both been called the "greatest rock 'n' roll band of all time," the prize should go to the Rolling Stones. While both bands have had a huge influence on popular music, the Beatles broke up in 1970, and the Rolling Stones went on recording and performing for over 50 years.

2 Both the Beatles and the Rolling Stones began as four-member British bands that first became popular in the 1960s. The two bands released their first records within a year of each other, and both featured a pair of talented songwriters: Paul McCartney and John Lennon for the Beatles, and Mick Jagger and Keith Richards for the Rolling Stones. Like the Rolling Stones, the Beatles were famous for their cutting-edge style at the time of their debut, and both bands were known for their energetic stage performances.

3 In the beginning, the Beatles were clean-cut boys with short hair who wore suits. In contrast, the Rolling Stones had a "bad boy" image – they dressed in funky clothes and acted like rebels. One of the Beatles' first major hits was the catchy love song "I Want to Hold Your Hand," but the Stones' first big hit was a rock song called "Satisfaction." While the Beatles were pop stars, the Rolling Stones were rockers.

4 It's true that the Beatles did amazing things during the short time they were together, and their innovations are still apparent in today's music. However, the Rolling Stones were the first band to offer the world "real" rock music, and even after all these years, their music still rocks. That says it all.

B Choose two bands, singers, or musical styles to compare and contrast, and make a list of similarities and differences. Then compose a thesis statement that expresses your view.

C Write a four-paragraph essay. Make sure it has an introduction with a clear thesis statement, two paragraphs describing similarities and differences, and an effective conclusion.

D **Pair work** Take turns reading your essays. Do not read your thesis statement. Can your partner guess your point of view?

1 STARTING POINT
Music success stories

A Read about these three music success stories. Do you know these singers? Do you know how any other famous singers began their music careers?

Bruno Mars

Bruno Mars, born Peter Gene Bayot Hernández Jr., grew up in a very musical family in Hawaii. At age four, he would play with his family's band five days a week. When he was only 17, he moved to L.A. to write and produce music. At concerts, you'll see this multi-talented musician sing and play the piano or the guitar with ease.

From a very young age, Adele would perform for her mother, impersonating her favorite singers. She went to a performing arts academy in her teens, and, while there, a friend posted some of her songs online. Two years later, recording companies started noticing her. Despite her fame, Adele will still sometimes suffer from stage fright before a performance.

Adele

Rihanna

As a girl in Barbados, Robyn Rihanna Fenty would sell clothes at a street stall. She loved to sing with neighbors and friends. True talent will always be noticed. In 2003, a visiting music producer discovered her. Today, superstar Rihanna will often reinvent her look with startling new hairstyles and clothes.

B **Pair work** What qualities and opportunities does a person need to have in order to be a success in the popular music industry? Share your ideas with a partner.

"I think it's important to have an established person in the business take an interest in your talent and help you get your start."

2 VOCABULARY

Breaking into the business

A Look at these expressions related to show business and fame. Write them in the chart below. Compare with a partner.

be a big hit	make it big	get your big break	break into the business
be a has-been	be washed up	make a comeback	make a name for yourself
be discovered	pay your dues	be a one-hit wonder	get your foot in the door

Just starting out	Currently successful	No longer successful
	be a big hit	

B **Pair work** Talk about famous people you know. How did they start out? Which ones are still successful? Which ones are has-beens?

"Mark Wahlberg has really made a name for himself. He went from singer to model to Oscar-nominated actor."

VOCABULARY PLUS *see page 135*

③ GRAMMAR

Will and *would* for habits and general truths

You can use *would* to express habitual actions in the past. *Would* is more formal than *used to* and is frequently used in past narratives. *Would* needs to be clearly associated with a time in the past.
From a very young age, Adele **would** perform for her mother.

You can use *will* to express personal habits or characteristic behavior in the present.
Today, superstar Rihanna **will** often reinvent her look with startling new hairstyles and clothes.

Will is also used to express facts that are generally true.
True talent **will** always be noticed.

GRAMMAR PLUS *see page 117*

A Look at the Starting Point on page 48 again. Which other habitual actions are expressed using *would* and *will*?

Habit - will

B Complete these sentences using the verb in parentheses and *would* or *will*.

1. In my younger days, I ___***would play***___ (play) in a band at local clubs.
2. I love playing the piano. I _will practice_ (practice) every chance I get.
3. After he went deaf, Beethoven _would compose_ (compose) music in his head.
4. My son loves to play his electric guitar. Whenever he can, he _will plug_ (plug) it in and play a few songs.
5. When she was only 11 years old, Japanese violinist Midori Goto _would_ (perform) in front of large audiences with confidence.
6. As a young man in Britain, singer-songwriter James Morrison _will gain_ (gain) valuable experience by performing for people on the street.

C Read these descriptions of people. Then use your own ideas to write sentences describing their habitual actions with *would* or *will*.

1. When Ricky was a little boy, he was crazy about his violin.
   He would take it with him wherever he went.
2. Evan is really interested in learning all he can about today's top musicians.
3. Our teacher used to have lots of good ideas to pass the time on monotonous school bus trips.
4. The music Helen listened to as a teen was very different from what's popular these days.
5. The key to Jennifer's successful music career is that she teaches and performs.

D **Pair work** Complete these statements with true information. Then write a follow-up sentence using *would* or *will*. Share your answers with a partner.

1. I really enjoy listening to . . .
2. When I was young, I loved . . .
3. It's true that musicians today . . .

"I really enjoy listening to techno music. I'll listen to it when I'm feeling tired or sad, and it will always make me feel better."

4 LISTENING
Guitar blues

A Pair work You are going to listen to Paul, a young musician, talk to Theresa about his career. What do you think some of his concerns might be? Tell your partner.

B Now listen to the conversation between Paul and Theresa. What's Paul's biggest problem?

C Listen again. What advice does Theresa give Paul regarding each of these four areas? Complete the chart.

	Theresa's advice
1. His parents	
2. His opinion of himself	
3. His appearance	
4. The possibility of failure	

5 DISCUSSION
The secrets of success

A Group work Discuss the following questions with your group.

1. What are some of the ways that some actors and singers have made it big?
2. What are some of the things that successful people have in common?
3. What is your definition of *success*?

B Read the advice for success below. Choose the three pieces of advice that you think are most useful.

Advice *for* Success

○ **1. Don't be afraid to dream.** You don't need to accept limitations others put on you.

○ **2. Don't talk about your plans too much.** Spend that energy making things happen.

○ **3. Take yourself seriously.** Pursue your dreams with conviction.

○ **4. Don't try to do it all alone.** Seek out the people and resources you need.

○ **5. Always appear confident** – even if you don't always feel that way inside.

○ **6. Think positively.** Don't let yourself have negative thoughts for very long.

○ **7. Don't be afraid to fail.** All successful people will fail – and learn a lot from it.

○ **8. Dress for success.** Figure out how you need to look to get what you want.

C Group work Tell your group which three pieces of advice you chose. Explain why you think they are useful.

A **Pair work** How could a musician possibly become famous without knowing it? Discuss with a partner. Then read the article.

ON THE TRAIL OF SIXTO RODRIGUEZ

Sixto Rodriguez, a Mexican-American construction worker from Detroit, used to perform his songs in the city's small clubs in the late sixties. Known simply as Rodriguez, he would perform with his back to the audience. "There was something mysterious about him," says one local who saw him back then.

During that period, Rodriguez recorded and released two albums – *Cold Fact* and *Coming From Reality*. Sales, though, were small, and the albums disappeared without a trace. Since he'd never had a big hit, no one in the United States thought much more about Rodriguez after that.

But in South Africa, a bootleg copy of *Cold Fact* wound up being distributed on a small South African record label and some songs got played on the radio. Those songs became incredibly popular, and Rodriguez's reputation spread – along with the myths about him.

In those pre-Internet days, there was no information from the United States about this long-forgotten artist. Most people thought he had died, and the mystery surrounding Rodriguez just increased his incredible popularity in South Africa.

Documentary filmmaker Malik Bendjelloul stumbled on the Rodriguez story in 2006 while in Cape Town, where "every other person knew and loved Rodriguez," he recalls. "He was huge there – bigger than the Rolling Stones."

However, a decade earlier, two of his biggest South African fans, Cape Town record store owner Steve Segerman and music journalist Craig Bartholomew, had already set out to find out what had happened to Rodriguez.

The two men studied every Rodriguez lyric to establish where he might have lived and then found the producer of Rodriguez's album *Cold Fact*. Finally, the truth was revealed: Rodriguez was alive, had three adult daughters, and was still living in the same house in Detroit and doing construction work. Rodriguez knew nothing of his astonishing popularity in South Africa.

Segerman finally spoke with Rodriguez from Cape Town. The next step was for Rodriguez to perform there. He flew from the States with his daughters and was astonished to find a limousine waiting for him. On that first tour, Rodriguez played six sold-out concerts in a 5,000-seat hall. Crowds went wild, and *Cold Fact* went platinum, selling half a million copies in South Africa.

Footage of those first concerts, and the fan frenzy they inspired, can be seen in *Searching for Sugar Man*, Bendjelloul's documentary that tells the story of Rodriguez. Finally, his work will be heard widely.

Source: "Sixto Rodriguez: On the Trail of the Dylan of Detroit," by David Gritten, *The Telegraph*

B Read the article again. Are these statements true (*T*), false (*F*), or is the information not given (*NG*)? Correct the false statements to make them true.

____ 1. In the United States, Rodriguez's recordings were not commercially successful in the 1960s.

____ 2. *Cold Fact* sold more copies in the United States than *Coming From Reality* did.

____ 3. Rodriguez's songs helped Segerman and Bartholomew find the musician.

____ 4. Bendjelloul had heard about Rodriguez before he went to South Africa.

____ 5. Rodriguez was not really surprised about how he was greeted in Cape Town.

____ 6. Tickets for the first Rodriguez tour of South Africa were incredibly expensive.

C **Group work** How do you think instant fame affects people? Does age matter? How do you think Rodriguez's life changed after his trip to South Africa? Discuss your answers.

COMMUNICATION REVIEW

UNITS 4–6

1 DISCUSSION
My kind of show

A Think of an example of each type of television show. For each show, write at least one good point about it and one change that would improve it.

Type of show	Example	Good points	Changes you'd make
game show			
reality TV show			
soap opera			
talk show			
drama series			

B **Pair work** Compare your ideas with a partner. Use sentence adverbs.

"For me, CSI is unquestionably the best TV show ever."
"I like it, too. Apparently, some of the episodes are based on real crimes. But one thing I'd change is . . ."

2 DISCUSSION
You have to see this!

A Think about your movie-viewing habits. Give an example for each of these topics.

1. a movie you would recommend
2. the most interesting character you've ever come across in a movie
3. a book you would like to see made, or that has already been made, into a movie
4. a movie that you would rather see in a theater than at home

B **Pair work** Discuss your ideas with a partner.

"I recommend Life of Pi. It's so moving that it actually made me cry."

A You are going to listen to a show about superstitions in the acting profession. Why do you think actors might be more superstitious than non-actors?

B Now listen to the program. What is the main reason Jeffrey gives for superstition among actors? Choose the correct answer.

- ☐ a. They used to feel isolated from the rest of society.
- ☐ b. They are insecure.
- ☐ c. They travel a lot.

C Listen again. Choose the theater superstition you hear in each pair.

1. ☐ a. Black cats are considered lucky.
   ☐ b. Black cats are considered unlucky.

2. ☐ a. A costume is unlucky if a cat has slept on it.
   ☐ b. A costume is unlucky unless a cat has slept on it.

3. ☐ a. The number 13 is believed to be lucky.
   ☐ b. The number 13 is believed to be unlucky.

4. ☐ a. It is unlucky to act in the play *Macbeth*.
   ☐ b. It is unlucky to say the name of the play *Macbeth*.

SPEAKING
Hit songs

A **Pair work** What are the five best songs from the last three years? Support your choices with reasons. Make a list of five songs you both agree on.

B **Group work** Join another pair and share your lists. Then discuss which three songs are the very best. Create a new list you all agree on and share it with the rest of the class. Is there one song that appears on all the lists?

"How do you feel about . . . ?"

"Well, the more I hear it, the more I like it. It's pretty evocative. But I'm also into music with a mellow and soothing sound. What do you think about . . . ?"

7 CHANGING TIMES

LESSON A ▶ *Lifestyles in transition*

1 STARTING POINT
How we are changing

A People's lifestyles are changing more quickly than ever before. Have you noticed any of these trends in your community?

Lifestyle Trends

1 Social exercise programs that offer fun group workouts are on the rise. Enrollment in cycling, strength-training, dance, and yoga classes has never been higher.

2 Hybrid cars, powered by both gas and electricity, are an option that more people are choosing in order to save money and reduce pollution.

3 More professionals whose managers allow it are opting to telecommute, or work from home.

4 More and more shoppers are looking for recyclable products that companies can manufacture sustainably.

5 Children are learning foreign languages at earlier ages than ever before. Some elementary schools now offer classes for children whom they once considered too young.

6 A growing number of people who are concerned with the effects of pesticides on the environment are buying organic produce.

7 These days, people who are not happy with their bodies are more likely to resort to cosmetic surgery.

8 Tourists whose destinations are foreign countries are taking more trips, traveling greater distances, and spending more money.

B Pair work Discuss the good points and bad points of each trend. Which trends do you think are the most beneficial?

"Social exercise programs are great because they encourage more people to get fit."

"I think many people get a better workout by themselves. They exercise more and socialize less!"

2 DISCUSSION
Current trends

A Pair work Think of a current trend in your country, community, or among people you know for as many of these areas as you can.

- education / schools
- nature / environment
- shopping / stores
- food / restaurants
- health / fitness
- travel / tourism
- science / technology
- appearance / fashion

B Group work Join another pair. Share your ideas and choose the three most significant trends. Then prepare a short presentation for the class explaining the trends and why you think they are the most important.

"One trend we discussed is that a lot of people are into ecotourism lately. This is certainly an important and beneficial trend because . . . "

GRAMMAR

Optional and required relative pronouns

In defining relative clauses, when the relative pronoun is the subject of the clause or it shows possession, the relative pronoun is required. When it is the object, it is usually optional.

Subject of clause (relative pronouns *that*, *which*, or *who* required)
People **who / that** are concerned with the effects of pesticides on the environment are buying organic produce.
Social exercise programs **that / which** offer fun group workouts are on the rise.

Showing possession (relative pronoun *whose* required)
More professionals **whose** managers allow it are opting to telecommute, or work from home.

Object of clause (relative pronouns *that*, *which*, *who*, or *whom* optional)
Hybrid cars are an option (**that / which**) more people are choosing.
Some elementary schools now offer classes for children (**who / whom / that**) they once considered too young.

GRAMMAR PLUS *see page 118*

A Look at the Starting Point on page 54 again. In which sentences is the relative pronoun required?

B Choose the sentences in which the relative pronoun is optional. Which sentences are true for your community?

☐ 1. Young families who dream of owning a house are finding they can't afford one.

☐ 2. The pressure that students feel to succeed in school is increasing.

☐ 3. People who used to go to theaters to watch movies now watch them at home.

☐ 4. People want exercise programs that are designed for their specific age group.

☐ 5. People are devoting more time to others who are less fortunate.

☐ 6. People are recycling many things which they would have thrown away in the past.

☐ 7. A lot of people who have grown tired of city life are moving to the country.

☐ 8. More college students are choosing majors that they think will lead to high-paying jobs.

C Is the relative pronoun in these sentences the subject of the clause (*S*), the object of the clause (*O*), or does it show possession (*P*)? Write the correct letter.

_____ 1. Is the number of young people **who** opt for cosmetic surgery growing or shrinking?

_____ 2. Who are some celebrities **whose** style has affected fashion or other trends?

_____ 3. How have the foods **that** fast-food restaurants offer changed in recent years?

_____ 4. What brand names **that** once were very popular are no longer as relevant?

_____ 5. Are there any alternative therapies **that** you think are ineffective or even dangerous?

_____ 6. Is it becoming more difficult for people **who** don't speak a foreign language fluently to get a job?

D Pair work Interview each other using the questions in part C.

A The antonyms of these adjectives can be formed by adding the prefix *il-*, *im-*, *in-*, or *ir-*. Write the correct prefix in front of each adjective.

a. ____considerate   c. ____decisive   e. ____mature   g. ____responsible

b. ____consistent   d. ____logical   f. ____proper   h. ____tolerant

B Complete each opinion with one of the antonyms in part A. Write the correct letter.

1. "You can be 40 and still be ____ if you refuse to grow up and have the expected behavior for a person your age."

2. "People today just don't care about following correct rules or manners. They have such ____ behavior."

3. "Today's politicians are so ____. They just change their opinions and statements from one day to the next."

4. "Selfish people are often ____ of others and don't care about their feelings."

5. "____ people refuse to accept ideas and behavior different from their own."

6. "Many accidents happen when people are ____ and don't give careful thought to the results of their actions."

7. "Because young people lack wisdom and reason, they often make ____ decisions."

8. "Many young people are ____ about their future and unable to choose a course of action."

C Pair work Do you agree with the opinions? Discuss with a partner.

VOCABULARY PLUS *see page 136*

5 LISTENING
Generation Y

🔊 **A** Listen to a presentation by a corporate executive about two generations of employees. What audience is the presentation addressed to? What is the purpose?

🔊 **B** Listen again. Write the attitudes Generation Y has regarding each area in the chart. Then write what the company is planning to do to address each attitude.

	Generation Y's attitude	Plan
1. work and free time		
2. relationship to boss		
3. community involvement		

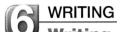

WRITING

Writing about a personal experience

A personal-experience composition usually begins with an introductory paragraph containing a thesis statement and some observations or comments. The body of the composition provides background information and gives details about what happened. The conclusion usually restates the thesis and presents the writer's feelings.

A Underline the thesis statement. Then read the composition and answer the questions below. Compare answers with a partner.

> Last month I took a giant step and finally moved to a new apartment. I had been sharing a two-bedroom apartment for two years with a friend who I'd known since childhood, and I decided that it was time to have my own place. In the beginning, I was a little scared because I would be assuming a great deal of financial responsibility. I was also a little concerned about feeling lonely, but I knew it was important to have the experience of being totally on my own.
>
> The first thing I wanted to do before making a final decision was to talk things over with my roommate. We had first moved in together because neither of us could afford . . .
>
> I looked at many apartments before making up my mind. I finally found one that I liked – an affordable one-bedroom in very good shape, with a lot of light. The apartment is . . .
>
> My new apartment is beginning to look like a home now. I've been looking at a lot of interior design websites, and I've managed to decorate my apartment. . . .
>
> Looking back, I definitely think that I made the right decision. I feel really good about having a place I can call my own. I feel more independent and responsible. Sometimes I feel a little lonely, but for the most part, I enjoy the privacy.

1. What observations or personal comments does the writer make in the first paragraph?
2. What details and background information does the body of the composition provide?
3. What additional information do you think the writer gives to complete the body paragraphs?

B Write a composition about something that has happened to you recently. Make sure to include an introductory paragraph, three body paragraphs with details, and a conclusion.

C Pair work Exchange papers and answer these questions.

1. Does your partner's introductory paragraph have a thesis statement?
2. Do all the details in the body of the composition support the thesis statement?
3. What other points or examples could be added?

LESSON B ▶ *A change for the better*

1 STARTING POINT
Contemplating a change

A **Pair work** Read about the changes these people are thinking about. Do you think they'd be happy if they made the changes? Why or why not?

My public-relations job is secure and high paying. Still, I feel as though something is missing. My real passion is skiing, and today I saw an ad for a PR consultant at a ski resort. It seems like the job was made for me! I'd have to take a big pay cut, but it might be worth it.

My parents expect me to go to a four-year college the way they did. I'm not really sure that's for me. I mean, why go away for an education when there are so many online courses? It's as if my computer is a university! For some jobs I'm interested in, I only need a professional certificate, which I could earn online in less than a year.

I'm making ends meet thanks to my part-time jobs, but I guess I'm looking for more meaning in my life. I'm thinking of joining a volunteer program to help build houses for the needy as a few of my friends have. I'd get to travel, meet new people, and do something for others.

B **Group work** Tell your group about a change you are thinking of making. Respond to each other's ideas with advice about the changes and other suggestions.

"I'm thinking about changing careers and getting into fashion design."

"That's cool! Maybe taking online courses in fashion would be a good place to start."

2 LISTENING
Volunteering for a change

A You are going to listen to Jody speak to Mr. Turner about volunteering in a program called Houses for All. What kind of program do you think it is?

 B Now listen to the conversation. Which of these things is Jody concerned about? Choose the correct answers.

☐ airfare   ☐ food   ☐ making friends
☐ culture shock ☐ job skills ☐ visiting home

 C Listen again. Write the three ways that Jody is hoping to benefit from the program.

1. _____

2. _____

3. _____

③ GRAMMAR

As if, as though, as, the way, and like

As if and *as though* often introduce clauses that describe impressions about feelings or behavior after verbs such as *act, behave, feel, look, seem,* and *talk.*
Still, I feel **as if / as though** something is missing.

As and *the way* introduce clauses that express a comparison.
I'm thinking of joining a volunteer program to help build houses for the needy **as / the way** a few of my friends have.

In informal English, the word *like* can be used instead of *as if / as though* and *as / the way.*
It seems **as though** the job was made for me!
It seems **like** the job was made for me!

GRAMMAR PLUS *see page 119*

A Look at the Starting Point on page 58 again. Can you find another expression you can rewrite with *like*?

B Rewrite these sentences to make them more formal using *as if, as though, as,* or *the way.* Compare your answers with a partner. More than one answer is possible.

1. Lately, I'm trying to think more positively, like I did when I was younger.
   Lately, I'm trying to think more positively, the way I did when I was younger.

2. My father is trying to exercise more like his doctor advised.

3. Sometimes I feel like the world is changing too fast.

4. To become a better listener, listen to people like everything they say is important.

5. My uncle needs to stop dressing like time has stood still for 20 years.

6. A friend of mine is teaching me to bake bread like they do in France.

C Pair work Complete these sentences so that they are true for you. Add another sentence with your own information, and compare with a partner.

1. I feel as though I don't have enough time to . . .
   cook healthy food.
2. I don't feel the need to . . . as so many people do these days.
3. Young people today feel as though . . .
4. I wish I could still . . . the way I used to when I was younger.
5. People today would find it difficult to . . . as was necessary long ago.
6. _____

D Group work Join another pair and share your answers.
Ask for more specific information, and give your opinions.

"I really feel as if I don't have enough time to cook healthy food."
"What makes you say that?"
"Well, I'm so busy that there's too little time to go food shopping and make proper meals. It's easier just to grab fast food."

Useful expressions

Asking for more specific information
What makes you say that?
Why do you think that?
In what way(s)?

4 VOCABULARY & SPEAKING
Collocations with *change*

A Look at the expressions with *change*. Match each expression with its definition.

1. anticipate ____
2. avoid ____
3. bring about ____
4. cope with ____   (a) change
5. go through ____
6. resist ____
7. welcome ____

a. experience a change
b. expect a change
c. successfully deal with a change
d. fight against a change
e. escape or stay away from a change
f. cause a change
g. invite and be happy about a change

B Pair work Use the expressions to discuss with your partner changes you would (not) . . .

1. avoid.   2. be able to cope with.   3. resist.   4. welcome.   5. bring about if you could.

"I'd try to avoid changes to my current lifestyle. I'm really happy with my life right now."

"That's good to hear. But would you also avoid changes that could make your life even better?"

VOCABULARY PLUS *see page 136*

5 DISCUSSION
How do you cope?

A Complete the survey. How true is each statement for you? Choose a number from 1 to 5. Then discuss the survey with a partner.

DO YOU **RESIST** OR **WELCOME** CHANGE?	Not true at all ⟵		⟶		Very true
1. I set realistic goals for myself and take steps to achieve them.	1	2	3	4	5
2. I am a curious person and enjoy new experiences.	1	2	3	4	5
3. I live in the present, appreciate the past, and focus on the future.	1	2	3	4	5
4. I listen to others and seek understanding.	1	2	3	4	5
5. When solving a problem, I seek advice and support from friends and family I trust.	1	2	3	4	5
6. I am highly flexible and easygoing.	1	2	3	4	5
7. I am creative and brainstorm solutions to challenges.	1	2	3	4	5
8. I stand up for myself and say "no" when I need to.	1	2	3	4	5
9. When I fail at something, I see it as a learning experience.	1	2	3	4	5
10. I try to find humor in all situations.	1	2	3	4	5

SCORE	10–20	21–30	31–40	41–50
	You tend to avoid change. You need to learn to welcome change in your life.	You often resist change. Friends and family can help you cope with it.	You respond to change well. However, there is always room for improvement.	You are exceptionally adaptable. You bring about positive changes in your life.

B Pair work Think of a big change in your life. Tell your partner about your feelings and reactions at the time and how your life today is different because of it.

"Getting my driver's license was a welcome change. I felt independent and was thrilled to finally be able to go where I wanted when I wanted. . . ."

Return to simplicity

A Pair work Would you reduce your income by half in exchange for more free time and less stress? Discuss with a partner. Then read the article.

LEAVING THE
Rat Race
FOR THE
Simple Life

Time is more precious than money for an increasing number of people who are choosing to live more with less – and welcoming the change.

Kay and Charles Giddens, a paralegal and a trial lawyer, respectively, sold their home to start a bed and breakfast. Four years later, the couple was dishing out banana pancake breakfasts, cleaning toilets, and serving homemade chocolate chip cookies to guests in a bed and breakfast surrounded by trees on a mesa known for colorful sunsets.

"Do I miss the freeways? Do I miss the traffic? Do I miss the stress? No," said Ms. Giddens. "This is a phenomenon that's fairly widespread. A lot of people are re-evaluating their lives and figuring out what they want to do."

Simple living ranges from cutting down on weeknight activities to sharing housing, living closer to work and commuting less, avoiding shopping malls, borrowing books from the library instead of buying them, and taking a cut in pay to work at a more pleasurable job.

Vicki Robin, a writer, tells us how she copes with the changes in her budget, now far less than she used to make.

"You become conscious about where your money is going and how valuable it is," Ms. Robin says. "You tend not to use things up. You cook at home rather than eat out. Your life is less frazzled, and you discover your expenses have gone way down."

Janet Luhrs, a lawyer, quit her practice after giving birth and leaving her daughter with a nanny for two weeks. "It was not the way I wanted to raise my kids," she says. "Simplicity is not just about saving money, it's about me sitting down every night with my kids to a candlelit dinner with classical music."

Mrs. Luhrs started editing a magazine called *Simple Living* and publishing tips on how to buy recycled furniture and shoes, organize potluck dinners instead of fancy receptions, and advocating changes in consumption patterns.

"It's not about poverty or deprivation," Mrs. Luhrs explains. "It's about conscious living and creating the life you want. The less stuff you buy, the less money goes out the door, and the less money you have to earn."

Source: "Living the Simple Life – and Loving It," by Julia Duin, The Washington Times

B Complete the summary of the article. Fill in each blank with words or phrases from the article.

Many people have come to think that time is (1) _____ than money.
The Giddenses gave up their law careers to run a (2) _____, and they are
happy they did. Others have chosen to simplify their lives by (3) _____ their
activities and expenses. Janet Luhrs quit her job as a lawyer to spend more time with
(4) _____. She started editing a (5) _____ called *Simple
Living*. She understands that the less stuff you (6) _____, the less
(7) _____ you need to earn.

C Group work Discuss these questions. Then share your answers with the class.

1. Do you think the people in the article have improved their lives? Why?

2. What changes would you make to live more simply? How would these changes simplify your life?

8 CONSUMER CULTURE

LESSON A ▶ *What's new on the market?*

---

1 STARTING POINT
Smart shoppers

A Pair work Read about these four ways to find bargains. Which ones have you or your partner tried?

$MART $HOPPERS
How do you find the best bargains?

Rick, 24
"I'm really into online auctions. Members sell each other all kinds of stuff. I really get excited about the bidding – sometimes there's lots of competition. But sometimes you're the only bidder. See this hat? It only cost me two dollars!"

Carla, 32
"When I go shopping, I use this cool sale-locator app. It provides information about in-store sales to bargain hunters free of charge. The app collects information from thousand of stores, and you can also send information about deals you find to other shoppers."

Norma, 21
"Do you get tired of clothes quickly? Do you always want to buy something new for yourself? Let me give you a tip. I buy secondhand clothes at thrift shops. I can always find something I like -- even designer brands – at a greatly reduced price!"

Ling Wei, 43
"For food and everyday items, I recommend wholesale clubs to everyone I know. For a small membership fee, you can go to a big warehouse-like store that sells everything in bulk – in large quantities. The rule there is: the more you buy, the more you save."

B Pair work What other ways do you find bargains? Can you remember an item you bought at a reduced price?

"There are some great discount websites that sell electronics, and you can find some awesome bargains. I got a great camera for half price from one of those sites."

---

2 LISTENING
Shopping preferences

🔊 **A** Listen to Ben and Anna talk about shopping online and in stores. Choose their preference and write three positive aspects they mention about it.

	Ben		Anna	
Shopping preference	☐ online	☐ in stores	☐ online	☐ in stores
Positive aspects				
Negative aspects				

🔊 **B** Listen again. Write two negative aspects they mention in the chart.

C Pair work Do you prefer shopping online or in stores? Explain your preference.

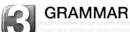

GRAMMAR

Placement of direct and indirect objects

For most verbs in English, including *get*, *give*, *lend*, *offer*, *sell*, *send*, *show*, *teach*, and *tell*, direct and indirect objects follow these patterns:

Pattern A
direct object + *to / for* + indirect object
You can send **information to other shoppers**.
You can send **information to them**.
You can send **it to other shoppers**.
You can send **it to them**.

Pattern B
indirect object + direct object
You can send **other shoppers information**.
You can send **them information**.

With verbs such as *announce*, *describe*, *explain*, *mention*, *provide*, *recommend*, *return*, and *say*, the indirect object cannot precede the direct object. Sentences follow Pattern A above.
It provides **information** about in-store sales **to bargain hunters** free of charge.
It provides **it to them** free of charge.

With verbs such as *allow*, *ask*, *cause*, and *cost*, the indirect object precedes the direct object and takes no preposition. Sentences follow Pattern B above.
It only cost **Rick two dollars**!
It only cost **him two dollars**!

GRAMMAR PLUS *see page 120*

A Look at the Starting Point on page 62 again. Find more sentences containing both a direct and an indirect object. Which pattern do they follow?

B Complete these sentences using the words in parentheses. Whenever possible, write the sentence in two different ways.

1. Many companies use cartoon characters to sell . . . (products / children)
   products to children. / children products.

2. If I'm not satisfied with a product, I never hesitate to return . . . (it / the store)

3. The Internet has made shopping much easier, but delivery costs . . . (more money / people)

4. At restaurants, my wife thinks I ask . . . (too many questions / the waiter)

5. At discount stores, when they lower prices, they always announce . . . (it / the shoppers)

6. When I told the baker the bread smelled good, he gave . . . (a free sample / me)

7. In most malls, there is a directory that shows . . . (the locations of all the stores / the shoppers)

8. Good salespeople convincingly explain . . . (the benefits of a product / their customers)

C **Pair work** Use the verbs below to talk about things you've bought recently. Ask follow-up questions.

ask	describe	give	return
cost	explain	recommend	tell

"A friend recommended a new discount store to me, and I finally went there last weekend."
"What kinds of things do they sell?"
"Mainly high-tech electronics and stuff like that."
"Did you buy anything?"
"Yeah. I bought a toy robot for my nephew."

4 VOCABULARY & SPEAKING
Shopping experiences

A Pair work Match each expression with its meaning. Then compare with a partner.

1. go over your credit limit __g__
2. be a bargain hunter ____
3. be a compulsive shopper ____
4. have buyer's remorse ____
5. make an impulse buy ____
6. bid on an item ____
7. go on a shopping spree ____
8. go window-shopping ____

a. have regrets after making an unwise purchase
b. be unable to control your need to buy things
c. buy something suddenly without having planned to
d. spend lots of money shopping for pleasure
e. look at goods in stores without buying any
f. be a person who looks for low-priced products
g. charge more to your credit card than the allowed amount
h. offer money to buy an item at an auction

B Group work Which of these experiences related to shopping have you had? Share your experiences with the group. Use the expressions in part A where appropriate.

- You made an impulse buy.
- You resisted buying something you wanted.
- You bought something and later wished you hadn't.

"I'm usually a bargain hunter, but this outfit looked so good on the store mannequin that I just had to buy it."

VOCABULARY PLUS *see page 137*

5 DISCUSSION
Are you a compulsive shopper?

A Pair work Which statements are true for you? Choose *yes* or *no* for each statement. Then discuss your answers with a partner.

What Are Your SHOPPING HABITS?

	Yes	No
1. I can never go shopping without making an impulse buy.	○	○
2. I often buy things that I end up never wearing or using.	○	○
3. At home, I frequently feel tempted to go online and buy something.	○	○
4. When I visit a new city, I spend most of my free time shopping.	○	○
5. I always have buyer's remorse after going on a shopping spree.	○	○
6. I have gone over my credit limit at least once.	○	○
7. As soon as new fashions appear in the stores, I have to buy them.	○	○
8. After buying things, I sometimes lie to relatives and friends about the price.	○	○
9. I sometimes go shopping to forget my troubles.	○	○

B Group work Discuss these questions. Then share your ideas with the class.

1. What are some other characteristics of a compulsive shopper?
2. What other problems do compulsive shoppers face?
3. What would you do to help a compulsive shopper?

WRITING
Supporting an opinion

When writing a composition that supports an opinion, first present the opinion in the thesis statement. Then support it in subsequent paragraphs with examples and details.

A Read the composition and discuss your answers to the questions.

1. What is the writer's opinion?
2. What are the reasons given to support the opinion?

   Having almost unlimited credit is certainly one of the many advantages of using credit cards. However, this benefit can easily turn into a major problem. With unlimited credit, people spend too much money. I think there should be a limit to the total amount of credit people can have. This way, the total amount of credit on all of their credit cards together could never go over a certain percentage of their income.

   Many compulsive shoppers run up such high debts that they go bankrupt, creating problems for their families as well as for the people to whom they owe money. Currently, it is easy for people to accumulate many credit cards. Although the credit cards have limits, the number of credit cards is not limited. People with 10 credit cards, each with a $5,000 limit, have $50,000 of credit, even though they might not be able to pay all of their bills. Such a situation can quickly lead to bankruptcy.

   People need to be given an absolute credit limit. If people were not permitted to go over this limit, they would have to be more responsible with their money and evaluate which purchases were most important to them. I think that the actual limit on credit card spending should be based on income so that credit would be based on the ability to pay.

B Complete one of these opinions on shopping or use one of your own. Then present your opinion in a thesis statement.

1. No one under 18 should be allowed to . . .
2. People with a lot of debt should . . .
3. Stores should never give cash refunds for . . .
4. Customers who break an item in a store should . . .
5. Shoplifters should do community service by . . .

C Make a list of details or examples to support your thesis statement. Then write a composition with an introductory paragraph containing your opinion, and at least one paragraph with supporting examples or details.

D **Pair work** Take turns reading each other's compositions. Can you think of additional examples or details your partner could use to be more persuasive?

LESSON B ► *Consumer awareness*

1 STARTING POINT
Print advertisements

A Pair work Look at the three advertisements. Which kind do you think is the most effective? Where else do you see advertisements?

magazine ads   *company logos*   *billboards*

B Pair work Read these opinions about advertisements. Do you agree with them? What do you think makes a good advertisement?

- "I think consumers need to insist that advertisements be truthful in every respect."
- "It seems to me that a good ad is a memorable ad – one that sticks in your head."
- "I believe it is essential that an ad be clever and witty in order to be effective."
- "Some ads seem to demand that the customer buy the product. I don't like a 'hard-sell' approach."
- "I think it's crucial that an ad clearly communicate the benefits of the product it is selling."

2 LISTENING
Radio ads

A Pair work What types of products or services are typically advertised on the radio? Do you think radio is an effective advertising medium?

◄)) B Listen to three radio advertisements. What products are they for? Write the name and type of each product in the chart in part C.

◄)) C Listen again. What benefits of the products are highlighted in the ads? Complete the chart.

	Name of product	Type of product	Benefit(s)
1.			
2.			
3.			

3 GRAMMAR

Verbs in the subjunctive

Certain expressions and verbs such as *demand, insist, propose, recommend, request,* and *suggest* are followed by the subjunctive. The subjunctive uses the base form of the verb. It is generally used in formal language to express a wish or necessity.

I think consumers need to insist (that) **advertisements be** truthful in every respect.
Some ads seem to demand (that) **the customer buy** the product.

These expressions are frequently followed by the subjunctive:

it is crucial	it is imperative	it is important
it is essential	it is vital	it is critical

I believe it is essential that **an ad be** clever and witty in order to be effective.

GRAMMAR PLUS *see page 121*

A Look at the Starting Point on page 66 again. Which opinion does not use the subjunctive?

B Use verbs followed by the subjunctive instead of *should* or *must* to rewrite these sentences without changing the meaning.

1. Companies should advertise more to increase sales. (I / suggest)
   I suggest that companies advertise more to increase sales.
2. Advertising agencies should use humor in their ads. (It is important)
3. Cities should tear down billboards that obstruct city views. (I / demand)
4. The government must regulate ads on the Internet. (It is essential)
5. Viewers should skip the ads that precede online video clips. (I / recommend)
6. The advertising of harmful products must stop. (It is crucial)
7. False advertising should be treated as a serious crime. (I / propose)
8. Public television should remain commercial free. (It is vital)

C Group work Use the verbs and expressions in the box below to give these people advice on their problems. Do you ever have similar problems? Ask your group for advice.

insist	it is crucial	it is essential
propose	recommend	suggest

Useful expressions

Asking for advice

What do you think I should do?
What would you do if you were me?
What would you do if you were in my position?

❶ "The fast food in commercials and posters always looks great. It looks so good I can't resist buying some, but what they actually give me looks pretty bad and really unappetizing."

❷ "I saw a clothing store with a big 'Going Out of Business' sign in the window last year, so I went in and bought a lot of clothes. Now, it's a year later, and the sign is still there."

❸ "Several friends told me they have received spam emails from me offering to sell them diet pills. The thing is, I didn't send the emails. Someone must have hacked my email account!"

4 VOCABULARY
Marketing strategies

A Look at the list of marketing strategies. Write the correct letter to complete the sentences below.

a. a free sample
b. coupon codes
c. product placement
d. comparative marketing
e. search-engine marketing
f. a celebrity endorsement
g. a loyalty program
h. word-of-mouth marketing

1. ____ gets attention for products when they are shown in movies or on TV shows.

2. ____ links the name and image of a famous person to a product.

3. ____ lets people try a product they weren't planning on buying.

4. ____ promotes a product or service related to your search on the results page.

5. ____ rewards customers for repeatedly purchasing products from one retailer.

6. ____ occurs when satisfied customers tell others about their positive experience.

7. ____ can be obtained at many websites and entitle customers to discounts.

8. ____ points out the superiority of a product over its competitors.

B Pair work With your partner, brainstorm an example from real life for as many of the marketing strategies as you can. How effective do you think they were?

VOCABULARY PLUS *see page 137*

5 DISCUSSION
The ethics of undercover marketing

A Pair work Look at the expressions in Exercise 4. Which of them describe undercover marketing strategies, in which people are not aware that they are being marketed to? Discuss your answers with your partner.

B Group work Read about undercover marketing. Then discuss the questions below with your group.

> **Undercover marketers** (also called "stealth marketers") try to find ways to introduce products to people without actually letting them know that they are being marketed to. Here are three actual techniques that have been used for undercover marketing.
>
> The product is a video gaming glove that allows gamers to control games with small finger movements. Unknown actors go into coffee shops and enthusiastically use the glove. This attracts interested people. The actor lets them try it out, never saying who he is.
>
> A top cell phone company sent 60 actors to 10 cities with its latest model. The actors pretended to be tourists and asked people to take their picture with the phone. In this way, they put the new phone in people's hands and let them interact with it.
>
> To attract attention and appear well established, a young firm had fake newspapers printed that had full back-page ads for the company. They then paid people to ride the subways in a major city, pretending to read the newspapers while holding up the ads for all to see.

1. Which of these three marketing techniques seems the most unethical to you? Why?

2. Do you think undercover marketing should be controlled by the government? Why or why not?

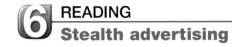

READING

Stealth advertising

A **Pair work** What influences you most to try a new brand or product?
How likely are you to use the same brands and products your friends use?
Discuss with a partner. Then read the article.

Word-of-Mouth MARKETING

It was close to midnight as one truck after another crept down a quiet street in Laguna Beach, one of the most beautiful, affluent, and expensive communities in Southern California. Considering the time of night, it was unusual to see vehicles on the road. Yet several trucks stood silhouetted in the driveway and along the front curb as workers silently unloaded camera equipment and cardboard boxes, and then carried them inside the Morgenson family home.

What took place over the next eight weeks was inspired by a Hollywood movie called *The Joneses* about a family of stealth marketers who move into an upper-middle-class neighborhood to **peddle** their wares to unsuspecting neighbors. The idea was both simple and ambitious: to test the power of word-of-mouth marketing. By filming a "real" family in spontaneous, unscripted situations, my team and I would document how the Morgensons' circle of friends responded to specific brands and products the Morgensons brought into their lives. Would they want all the things that family has? Would this influence be so powerful as to make them actually go out and buy those things?

With the help of 35 video cameras and 25 microphones **tucked away** inside the furniture and fixtures, the clandestine operation revealed

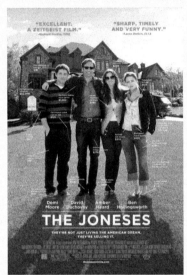

something shocking. The most powerful hidden persuader of all isn't in your TV or on the shelves of your supermarket or even lurking in your smartphones. It's a far more **pervasive** influence that's around you virtually every waking moment: your very own friends and neighbors. There's nothing quite so persuasive as observing someone we respect or admire using a brand or product.

Our analysis also found that the brands the Morgensons advocated went viral faster. Roughly one third of the Morgensons' friends began promoting these same brands to *their* friends and acquaintances. We also found that the brands their peers were most likely to buy at the Morgensons' subtle suggestion were the bigger and better-known ones. This confirmed my theory that conventional marketing and the more **covert** variety work well together. The most persuasive advertising strategies become that much more so when **amplified** by word-of-mouth advertising.

Whenever I meet with company executives, I remind them that the people who hold the *real* marketing power are **hyperconnected**, mouse-clicking consumers and their wide circles of virtual and real-life friends and acquaintances. In other words, the people who hold the real power are *us.*

Source: "Word-of-Mouth Marketing: We All Want to Keep Up with the Joneses," by Martin Lindstrom

B **Pair work** Write the expressions and words in boldface from the article next to their meanings.

1. undercover _____
2. strengthened _____
3. hidden _____
4. sell _____
5. always online _____
6. widespread and invasive _____

C **Group work** Discuss these questions. Then share your answers with the class.

1. In your opinion, what were the most interesting findings of the experiment described in the article?

2. Do you agree that there's nothing quite as persuasive as seeing people we admire and respect using a brand or product? Why or why not?

3. How ethical do you think covert word-of-mouth marketing is? Does the experiment described in the article present any dilemmas or limitations? Explain.

1 STARTING POINT
Amazing animals

A Read about these three famous animals. Have you heard of any of them before? Which do you think is the most impressive?

Ruby

Ruby was one of many elephants that learned to paint at the Phoenix Zoo. Wherever there are elephants painting, people are fascinated. Ruby was even more intriguing because she chose her own colors when she painted. Her works raised about $500,000 for the zoo.

Bart the Bear

Bart the Bear was a nine-foot Alaskan Kodiak bear. When he was a cub, he was raised by humans and trained to act in films. Whenever actors worked with him, they were always impressed. He worked with stars such as Brad Pitt and Steven Seagal.

Alex

Alex's name is usually mentioned whenever experts talk about language use by animals. It is claimed that this African grey parrot could categorize about 150 words, count numbers, and distinguish colors and shapes. He showed some of his skills on several nature shows on TV.

B Pair work Discuss these questions and share your ideas with the class.

1. Do you think animals should be trained for entertainment? Is it ethical?
2. What other interesting talents or skills do animals have?

"I think it's OK to train animals as performers, provided they don't suffer in any way when trained."

2 LISTENING
Helping hands

A Listen to these news reports on animals that help people. What kinds of people does each animal help?

B Listen again. How does each animal help the people? Write *M* for monkey, *D* for dog, or *NG* for information not given.

____ 1. fetching objects

____ 2. picking things up off the floor

____ 3. helping them to cross streets

____ 4. taking them places

____ 5. doing tricks to make them laugh

____ 6. sparking memories of pets

____ 7. giving them something to take care of

____ 8. scratching an itchy nose

____ 9. giving them something to look forward to

GRAMMAR

Whenever and *wherever* contrasted with *when* and *where*

Whenever and *wherever* mean "at any time" and "in any place." They are used to introduce adverbial clauses. Notice their position in the sentences.

Whenever experts talk about language use by animals, Alex's name is usually mentioned.
Alex's name is usually mentioned **whenever experts talk about language use by animals**.
Wherever there are elephants painting, people are fascinated.
People are fascinated **wherever there are elephants painting**.

When and *where* can replace *whenever* and *wherever* when they have the sense of "at any time" or "in any place."
Whenever / When actors worked with Bart the Bear, they were always impressed.
Wherever / Where there are elephants painting, people are fascinated.

Whenever and *wherever* cannot be used if the sentence refers to a specific time or location. In these cases, *when* and *where* are used.
Whenever actors worked with him, they were always impressed. *(any time)*
When Brad Pitt worked with Bart in *Legends of the Fall*, he was very impressed. *(specific time)*
Wherever there are elephants painting, people are fascinated. *(any place)*
There were a lot of people **where** the elephants were painting today. *(specific place)*

GRAMMAR PLUS *see page 122*

A Look at the Starting Point on page 70 again. In which sentences can *whenever* and *wherever* be used interchangeably with *when* and *where*?

B Complete the sentences with *whenever* or *wherever*. If the time or place is specific, use *when* or *where*.

1. Large animals, like tigers and bears, need to be trained _____ they are still very young.

2. Though large, trained elephants are obedient. They will usually go _____ they are led.

3. _____ someone has an unusual pet, serious problems can arise.

4. _____ you see a cat flatten its ears, you should assume it's upset.

5. _____ my sister and her family live now, tenants aren't allowed to have pets.

6. _____ a messenger pigeon is taken somewhere and released, it almost always find its way home.

C Match the clauses on the left with clauses on the right. Make logical sentences using *when*, *whenever*, *where*, or *wherever*.

1. We were very startled last night __*c*__
2. Parrots become very sad ____
3. The sheep population grows quickly ____
4. A guide dog always stops ____
5. Police officers ride horses ____
6. Our helper monkey wakes us up ____

a. the traffic light is red.
b. cars can't conveniently go.
c. a bat flew into the window.
d. there is plenty of grass to eat.
e. the sun comes up in the morning.
f. they are separated from their owners.

We were very startled last night when a bat flew into the window.

VOCABULARY
Physical features of animals

A Pair work Look at this list of animal features. Which type(s) of animal do they belong to? Write them in the correct column(s) in the chart.

| beaks | fangs | fins | gills | horns | scales | tusks |
| claws | feathers | fur | hooves | paws | tails | wings |

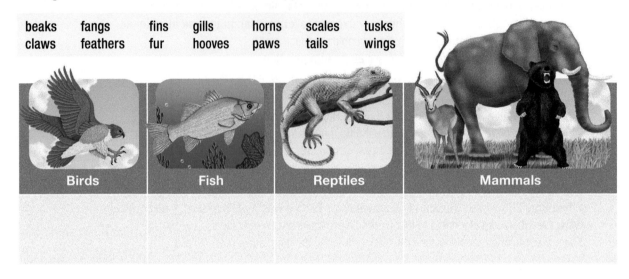

| Birds | Fish | Reptiles | Mammals |

B Pair work Which animal features in part A do people make use of? Which animals do they come from, and what are the uses?

"Feathers are used in various ways. For example, many pillows are stuffed with duck or goose feathers."

VOCABULARY PLUS *see page 138*

DISCUSSION
Is it right to do that?

A Look at these ways humans use animals. How acceptable do you think they are? Add one idea of your own, and complete the chart.

ANIMAL ETHICS	I'm against it.	It depends.	I'm OK with it.
1. using ivory from elephant tusks in jewelry	☐	☐	☐
2. using rhinoceros horns for medicines	☐	☐	☐
3. using animals for medical research	☐	☐	☐
4. wearing animal fur and leather	☐	☐	☐
5. serving wild animal meat in restaurants	☐	☐	☐
6. using animals to test cosmetics	☐	☐	☐
7. training animals to perform in circuses	☐	☐	☐
8. _____	☐	☐	☐

B Group work Share your answers with the group, and explain your reasons. Who in your group seems to be the most "animal-friendly"?

"For me, using ivory from elephant tusks in jewelry depends on whether or not the ivory was taken from elephants that were killed illegally."

A classification essay organizes information into categories. The first paragraph introduces the overall topic of the essay, includes a thesis statement, and gives an overview of the categories the writer will focus on. Each subsequent paragraph provides detailed information about one of the categories. A conclusion gives an additional perspective on the overall topic.

A Read this classification essay. What special kind of dog is the main topic of the essay? What three categories of this type of dog does the writer provide more information about?

Although most dogs offer their owners little more than companionship, assistance dogs are specially trained to assist people with disabilities or special needs. These dogs devote themselves to helping their owners live more independent lives. There are several types of assistance dogs, but the most common are guide dogs, hearing dogs, and service dogs.

Guide dogs help blind or visually impaired people get around their homes and communities. Most guide dogs are large breeds like Labrador retrievers and German shepherds, which wear a harness with a U-shaped handle to allow the dog and its human partner to communicate. The owner gives directional commands, and the dog's role is to ensure the human's safety, even if it means disobeying an unsafe command.

Hearing dogs alert a person who is deaf or hearing-impaired to sounds like doorbells, a baby's cries, and smoke alarms. They're trained to make physical contact and lead their owner to the source of the sound. Hearing dogs may be any size or breed, but they tend to be small to medium-sized mixed breeds because they are rescued from shelters. Hearing dogs can all be identified by their orange collar and vest.

Service dogs usually assist people who are confined to a wheelchair. The dogs are trained to pick up dropped objects, open and close doors, help in getting a person into or out of a wheelchair, and find help when needed. Because many of these tasks require strength, most service dogs are large breeds such as golden or Labrador retrievers. These dogs usually wear a backpack, harness, or vest.

Guide dogs, hearing dogs, and service dogs have one thing in common, however. Before being matched with a human partner, each type of assistance dog undergoes a one- to two-year training program. Once the dog and owner are matched, they begin to form a bond of trust with each other and often become an inseparable team.

B Choose one of these topics or one of your own. Brainstorm ways to classify your topic into at least three categories, and make a list of ideas for each.

- types of cats
- types of pets
- types of pet owners
- people who work with animals

C Write a classification essay that includes an introduction, three or more paragraphs – each one about a different category – and a conclusion.

D **Pair work** Read your partner's essay. Is the thesis statement clear? Are the categories distinct? Is each category described adequately? What other information would you want to have included?

1 STARTING POINT
Careers in nature

A Read the job postings on this website. Do you know anyone who has one of these jobs? What else do you know about the jobs?

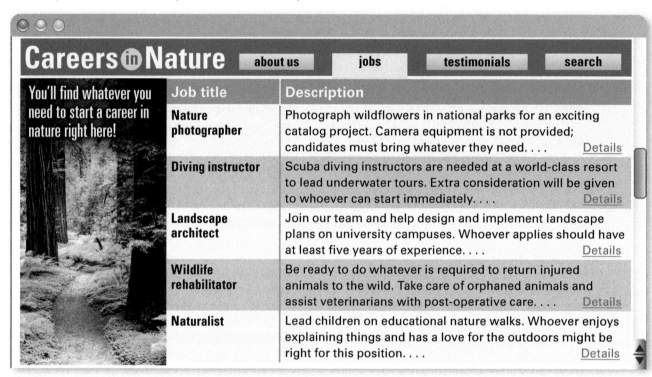

	Job title	Description
Careers in Nature		
about us / jobs / testimonials / search		
You'll find whatever you need to start a career in nature right here!	**Nature photographer**	Photograph wildflowers in national parks for an exciting catalog project. Camera equipment is not provided; candidates must bring whatever they need. . . . Details
	Diving instructor	Scuba diving instructors are needed at a world-class resort to lead underwater tours. Extra consideration will be given to whoever can start immediately. . . . Details
	Landscape architect	Join our team and help design and implement landscape plans on university campuses. Whoever applies should have at least five years of experience. . . . Details
	Wildlife rehabilitator	Be ready to do whatever is required to return injured animals to the wild. Take care of orphaned animals and assist veterinarians with post-operative care. . . . Details
	Naturalist	Lead children on educational nature walks. Whoever enjoys explaining things and has a love for the outdoors might be right for this position. . . . Details

B Pair work Choose one of the jobs on the website or another nature-related job you might be interested in trying. Tell your partner what interests you about it.

2 LISTENING
An eco-resort

A Listen to a conversation with the manager of an eco-resort. Who is the manager speaking with? Choose the correct answer.

☐ a guest ☐ a job applicant ☐ a journalist ☐ a nature guide

B Listen again. What is special about these features of the eco-resort? Complete the chart.

Eco-resort feature	Reasons it is special
1. Resort design	
2. Nature guides	
3. Spa	
4. Zip lines	

C Pair work If you were designing an eco-resort, which of the features in part B would you include in your resort? Why? What other features would you include?

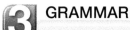

3 GRAMMAR

Noun clauses with *whoever* and *whatever*

Whoever and *whatever* can begin noun clauses and function as either the subject or object of the clause.

Whoever = the person who / anyone who / everyone who
Whoever applies should have at least five years of experience.
Extra consideration will be given to **whoever** can start immediately.

Whatever = anything that / everything that
Be ready to do **whatever** is required to return injured animals to the wild.
You'll find **whatever** you need to start a career in nature right here!

GRAMMAR PLUS *see page 123*

A Look at the Starting Point on page 74 again. In which sentences are *whoever* or *whatever* used as the subject of a clause? In which are they the object of a clause?

B Complete the sentences with *whoever* or *whatever*. Then compare your answers with a partner.

1. Here's a warning to _____ is thinking about becoming a beekeeper: You *will* be stung!

2. The birds on that island are curious about people and approach _____ they see coming.

3. Nature photographers take pictures of landscapes and _____ they see in the wild.

4. It's a forest ranger's duty to immediately report _____ looks like smoke or fire.

5. _____ took this photo of Mount Everest is a talented nature photographer.

6. I'm sure a relaxing trip to the mountains will take your mind off _____ is bothering you.

7. Visitors must follow the rules and are not allowed to do _____ they want in nature reserves.

8. Wildflowers are protected by law in many places; _____ picks them is subject to a fine.

C Group work Complete the statements with your own ideas. Compare and discuss your ideas with your group.

1. Whoever has a strong desire to help animals . . .
   should consider volunteering some of their time at a wildlife center.
2. Whatever humans really need is provided by nature. For example, people can get . . .
3. Hiking is a great pastime for whoever . . .
4. It's a bad idea to feed a pet whatever it wants. Instead, . . .
5. Whoever is planning an excursion in nature . . .

4 VOCABULARY
Nature-related idioms

A Match the idioms in boldface with their meanings.

1. Her ideas are **a breath of fresh air** among so many outdated ones. __*e*__
2. Our contribution to the wildlife fund was just **a drop in the ocean**, but even small donations help. ____
3. His report on the wildfire is **as clear as mud**. I can't understand it. ____
4. This project is **a walk in the park**. The other one was so complex. ____
5. These are just initial ideas for the campaign. Nothing is **set in stone**. ____
6. This is just **the tip of the iceberg**. Things are much worse than that. ____
7. My son is **under the weather** today, so he can't go on the field trip. ____
8. The plans are still **up in the air**. Nothing has been decided yet. ____

a. easy
b. confusing; unclear
c. unchangeable
d. not feeling well
e. new, different, exciting
f. less/fewer than needed
g. undecided; uncertain
h. a small perceptible part of a much bigger problem

B **Pair work** Use the idioms to talk to your partner about nature-related issues.

"The new plan of turning that run-down area of the city into a park is a breath of fresh air. The previous plans were not very interesting."

VOCABULARY PLUS *see page 138*

5 DISCUSSION
The importance of nature

A How in touch with nature are you? Complete the survey to find out.

Are You in Touch with Nature?	Agree	⟷	Disagree
1. Human beings are a part of nature, and therefore must interact frequently with nature to be healthy.	2	1	0
2. It's important to work or study in a space with indoor plants and large windows that let in sunlight.	2	1	0
3. Everyone needs at least one hobby, such as horseback riding or gardening, to keep in touch with nature.	2	1	0
4. When it comes to clothing and body care, it's best to wear natural fibers and use natural soaps and shampoos.	2	1	0
5. When I'm under the weather, I prefer to use all-natural treatments instead of synthetic drugs.	2	1	0
6. I would have been happier living in harmony with nature in a time before industry and technology.	2	1	0
7. Given a choice, I'd buy free-range poultry and meat products. I'd also buy wild fish instead of farmed varieties.	2	1	0
8. I recycle everything I can. Although my efforts might be just a drop in the ocean, I think I'm helping to preserve our natural resources.	2	1	0

SCORE

0–4 Like much of modern society, you may be out of touch with the natural world.

5–8 While nature isn't a priority for you, you do appreciate it when you experience it.

9–12 You see nature as an important part of your life and necessary for your well-being.

13–16 You're a nature lover who needs to be in constant contact with the natural world.

B **Group work** Discuss your answers to the survey. Talk about the reasons for your choices and whether or not you agree with your score.

A **Pair work** What are some of the daily tasks a park ranger might have to do in a city park? Discuss with a partner. Then read the article.

A SUMMER JOB that's a walk in the park

Every summer, curious creatures infiltrate New York City's biggest parks. They number in the dozens, walk on their hind legs, are khaki in color, and exceedingly amiable by nature. Their most distinguished markings are their wide-brimmed Smokey Bear hats.

They are Urban Park Ranger fellows, possessors of what may be the best, if not the most unusual, summer jobs in New York. "It's pretty laid back – kind of therapeutic," said Mohammed Alomeri, 22, who is from Midwood, Brooklyn, and works as a summer ranger at Fort Greene Park. "Every day, literally, is a walk in the park."

The summer fellows supplement the corps of year-round Urban Park Rangers – who also wear the Smokey Bear hats, but also carry nightsticks and can issue summonses – during the parks' busiest season. ...

Daily tasks can include, but are not limited to, giving nature walks, history talks, and children's craft classes; guiding people who have gotten lost; asking people to leash their dogs; getting outdoor chefs to move their barbecue grills away from trees; talking about why feeding chicken nuggets to birds is unhealthy; explaining that, yes, they are rangers, just like the ones in national parks; and posing for tourists' cameras. ...

Rangers field hundreds of calls from park visitors who are concerned about the behavior of wildlife, often when the animals in question are behaving naturally. They get reports from people who are unnerved by the sight of raccoons, or who mistakenly assume that pigeons sunning themselves have broken wings, or who grow vexed whenever an animal wanders onto a jogging path. The sight of hawks hunting smaller birds will invariably yield dozens of concerned calls.

"They call and say, 'You gotta get in there and get that pigeon out,'" said Richard Simon, who is citywide ranger captain and oversees the fellowship program. "That's when we explain, 'This is the food chain.'" ...

The rangers also get reports about animals that truly are hurt or in the wrong place. They are handed injured baby birds, alerted to exotic animals that have been dumped by their owners, or led to stunned squirrels that have fallen from trees. "They fall out of trees all the time," said Kathy Vasquez, a full-time, year-round ranger. "They usually land on their feet, but sometimes not so much." ...

The summer rangers program ends on Saturday, which means a return to a life indoors for most of the five dozen fellows. Mr. Alomeri, however, plans to apply for a position as a full-time ranger. He has only one semester left at Brooklyn College, where he is studying physics, and wants to put off graduate school. He has fallen in love with being a ranger, and delights at the way he can now identify trees and birds. ...

Source: "A Summer Job That Promises Nature Walks for Pay," by Cara Buckley, *The New York Times* (The ellipses indicate passages omitted from the original article.)

B **Pair work** Find the words in the article that match the meanings below.

1. friendly (paragraph 1) _____
2. healing (paragraph 2) _____
3. respond to (paragraph 5) _____
4. agitated (paragraph 5) _____
5. lead to (paragraph 5) _____
6. abandoned (paragraph 7) _____

C **Group work** Discuss these questions. Then share your answers with the class.

1. How do the Urban Park Ranger fellows help park visitors connect with nature?
2. What evidence from the article might lead you to assume that many park visitors are not familiar with nature? Is the same true about city dwellers where you're from? Explain.
3. Do you agree that being an Urban Park Ranger fellow would be laid back and therapeutic? Why?

COMMUNICATION REVIEW

SELF-ASSESSMENT

How well can you do these things? Choose the best answer.

I can . . .	Very well	OK	A little
▶ Take part in a discussion about recent trends and life choices (Ex. 1)	☐	☐	☐
▶ Take part in a decision-making discussion about marketing a new product or service (Ex. 2)	☐	☐	☐
▶ Give a persuasive presentation about a new product or service (Ex. 2)	☐	☐	☐
▶ Take part in a discussion about animals as pets (Ex. 3)	☐	☐	☐
▶ Understand an interview about animal caretaking (Ex. 4)	☐	☐	☐

Now do the corresponding exercises. Was your assessment correct?

1 DISCUSSION

Trends and attitudes

A **Pair work** Read what these people have to say about some trends. Who do you agree with the most, and who do you agree with the least? Discuss your ideas with a partner, and give reasons for them.

CARLOS

"I think it's great that so many companies allow employees to telecommute. It's illogical, even irresponsible, for companies to require employees who don't live nearby to come in to work every day."

HUI LIN

"Something that worries me is the way people risk their health by experimenting with alternative medicines and therapies that haven't been properly tested. No one really knows how safe they are."

STEPHANIE

"I'm hoping attitudes toward consumption – like constantly buying new clothes – are changing. Celebrities like actors, musicians, and athletes, whom young people look up to, need to set the right example and help bring about change."

"I disagree with Hui Lin. I don't think alternative medicines are dangerous. Many of them are traditional medicines that have been used for years. However, I agree with . . ."

B **Group work** Discuss how you feel about these life choices. Then share your answers with the class.

- adult children returning home to live with their parents
- people choosing to get married at a later age
- people socializing more online than they do in person
- senior citizens going back to school to earn degrees
- people choosing to spend more of their free time doing volunteer work

2 DISCUSSION
New products and marketing plans

A Group work Think of a new product or service you think would be successful. What is it? Who is it for? How does it work? What's the best way to advertise and promote it?

"Well, I'm thinking about a concierge service for people who are new in town. The concierge could provide the same services as a concierge in a hotel."

"I suggest we offer information and advice to help them cope with all the changes."

"Good idea. I recommend we advertise on the town's website. . . ."

B Class activity Present your product or service and marketing plans to the class. Which group has the best ideas?

3 SPEAKING
Suitable pets?

A Would you consider having any of these animals as pets? Why or why not?

tropical fish

boa constrictor

chimpanzee

B Pair work Compare your ideas with a partner. Explain your reasons.

"I really love tropical fish. Whenever I get the chance, I go snorkeling. I wouldn't have them as pets, though. I would rather see them in the ocean than in an aquarium."

4 LISTENING
Bird talk

 A Listen to an interview with a parrot expert. She mentions three things that are important for a person to have before getting an African grey parrot. Choose the three basic requirements she mentions.

☐ a. time   ☐ c. space   ☐ e. children
☐ b. videos   ☐ d. interest in parrots   ☐ f. other birds

 B Listen again. Are these statements true or false? Choose the correct answer.

	True	False
1. It is illegal to import wild African grey parrots.	☐	☐
2. Parrots cause asthma.	☐	☐
3. Parrots are intelligent and unpredictable.	☐	☐
4. Parrots need some time outside of their cage each day.	☐	☐
5. Research has been done on African grey parrots talking.	☐	☐
6. Parrots can eat all fruits and vegetables.	☐	☐

1 STARTING POINT
Effective communicators

A Read about these effective communicators. What else do you know about them?

Steve Jobs, the former CEO of Apple, is remembered for his contributions to communications technologies, such as smartphones and music players. Many of his design innovations are still being imitated by competitors. Jobs will also be remembered as an inspiring public speaker, as when he told Stanford University graduates: "Your time is limited, so don't waste it living someone else's life." Business presentations have been forever transformed by his simple but engaging style.

No one should have been surprised when **Nelson Mandela** was awarded the Nobel Peace Prize in 1993. Even while in prison for 27 years, his fight to end apartheid in South Africa was being kept alive by activists around the world. Mandela is always going to be remembered for his great speeches and eloquent quotations, such as, "Education is the most powerful weapon which you can use to change the world." In 2005, for his contribution to international understanding, he was designated Goodwill Ambassador by UNESCO.

B Pair work Who are some effective communicators you know? What qualities make them effective?

2 DISCUSSION
Fear of public speaking

A Studies have shown that public speaking is many people's biggest fear. Do you share this fear? Complete the survey. Add a statement of your own.

Are you **AFRAID** to talk?	Always true	Sometimes true	Never true
1 I can't sleep the night before a presentation.	☐	☐	☐
2 I rarely participate in discussions at work or in class.	☐	☐	☐
3 I avoid situations in which I might have to give an impromptu speech.	☐	☐	☐
4 When talking to others, I find it hard to look people in the eye.	☐	☐	☐
5 I can speak only from a prepared speech.	☐	☐	☐
6 I am intimidated by job interviews.	☐	☐	☐
7 I'd rather go to the dentist, pay taxes, or clean closets than give a presentation.	☐	☐	☐
8 _____	☐	☐	☐

Source: Schaum's Quick Guide to Great Presentation Skills

B Pair work Compare and explain your answers using examples from your life whenever possible. What do you have in common? How are you different?

GRAMMAR

Overview of passives

Passive sentences focus on the receiver of the action by making it the subject of the sentence. The agent that performs the action can be omitted or follow *by* after the verb.

Passive = subject + form of *be* + past participle (+ *by* + agent)

Simple present: Steve Jobs **is remembered** for his contributions to communications technologies.

Present continuous: Many of his design innovations **are** still **being imitated** (by competitors).

Present perfect: Business presentations **have been** forever **transformed** by his simple but engaging style.

Simple past: Nelson Mandela **was awarded** the Nobel Peace Prize in 1993.

Past continuous: Mandela's fight **was being kept** alive (by activists) around the world.

Future with *going to*: Mandela **is** always **going to be remembered** for his great speeches.

Modals: Jobs **will** also **be remembered** as an inspiring public speaker.

Past modals: No one **should have been surprised**.

GRAMMAR PLUS *see page 124*

A Look at the Starting Point on page 80 again. Can you find another example of the passive? What verb form is it in?

B Change these active sentences to the passive. Keep or omit the agent as appropriate.

1. The Internet has changed the way the world communicates.
   The way the world communicates has been changed by the Internet.

2. People should deliver presentations confidently and cheerfully.

3. Someone should have told the students to speak louder during their speeches.

4. Counselors are advising married couples to communicate more openly.

5. Long ago, people used smoke signals to send simple messages in China.

6. After the ceremony, the president is announcing the scholarship recipients.

7. Translators are going to translate the president's speech into 35 languages.

8. The principal was making an announcement when the microphone went dead.

C Complete these sentences with information about language that is true for you. Then add another sentence of your own using a passive verb form.

1. I've been told by many people that . . .
   my English sounds quite formal.

2. My classmates and I are encouraged to . . .

3. I hope that someday I will be complimented on . . .

4. Students should / shouldn't be forced to . . .

5. Languages should be taught . . .

6. I've been advised . . .

7. Not long ago, I was told that . . .

8. _____

4 VOCABULARY
Discourse markers

A Discourse markers are expressions that make communication flow more smoothly. Match each expression below with a function it serves. Sometimes more than one answer is possible.

a. to open a presentation   c. to add information   e. to introduce contrasts

b. to sequence information   d. to introduce similarities   f. to close a presentation

____ 1. in conclusion   ____ 5. nevertheless   ____ 9. likewise

____ 2. next   ____ 6. in addition   ____ 10. yet

____ 3. similarly   ____ 7. to sum up   ____ 11. first / second / third

____ 4. to begin   ____ 8. first of all   ____ 12. furthermore

B Pair work Complete each sentence with an expression from part A. Sometimes more than one answer is possible.

(1) _____, let me thank everyone for your interest and attention as I speak on the topic of petroleum dependency – our dependency on oil for our energy needs.

There are important reasons why we should be concerned about our dependency on petroleum. (2) _____, petroleum-based fuels contribute to both air pollution and global warming, two very serious problems today. (3) _____, there is a limited supply of oil in the world; therefore, we must reduce fuel consumption and be prepared to replace petroleum with other sources of energy.

There are many ways in which to do this on a large scale. First, we must produce fuel-efficient cars; (4) _____, we must encourage the use of public transportation. Finally, tax breaks could be offered to businesses that conserve fuel. (5) _____, homeowners could also be offered tax incentives for fuel conservation. It's true that cutting down on consumption is beneficial to the environment; (6) _____, we should keep in mind that cutting down too quickly could have a negative effect on the economy.

(7) _____, this problem has no simple answers, but if the government, corporations, and private citizens all work together, I feel we can solve the problem.

VOCABULARY PLUS see page 139

5 LISTENING
Getting your message across

🔊 **A** Listen to advice about speaking in public. Choose the items the speaker mentions.

	Advice			Advice
☐ the audience			☐ posture	
☐ the outline			☐ eye contact	
☐ pronunciation			☐ voice	
☐ practicing			☐ questions	
☐ humor			☐ speed	

🔊 **B** Listen again. Complete the chart with the advice you hear.

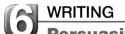

In persuasive writing, you take a position on an issue and try to convince the reader that your position is correct. To do so, you present both sides of the issue, providing arguments, reasons, and examples that support your point of view and show weaknesses of the opposing point of view.

A Read the article. What is the writer's position? What are the arguments for the opposing view? What arguments, reasons, and examples does the writer give to support his position and to show the weakness of the opposing viewpoint?

Every Student Should Be Required to Study a Foreign Language
by Leo Fernández

Recently, a student organization at our university proposed that we do away with our foreign language requirement, which mandates that all students complete two years of foreign language study. The main reason for this proposal seems to be to eliminate unnecessary courses; however, the proponents of this change are overlooking the great benefits foreign language study provides to students of any major.

Students who oppose the language requirement argue that university study should be more career focused. They feel that the language requirement steals time that could be spent on courses directly related to a student's major. This is a shortsighted position. Statistics suggest that candidates proficient in two languages have an increased chance of finding work. For example, . . .

Another point often made by the proponents of the change is that a large number of students who study a language for two years rarely use it again in their lives. While this may be true in some cases, study of a foreign language has been shown to further develop native language skills. In addition, the understanding of oneself and one's own culture is increased through contact with another language and its culture. Students who . . .

In conclusion, it is crucial that we keep the foreign language requirement. To eliminate it would be doing a great disservice to our university and its students. Foreign language learning benefits us in concrete and subtle ways as it broadens our minds and expands our opportunities.

B **Pair work** With a partner, take a position on one of these issues related to language, or use your own idea. Then brainstorm reasons supporting your position and weaknesses of the opposing view. Which reasons are the strongest?

- Schools should teach a second language starting in kindergarten.
- Every foreign language student should be required to study abroad.
- Institutions should be created to preserve dying languages.

C Write an article of at least four paragraphs supporting your position. Use the best reasons you have brainstormed to support your position. Make sure you argue against the opposing view.

D **Pair work** Exchange articles. Discuss ways the writing could be made more persuasive and the arguments stronger.

STARTING POINT

What's correct language?

A Read these statements about language. Choose the statements you agree with.

Proper English

- [ ] **1.** Most people don't need to write well. Speaking is more important.
- [ ] **2.** The majority of teenagers use too much slang.
- [ ] **3.** Three-quarters of email messages contain grammar errors.
- [ ] **4.** No one expects email to be correct.
- [ ] **5.** There are plenty of people with foreign accents who speak English well.
- [ ] **6.** None of us has the right to correct other people's grammar.
- [ ] **7.** All varieties of English are equally valid. Every variety is correct.
- [ ] **8.** A lot of advanced grammar is complicated even for native speakers.
- [ ] **9.** Only a minority of my friends cares about speaking correctly.

B **Pair work** Discuss your opinions with a partner.

"I disagree with the first sentence. A lot of people need to write well for their jobs."

 DISCUSSION

Text speak

A **Pair work** Read about "text speak." Then try to figure out what the six examples of text speak mean, and write the meanings. (For the answers, see page 142.)

"Text speak" refers to shortened forms of words commonly used in text messaging. When texting began, telephone companies would charge by the word, so fewer words and letters meant cheaper messages. These days, many people find text speak convenient and cool, and it is creeping into less informal types of writing. See some examples of text speak in the box.

b4	*before*
ruok?	_____
cul8r	_____
xlnt	_____
gr8	_____
2nite	_____

B **Group work** Read these opinions about text speak. Which one do you most agree with? Discuss your opinions about text speak with the group.

I try not to use text speak – except when I'm online or texting, of course – because it's annoying. I think people who use it in schoolwork and formal emails look idiotic and immature. — Raphael

I really feel old when my kids – and even my wife! – write to me using text speak. Nevertheless, I know that language always evolves. Just think of the difference between our English and Shakespeare's! — Rob

Txt spk is gr8! It's much easier and quicker, and u can use it for email, taking notes in class, and even in some homework assignments. — Wendy

People are free to use text speak if they think it's more convenient – after all, it's a free country. But I do hope it remains an alternative style, and that grammar is maintained. — Su-jin

3 GRAMMAR

Subject-verb agreement with quantifiers

All (of), *a lot of*, *lots of*, *plenty of*, *some (of)*, *most (of)*, and fractions take a singular verb if the noun they modify is uncountable or singular. They take a plural verb if the noun they modify is plural.
A lot of advanced **grammar is** complicated.
Most people don't need to write well.
Three-quarters of email **messages contain** grammar errors.

Each of, *every one of*, *none of*, and collective nouns, such as *majority (of)* and *minority (of)*, typically take a singular verb, but often take a plural verb after a plural noun in informal speech.
None of us has / have the right to correct other people's grammar.
The **majority of** teenagers **use / uses** too much slang.
A **minority of** my friends **care / cares** about speaking correctly.

Everyone, *someone*, *anyone*, *no one*, *each* + noun, and *every* + noun are followed by a singular verb.
Every variety **is** correct.
No one expects email to be correct.

GRAMMAR PLUS *see page 125*

A Look at the Starting Point on page 84 again. Can you find other quantifiers? Are they followed by a singular or plural verb?

B Complete these sentences with the correct form of the verb in parentheses. Use the simple present.

1. A lot of people _____*agree*_____ (agree) that spelling and grammar shouldn't change.
2. All of the students in my class _____ (attend) English club meetings.
3. Most of the faculty at school _____ (speak) at least three languages.
4. A quarter of my classmates _____ (be) going to study abroad next semester.
5. The majority of people _____ (use) text speak in their emails.
6. None of the information in the email _____ (be) correct.
7. Every letter I receive usually _____ (contain) one or two spelling mistakes.
8. Over four-fifths of the world population _____ (be) able to read and write.

C Group work Complete these sentences with information about how people use language in different situations. Then discuss your answers.

1. Lots of the slang people use these days . . .
2. The majority of people my age . . .
3. Some of the language older people use . . .
4. None of my friends . . .
5. Most of the news anchors you see on TV . . .
6. Every one of my teachers . . .

"Lots of the slang people use these days comes from words they hear in popular music."

"That's true. In hip-hop slang, 'crib' means home, and 'bling' means flashy jewelry."

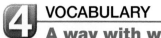

4 VOCABULARY
A way with words

A The expressions on the left can be used to comment on the way people speak.
Match them with their definitions on the right.

1. have a sharp tongue ____
2. have a way with words ____
3. stick to the point ____
4. talk around a point ____
5. talk behind someone's back ____
6. talk someone into something ____
7. talk someone's ear off ____
8. love to hear oneself talk ____

a. talk about something without addressing it directly
b. enjoy talking even if nobody is paying attention
c. talk about a person without him or her knowing
d. continue talking about a main idea
e. talk in a bitter, critical way
f. talk until the other person is tired of listening
g. convince a person to do something
h. have a talent for speaking

B Pair work Use expressions from above to comment on these people and the
way they are speaking.

1 | Klaus
"I wouldn't say I dislike the book, or at least I don't think so. I guess it's hard to say."

2 | Risa
"Why don't you want to go? Come on! It'll be fun, and it's cheap. I'll even drive!"

3 | Sandra
"Just be quiet! You don't know what you're talking about, so stop wasting my time!"

4 | Philip
"Diane got an F on her test. She tried to put it away quickly, but I saw it anyway!"

VOCABULARY PLUS *see page 139*

5 LISTENING & SPEAKING
Assert yourself!

A Listen to three one-sided conversations. Write the number of the conversation
next to the correct description.

____ a. One person is talking the other person's ear off.

____ b. One person is trying to talk the other person into doing something.

____ c. One person isn't sticking to the point.

B Listen again. Which expressions do you hear used in the conversations?
Write the number of the conversation next to the correct expression.

____ a. Could I say something?   ____ d. That's nice, but we really need to . . .

____ b. Thanks for asking, but . . .   ____ e. That's really nice of you, but . . .

____ c. I just wanted to say . . .   ____ f. Getting back to what we were talking about . . .

C Pair work Prepare a conversation similar to those from the listening. Use the
expressions in part B. Then perform the scene for the class.

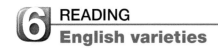

A **Pair work** Read the quote in the first line of the article. What do you think it means? Then read the article to compare your ideas to the author's.

SLANG Abroad

George Bernard Shaw said, "England and America are two countries separated by a common language." I never really understood the meaning of this quote until a friend and I stopped at a London convenience store. We had some trash to throw away, so I, in as polite a manner as I could muster, asked the clerk for a trash can. Then I asked him again, thinking he didn't hear me. And then I asked again, only this time while speaking the international language (loudly and slowly while pointing to the object I wanted to throw away). After this horribly rude display, he politely asked me what a trash can was. So I told him it was a place for my garbage. I guess this weak explanation worked. The clerk then produced a small trash can from behind the counter and in the most you-must-not-be-from-around-here tone he could muster said, "rubbish bin."

Different names for objects, however, are not the main problem. Anyone can learn a language. But to really be a speaker of the language, you need to understand its idioms and its slang. There is a distinct difference between someone who learned a language in a classroom and someone who is a native speaker. Using slang proves that the speaker has been in a country long enough to learn it, and that offers a benefit greater than just being able to converse on a casual level. It allows the two speakers to get much closer much more quickly.

Eventually, after living somewhere for a while you pick up a few things, and this new language education gives a credibility that just pronouncing a city address cannot. It shows a belonging and membership in the club of permanent residents and that one is not just a mere extended tourist. I know it sounds superficial, that by being able to understand words that may or may not be in a dictionary, we can fool people into thinking we belong, but it isn't. What knowing and using slang shows is a basic understanding of a culture. It offers both members of the conversation a common ground.

And that's the point. Britain and America are two countries separated by a common language, but then again so are Mexico and Spain, Brazil and Portugal, and France and Haiti. While these countries' languages may all seem the same on paper, they're not. Really learning the languages can only be done on the ground. And once that learning is done, something far greater is achieved than just not sounding like a fool.

Source: "Slang Abroad," by Ben Falk, *The Daily Colonial*

B Which of these statements would the author probably agree with? Compare and discuss your answers.

1. It's impossible for anyone learning a foreign language to ever sound like a native speaker.
2. Studying books about slang is an effective way to learn how it's used.
3. Despite how connected the world is, slang and idioms remain very local.
4. Really learning a language means knowing how people actually use it.

C **Group work** Discuss these questions. Then share your answers with the class.

1. Do you agree with the author's idea that one can only really learn a language by living in a country where it's spoken? Why or why not?
2. Have you or anyone you know ever had any experiences like the one in the first paragraph? What happened? Do you think such misunderstandings are common?

11 EXCEPTIONAL PEOPLE

LESSON A ▶ *High achievers*

1 STARTING POINT
They've had an impact!

A Read about the exceptional people below. Have you heard of any of them? What sort of impact have they had on other people?

MAHATMA GANDHI

(1869–1948) Gandhi was a great political and spiritual leader in India. Although he was educated in England, Gandhi is best remembered for his struggle for Indian independence, which had far-reaching effects. His epoch-making victories through peaceful means later inspired other great leaders, like Martin Luther King Jr. and Aung San Suu Kyi.

NATALIA VODIANOVA

(1982–) Born in Russia, this blue-eyed, brown-haired beauty was working at a fruit stand by age 11. At 17, she moved to Paris and soon after signed with a well-known modeling agency. She was well received and quickly became a popular fashion model. A kind-hearted superstar, she created the Naked Heart Foundation to build playgrounds for underprivileged children in Russia.

ANDRE AGASSI

(1970–) Andre Agassi's hard-driving father always planned to make him a tennis star. Intensely coached, he was practicing with pros by age five. During his career, Agassi won every important tournament at least once and earned over 100 million dollars. Now retired but socially engaged, he built a free school for youth in one of Las Vegas's poorest neighborhoods.

B Group work Think of people who have had an impact on the world. Discuss their achievements, and then choose the person who has had the biggest impact.

2 DISCUSSION
Exceptional values

A Group work Think about the people you talked about in the Starting Point. What values do you think were most important to each of them? Why?

"I think Gandhi valued patience. He had patience with people and patience to achieve his goal through nonviolent measures."

B Look at this list of life values. Choose the three that are the most important in your life. If your top values aren't here, add them to the list.

☐ achievement	☐ environmentalism	☐ spirituality
☐ compassion	☐ health	☐ wealth
☐ cooperation	☐ independence	☐ _____
☐ creativity	☐ responsibility	☐ _____

C Group work Explain your choices to the members of your group. Then make a list of the three life values that are the most important to your group as a whole.

GRAMMAR
Compound adjectives

Compound adjectives are modifying phrases made up of two or more words. They can be joined by a hyphen, appear as a single word, or appear as two separate words. Always check a dictionary before using compound adjectives in writing.

Three common patterns for compound adjectives in English are:

a. adjective + noun + *-ed* *(absent-minded, high-spirited, long-winded, soft-hearted)*
When preceding a noun, these compounds are usually written with a hyphen unless they are one word.

b. adverb + past participle *(much-loved, well-dressed, highly acclaimed, widely respected)*
Compounds with adverbs ending in *-ly* are never hyphenated.
Other adverbs are usually hyphenated before but not after the noun.

c. adjective, adverb, or noun + present participle *(easygoing, forward-thinking, thought-provoking)*
When preceding a noun, these compounds are usually written with a hyphen unless they are one word.

GRAMMAR PLUS *see page 126*

A Look at the Starting Point on page 88 again. Can you find more compound adjectives? Which patterns from the grammar box do they follow?

B Rewrite these sentences using the compound adjectives from the Starting Point to replace the words in boldface. Sometimes more than one answer is possible.

1. Roger Federer is an athlete **everybody knows**.
   Roger Federer is a well-known athlete.

2. The play was **praised** by most theater critics.

3. Many charities are set up to help children **who are poor**.

4. The **very generous** celebrity gave money to the homeless.

5. The work of Gandhi had effects **that reached around the world**.

6. The child **with blue eyes** was adopted by a celebrity.

VOCABULARY
Compound adjectives related to the body

A Combine the words from both boxes to create compound adjectives and match them with their synonyms below. Sometimes more than one answer is possible.

absent	cool	hard	narrow	soft	blooded	hearted
cold	empty	hot	open	warm	headed	minded

1. silly and brainless   *empty-headed*
2. quick to anger _____
3. uncaring or unkind _____
4. sweet and loving _____
5. stubborn and unyielding _____
6. tolerant and unbiased _____
7. intolerant and disapproving _____
8. forgetful _____
9. calm and unexcitable _____
10. friendly and kind _____

B **Pair work** Use the compound adjectives in part A and others you can create to describe exceptional people or characters from movies, television, or books.

"Sherlock Holmes is an open-minded detective who uses his powers of observation to catch cold-blooded killers."

VOCABULARY PLUS *see page 140*

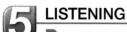

5 LISTENING
Do you want to be a high achiever?

A Listen to a speaker talk about the qualities of high achievers. Choose the four qualities he talks about.

	Suggestion		Suggestion
☐ lifelong learning		☐ positive attitude	
☐ high self-esteem		☐ risk-taking	
☐ responsibility		☐ creativity	

B Listen again. What does the speaker suggest people do in order to build the four qualities of high achievers? Write the suggestions in the chart.

6 DISCUSSION
Winning words

A **Pair work** Read these quotations from high achievers. Can you restate these quotations in your own words?

a

Mark Zuckerberg
entrepreneur
"The biggest risk is not taking any risk."

d

Andrea Jung
businesswoman
"If you feel like it's difficult to change, you will probably have a harder time succeeding."

b

Gloria Estefan
singer
"You don't have to give up who you are to be successful just because you're different."

e

Laird Hamilton
surfer and model
"Make sure your worst enemy doesn't live between your own two ears."

c

Donald Trump
businessman and TV personality
"If you're going to be thinking anyway, you might as well think big!"

Useful expressions

Describing what something means
What this means to me is that . . .
My understanding of this is that . . .
I interpret this to mean . . .

B **Group work** Which of the quotations in part A might be useful for the following kinds of people? Do you know any other sayings or quotations that might be helpful?

1. someone who wants to get rich in business
2. someone who wants success but worries about how much work or time it will take
3. someone who wants to study abroad but is afraid of not fitting in somewhere new
4. someone who is only working part-time and putting off starting a real career
5. someone who is hesitant to register for a class because of self-doubt

> A biographical profile usually begins with an introduction that includes a thesis statement about what makes the person interesting or special. The subsequent paragraphs are then usually arranged in chronological order.

A The paragraphs in this biographical profile about J. K. Rowling have been scrambled. Read the composition and put the paragraphs in order.

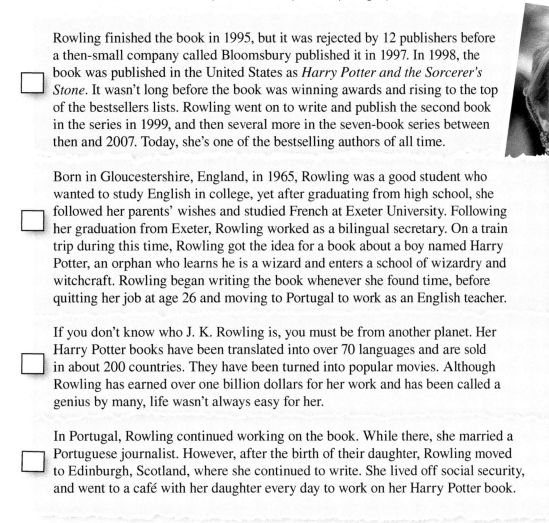

☐ Rowling finished the book in 1995, but it was rejected by 12 publishers before a then-small company called Bloomsbury published it in 1997. In 1998, the book was published in the United States as *Harry Potter and the Sorcerer's Stone*. It wasn't long before the book was winning awards and rising to the top of the bestsellers lists. Rowling went on to write and publish the second book in the series in 1999, and then several more in the seven-book series between then and 2007. Today, she's one of the bestselling authors of all time.

☐ Born in Gloucestershire, England, in 1965, Rowling was a good student who wanted to study English in college, yet after graduating from high school, she followed her parents' wishes and studied French at Exeter University. Following her graduation from Exeter, Rowling worked as a bilingual secretary. On a train trip during this time, Rowling got the idea for a book about a boy named Harry Potter, an orphan who learns he is a wizard and enters a school of wizardry and witchcraft. Rowling began writing the book whenever she found time, before quitting her job at age 26 and moving to Portugal to work as an English teacher.

☐ If you don't know who J. K. Rowling is, you must be from another planet. Her Harry Potter books have been translated into over 70 languages and are sold in about 200 countries. They have been turned into popular movies. Although Rowling has earned over one billion dollars for her work and has been called a genius by many, life wasn't always easy for her.

☐ In Portugal, Rowling continued working on the book. While there, she married a Portuguese journalist. However, after the birth of their daughter, Rowling moved to Edinburgh, Scotland, where she continued to write. She lived off social security, and went to a café with her daughter every day to work on her Harry Potter book.

B Choose a famous person you know a lot about. Make notes and list key events from this person's life in chronological order. Then use your notes to write a biographical profile.

C **Pair work** Exchange profiles with a partner, and answer these questions.

1. Does your partner's profile begin with an introduction and include a thesis statement?
2. Is the information in the profile arranged in chronological order?
3. Can you suggest any improvements to make the profile more interesting or effective?
4. What else would you like to know about the person your partner wrote about?

LESSON B ▶ *People we admire*

1 STARTING POINT
Role models

A Read these online posts about role models. What life values are reflected in each post?

YOUR SPACE TO SHARE FEELINGS AND IDEAS

Up for Discussion: **Tell us about the people you respect and admire.** + new post

 RobertD They may not be the smartest or the best-looking people in the world, but I'd say my friends are the people I most admire. We stick together and watch out for each other – and learn a lot from each other, too.

 Alena92 I've always looked up to my father. He's the hardest-working and the least narrow-minded man I know. He's always taught me that hard work is the surest way to be successful.

 OwnDrummer I'm not sure I have a role model. I mostly like to do my own thing. I think it's because I'm not the most easily impressed person when I meet someone new, and I'm pretty slow to trust people.

 Sporty_girl One person I really respect is my soccer coach. He's a tough competitor, and he's the best-trained soccer player I know. He's also one of the most warm-hearted.

 Thoughtful2 My philosophy professor is my role model, definitely. Her class is the most thought-provoking one I've ever attended. Someday, I'd like to be as well respected as she is.

 Amber334 I've always wanted to be more like my sister Tonya. While I tend to worry a lot, Tonya is the most easygoing person in our family. She never lets little problems bother her.

B Pair work Tell your partner about someone you consider a role model. Explain why you respect and admire that person. Your partner will then tell the class about the person.

"Bruno has an enormous amount of respect for his grandfather. He started his own business when he was 18 years old . . ."

2 LISTENING
People who make a difference

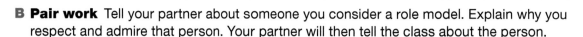 **A** Listen to Luisa talk about her grandmother and Chu Lan talk about his tennis coach. How do Luisa and Chu Lan feel about the people they are describing?

B Listen again. In what ways did these people influence Luisa and Chu Lan? Write two ways for each.

	How did Luisa's grandmother influence her?	How did Chu Lan's coach influence him?
1.		
2.		

GRAMMAR

Superlative compound adjectives

Superlative compound adjectives generally follow the same hyphenation rules as compound adjectives.

The superlative form of compound adjectives is most often formed by adding *the most* and *the least*. There is never a hyphen after *most* or *least*.
I'm not **the most easily impressed** person.
Tonya is **the most easygoing** person in our family.
He's **the least narrow-minded** man I know.

When the first word of a compound adjective is an adjective or adverb of one or sometimes two syllables, the superlative can also be formed by adding *the* and using the superlative form of the first word.
He is **the hardest-working** man I know.
They may not be the smartest or **the best-looking** people in the world.

Compound adjectives in their superlative form can also occur after the verb *be* without a noun.
Of all the men I know, he's **the hardest working**.

GRAMMAR PLUS *see page 127*

A Look at the Starting Point on page 92 again. How many superlative compound adjectives can you find?

B Rewrite these phrases using the superlative form of the compound adjective.

1. an awe-inspiring place
   the most awe-inspiring place
2. a widely read book
3. a good-looking man
4. a thirst-quenching beverage
5. a highly developed mind
6. a warm-hearted friend
7. a far-reaching plan
8. a thought-provoking novel
9. a well-defined project
10. a bad-intentioned person

C Complete these sentences with the superlative compound adjectives you wrote in part B and your own ideas. Share your answers with a partner.

1. . . . natural place I've ever been to is . . .
   The most awe-inspiring natural place I've ever been to is the Grand Canyon.
2. . . . magazine in the country is probably . . .
3. In my opinion, . . . actor / actress in the world is . . .
4. On a hot day, . . . drink is . . .
5. . . . movie I've ever seen is . . .
6. . . . person I know is . . .
7. . . . leader my country has ever had is / was . . .

4 VOCABULARY
Phrasal verbs

A Read the sentences below. Then match the phrasal verbs in boldface with their definitions.

a. take care of
b. defend or support
c. go see if someone is all right
d. rely on

e. confront
f. overcome
g. resemble (an older relative) in looks or character
h. achieve what is expected

____ 1. It's only natural for children to **look to** their parents for advice.

____ 2. Sometimes we need to **get through** difficulties in order to succeed.

____ 3. Before parents go to bed, they should **check on** their kids and see if they're OK.

____ 4. I expect my children to **look after** me when I reach old age.

____ 5. Parents need to teach their children to **face up to** their problems and solve them.

____ 6. When I argue with my sister, it seems like my parents **side with** her.

____ 7. The children of accomplished parents often find it difficult to **live up to** the high expectations people have for them.

____ 8. When it comes to finances, I **take after** my dad; he could never save money either.

B Pair work Discuss the sentences in part A with a partner. Comment on the statements, and talk about how they apply to your life.

"I find that the older I get, the more I look to my parents for advice."

VOCABULARY PLUS see page 140

5 DISCUSSION
Everyday heroism

A Pair work Read what Farah says about heroic behavior. What is her definition of a hero? Do you agree with the definition? Do you have other examples?

To me, heroes often aren't the most widely recognized people, and on the surface, their actions don't necessarily seem to be the most awe inspiring. A hero could be a parent who, after an exhausting day, helps a child with a difficult homework assignment. It could be a person on the street who picks up and returns something you didn't realize you'd dropped, someone who stops by to check on you when you're ill, someone who sides with you when you've been wronged, or someone who takes time out of a busy schedule to help you with a problem. A hero is not just a person who has the courage to take a risk; he or she is also a person who has the courage to always be kind to people no matter what they're going through.

Farah, 26

B Group work Discuss these situations. What would you do to make a difference?

a	b	c	d
Your next-door neighbor fell and broke her leg. She lives by herself.	The condition of your neighborhood park has deteriorated, and fewer and fewer people are using it.	Children in a nearby low-income neighborhood seem to have few opportunities for academic success.	A friend of yours has lost his or her job and can't seem to find another one.

"I would check on my neighbor from time to time and help her with some of her daily chores."

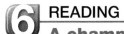

A champion for women in Africa

A Pair work Do you know any nongovernmental organizations (NGOs)? Discuss some of the ways they are making a change. Then read the article.

ANN COTTON,
SOCIAL ENTREPRENEUR }

The following is an interview with Ann Cotton, founder and chief executive of the Campaign for Female Education (Camfed), an NGO whose programs invest in the education of girls and young women and have benefited over two million children in the poorest areas of Africa.

How do you define a social entrepreneur? Someone who witnesses the pain and struggle in the lives of others and is compelled to act and to work with them.

What skills are needed to be a social entrepreneur? You need to be absolutely dogged. You need to listen to the people experiencing the problems, and their ideas need to crowd out the words of the "can't be done-ers."

How did your work as a former teacher and head of children's assessment help in setting up Camfed? There will always be children who don't fit the institution and whose sense of exclusion is reinforced day by day. Their experience shaped my approach to children and young people in Africa.

How did you learn how to run a successful charity? I learned by doing, and from others who were encouraging and generous in their help. I belonged to a community of activists that was inspirational.

How did you manage the growth of Camfed from supporting 32 girls, with £2,000 raised from selling your homemade cakes, to a £3,000,000 NGO? Lucy Lake [currently chief executive officer] and I built the whole model from the grassroots up. Donors could see it was working and began to get behind us in increasing numbers. We attract and retain outstanding individuals. In Africa, the early beneficiaries head the programs – young women who share a background of rural poverty, transformation through education, and the courage to bring about change.

What has been the key to the success of Camfed? Never take your eye off the ball. Always remember that you and everyone on the team are the servant of the cause – in our case, girls' education and young women's leadership in Africa.

What advice would you give tomorrow's social entrepreneurs? Be greedy for social change, and your life will be endlessly enriched. The only failure lies in not trying, or giving up.

What is the best piece of management advice you have received? Have faith in your intuition and listen to your gut feeling.

Source: "Leading Questions," interview by Alison Benjamin, *The Guardian*

B Are these statements about the reading true (*T*), false (*F*), or is the information not given (*NG*) in the interview? Write the correct letters.

____ 1. According to Ann Cotton, a social entrepreneur feels driven to help those who suffer in life.

____ 2. Ann Cotton's experience of being excluded in school has guided her approach to setting up Camfed.

____ 3. Today, Camfed continues to fund its programs through cake sales.

____ 4. Camfed's programs are run only by the most highly trained experts in management.

____ 5. Camfed's cause is to educate young women in Africa and encourage them to become leaders.

____ 6. Ann Cotton thinks managers should trust their instincts.

C Group work Discuss these questions with your group.

1. How does Ann Cotton explain the success of Camfed? Which of the factors mentioned do you think were the most important?

2. Do you think Ann Cotton is an exceptional individual, or could anyone have done what she did? Explain your answer.

1 STARTING POINT
Success stories

A Match these descriptions of successful companies with the company name.

____ 1. The Body Shop   ____ 2. Google   ____ 3. Sanrio

a. Larry Page and **Sergey Brin** started this innovative company in a dorm room at Stanford University. They didn't get along at first, and had they been unable to work together, the most widely used Internet search engine might never have been created. Should you ask about their company's goal, they'll probably smile and tell you it's to organize all of the world's information in order to make it accessible and useful.

b. Should you want to buy natural skin and hair care products, this company offers over 1,200 choices. **Anita Roddick** started the company to support her family. Had she been wealthy, she might not have gone into business. These stores communicate a message about human rights and environmental issues. The company is famous for its fair trade practices in impoverished communities.

c. In 1960, **Shintaro Tsuji** created a line of character-branded lifestyle products centered around gift-giving occasions. However, had this Tokyo-based company not created Hello Kitty, it wouldn't have become nearly so successful. Hello Kitty goods are in demand all over the world. They include purses, wastebaskets, pads and pens, erasers, cell phone holders, and much, much more.

B Pair work Discuss these questions.

1. What might be some reasons for the success of these companies?
2. Can you think of other successful companies? What do they offer?

2 LISTENING
Unsuccessful endeavors

A Group work Brainstorm some of the factors that can make a new business fail.

B Listen to two people discuss their unsuccessful attempts to start a business. What types of business did they try to get into? Why did they choose those types? Complete the chart.

	Type of business	Reason for choosing it
1.		
2.		

C Listen again. Write the main reasons why each attempt failed.

1. _____

2. _____

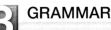

GRAMMAR

Subject-verb inversion in conditional sentences

In past unreal conditional sentences, people sometimes replace *if* by inverting the subject and the auxiliary *had*. This occurs mainly in more formal speech and writing.
If they **had been** unable to work together, the search engine **might never have been** created.
Had they **been** unable to work together, the search engine **might never have been** created.

The same construction is possible for negative sentences. Notice that negative forms are not contracted and *not* is separated from *had* in these sentences.
If this company **hadn't created** Hello Kitty, it **wouldn't have become** nearly so successful.
Had this company **not created** Hello Kitty, it **wouldn't have become** nearly so successful.

In present and future real conditionals, people often replace *if* by putting *should* at the beginning of the sentence. Note that this use of *should* does not express obligation.
If you **want** to buy natural skin care products, this company offers over 1,200 choices.
Should you **want** to buy natural skin care products, this company offers over 1,200 choices.

GRAMMAR PLUS *see page 128*

A Look at the Starting Point on page 96 again. Can you find other conditional sentences with subject-verb inversion?

B Combine these pairs of sentences using conditional clauses and subject-verb inversion. Then compare with a partner. Sometimes more than one answer is possible.

1. That company didn't take the competition into consideration. It went out of business.
   Had that company taken the competition into consideration, it wouldn't have gone out of business.

2. That fast-food chain hasn't offered any healthy food options. Its sales are down.

3. Terry didn't develop a serious business plan. She missed a number of opportunities.

4. I decided to go to business school. I started my own business.

5. The government doesn't encourage international business. The economy is slowing down.

6. My friends and I didn't know enough about the potential of the Internet. We didn't start an online business.

7. I knew it would take 10 years to pay off my college loans. I chose an affordable school.

8. I thought my friend's business idea would fail. I didn't lend her any money.

C Pair work Complete these sentences with your own information, and share them with a partner.

1. Had I saved more money when I was younger, . . .

2. Should all the students in the class start a small business, . . .

3. Had I not decided to take this English course, . . .

4. Had I followed my parents' advice, I would have . . .

5. Should I have the opportunity to start a business, I might . . .

6. Had I known five years ago what I know now, I'd probably . . .

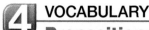

4 VOCABULARY
Prepositions following *work*

A The expressions on the left are composed of *work* and a preposition.
Match them with their definitions on the right.

1. work **against** your interests _____
2. work **around** a problem _____
3. work **for** a boss _____
4. work **toward** a goal _____
5. work **off** a debt _____
6. work **on** a task _____

a. be employed by
b. apply effort to
c. make it harder (for someone) to achieve something
d. work while avoiding (a difficulty)
e. work in order to achieve
f. work in order to eliminate

B Complete each statement with the correct preposition.

1. Entrepreneurs don't waste time trying to solve insolvable problems; they
work _____ them.

2. Inexperience can work _____ young people looking for jobs.

3. Workers are happier when they work _____ a variety of projects,
not just the same one.

4. My uncle lent me $4,000 to buy a car, but he's letting me work _____
part of the loan by painting his house.

> **VOCABULARY PLUS** *see page 141*

5 DISCUSSION
Too good to be true?

A Read these advertising messages for different job opportunities. Which do you
find the most believable? Which do you find the least? Why?

❶ Break into the fashion industry! Our classes are your first step to working toward your goal of becoming a glamorous fashion model.

❷ Start your career in real estate. You can buy houses for as little as $2,000 and resell them for a huge profit with our real-estate buying program.

Useful expressions

Expressing suspicion

That's a little hard to believe.
It sounds fishy to me.
It sounds too good to be true.

❸ Get paid for your time on social networking sites. Earn thousands every month just for posting comments!

❹ How would you like to get paid just for going shopping? Does it sound too good to be true? It's not. Ask us how!

❺ Invest like a professional.
Send us $50 for information on how to make millions in the stock market.

"In my opinion, the most believable one is number three. I read that companies pay people to write positive posts about their products. The one I found hardest to believe is . . ."

B **Group work** Discuss the questions with your group.

1. What would probably happen if you replied to an ad like one of those above?
2. What are some other examples of hard-to-believe advertisements?
3. Who do you think is attracted to these types of messages? Why?

WRITING
Formal letters

> Formal letters don't include personal information that is irrelevant to the topic. Unlike personal letters, formal letters tend to avoid contractions and idioms.

A Read this formal letter. Then label the five parts listed in the box.

1 The **heading** includes your address and the date. It typically goes in the top left corner. If you use letterhead stationery with an address, only the date is added.

2 The **inside address** is below the heading. It contains the addressee's name, title (if you know it), and address.

3 For the **greeting**, you should write "Dear" and "Mr." or "Ms." along with the person's family name. If you don't have a specific person to contact, write "Dear Sir or Madam." The greeting is usually followed by a colon (:).

4 The **body** of the letter follows. The first paragraph is used to state the reason for the letter. The paragraphs that follow should each focus on only one point. The letter generally concludes by thanking the reader in some way.

5 The **closing** includes a closing phrase, your signature, and your name and title (if you have one).

---

1 —

335 Henry St.
New York, NY 10002
July 10, 2014

DM
DONNA MALNICK

Mr. Jonathan Hayes, Director
Institute for Study Abroad
1472 Park Avenue
Summit, NJ 07091

Dear Mr. Hayes:

I am writing to request more information concerning your study abroad programs. Your programs sound extremely interesting, and I hope to participate in one of them next year. Your Study Abroad in Paris program sounds particularly fascinating.

I would like to sign up for the Paris program beginning in June. I'm still trying to decide whether to choose the homestay option or the dormitory option. Would it be possible to send me further information about those two choices in order to help me make a decision?

I realize that all the spaces in your Paris program may already be filled. In that case, my second choice would be the Study Abroad in Toulouse program. My third choice would be your Study Abroad in Strasbourg program.

Thank you very much for your help. I look forward to receiving the information.

Sincerely,

Donna Malnick

Donna Malnick

B Imagine that you are interested in learning more about a study program. Write your formal letter to the program director expressing interest and requesting information. Include all five parts of a formal letter.

1 STARTING POINT
Attitudes at work

A What kinds of working conditions would you like at your job? Choose the statements you agree with.

> ## What are you **looking for** in a **JOB?**
>
> ● **1** I would be happier and more productive if my workspace were neat and organized.
>
> ● **2** I would take almost any job provided that there were opportunities to learn.
>
> ● **3** I wouldn't care about a high salary if a job allowed me to balance my work, family, and social life.
>
> ● **4** I wouldn't mind working in an office, assuming that I had the freedom to be creative.
>
> ● **5** If the company I worked for dealt fairly with me, I would be loyal to it.
>
> ● **6** I would only take a job on the condition that it offered long-term security.
>
> ● **7** I would quit a job that required me to be dishonest, whether or not it were high paying.
>
> ● **8** Supposing I had the choice, I would prefer to work with a group rather than by myself.

B **Group work** Compare your answers with the members of your group. How are you different? Do you think you would make a harmonious group of co-workers?

2 DISCUSSION
The dream job

A Look at this checklist of considerations in choosing a job. Add two more items to the list. Then choose the three items that are the most important to you.

The ideal job . . .

☐ allows me to travel often.
☐ offers me a high salary.
☐ isn't stressful at all.
☐ doesn't require long hours.
☐ gives me the freedom to be creative.
☐ has a flexible schedule.

☐ lets me wear casual clothes.
☐ has an excellent health plan and benefits.
☐ has lots of opportunity for advancement.
☐ is close to my home or school.
☐ _____.
☐ _____.

B **Pair work** Share your ideas with a partner. Explain and compare your choices.

"For me, the ideal job should have a flexible schedule so that I always have time for family and a social life . . ."

3 GRAMMAR

Adverb clauses of condition

Conditional sentences do not necessarily use *if*. The following expressions are also used. The tense agreement in the clauses is the same as in conditional sentences with *if*.

Provided (that) and *on the condition (that)* introduce a condition on which another situation depends.
I would take almost any job **provided that** there were opportunities to learn.
I would only take a job **on the condition that** it offered long-term security.

Whether or not introduces a condition that does not influence another situation.
I would quit a job that required me to be dishonest, **whether or not** it were high paying.

Assuming (that) introduces an assumption upon which another condition depends.
I wouldn't mind working in an office, **assuming that** I had the freedom to be creative.

Supposing (that) introduces a possible condition that could influence another situation.
Supposing I had the choice, I would prefer to work with a group rather than by myself.

GRAMMAR PLUS *see page 129*

A Look at the Starting Point on page 100 again. Can you replace the sentences with *if* with another expression?

B Match the items to make logical sentences.

1. Whether or not you have a clear job description, ____
2. Assuming that you have an original idea, ____
3. On the condition that I didn't have to be away for more than two or three days, ____
4. Provided that I could find extra time, ____
5. Supposing a close friend wanted to start a business with you, ____
6. Whether or not I actually get the job, ____

a. you might be able to start a successful business.
b. I would be willing to travel on business.
c. would you jump at the opportunity?
d. I felt the interview process was a valuable experience.
e. you need to be flexible and cooperative.
f. I'd like to do some volunteer work.

C Pair work Complete these sentences with your own information. Then discuss them with a partner.

1. I would enjoy managing an office, assuming . . .
   I had responsible people working for me.
2. Provided a company paid for my commute, I . . .
3. Whether or not I have enough money in the bank, I . . .
4. I would take a reduction in salary on the condition that . . .
5. Supposing that I couldn't find a job, I . . .
6. I would agree to work overtime, assuming that . . .
7. On the condition that I were guaranteed two weeks' vacation a year, . . .

4 VOCABULARY & SPEAKING
Qualities essential for success

A Choose three qualities that are important to working alone successfully and three that are important to working well with others. Write them in the chart.

A **SUCCESSFUL** WORKER NEEDS TO . . . .

- have good communication skills
- have initiative
- be trustworthy
- have leadership ability
- have influence
- have charisma
- have specialized training
- have self-discipline
- be innovative
- be adaptable
- be optimistic
- be conscientious

To work alone successfully, you need to	To work well with others, you need to . . . .
have initiative	

B Pair work Discuss the qualities you chose. Why do you think they're important?

"I feel you can work alone successfully, provided you have initiative."

"I totally agree. You need to have a lot of initiative because you don't have a boss to tell you what to do."

> **VOCABULARY PLUS** *see page 141*

5 LISTENING
Can you really learn that?

🔊 **A** Listen to three people who participated in workshops for their jobs. What type of workshop did each person attend?

1. Anne: _____   2. Thomas: _____   3. Paulina: _____

🔊 **B** Listen again. What did each person learn from his or her workshop experience?

Anne: _____

Thomas: _____

Paulina: _____

C Pair work Would you like to take part in such workshops? Why or why not? Discuss your reasons.

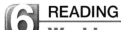

Working with others

A Pair work Do your friends tend to have similar values and temperaments?
Read the article and make a list of three categories that your friends would fit into.

THE VALUE OF DIFFERENCE

Every person is unique. We work with many people who are different from us. It is important to realize that differences are good and to appreciate that not all people are like us. On a team, the strengths of one worker can overcome the weaknesses of another. The balance created by such variety makes a team stronger.

There are three basic ways that people differ from one another: values, temperament, and individual diversity (gender, age, etc.).

Values are the importance that we give to ideas, things, or people. While our values may be quite different, organizational behavior expert Stephen Robbins suggests that people fall into one of three general categories:

Traditionalists: People in this category value hard work, doing things the way they've always been done, loyalty to the organization, and the authority of leaders.

Humanists: People in this category value quality of life, autonomy, loyalty to self, and leaders who are attentive to workers' needs.

Pragmatists: People in this category value success, achievement, loyalty to career, and leaders who reward people for hard work.

Another important way in which people differ is temperament. Your temperament is the distinctive way you think, feel, and react to the world. All of us have our own individual temperament. However, experts have found that it is easier to understand the differences in temperament by classifying people into four categories:

Optimists: People with this temperament must be free and not tied down. They're impulsive, they enjoy the immediate, and they like working with things. The optimist is generous and cheerful and enjoys action for action's sake.

Realists: People with this temperament like to belong to groups. They have a strong sense of obligation and are committed to society's standards. The realist is serious, likes order, and finds traditions important.

Futurists: People with this temperament like to control things and are also self-critical. They strive for excellence and live for work. The futurist focuses on the future and is highly creative.

Idealists: People with this temperament want to know the meaning of things. They appreciate others and get along well with people of all temperaments. The idealist is romantic, writes fluently, and values integrity.

Source: Job Savvy: How to Be a Success at Work, by LaVerne Ludden

B Match the categories from the article with the descriptions.

1. traditionalist ____
2. humanist ____
3. pragmatist ____
4. optimist ____
5. realist ____
6. futurist ____
7. idealist ____

a. generous and cheerful; enjoys action for action's sake
b. serious and likes order; has a strong sense of obligation
c. values quality of life; attentive to workers' needs
d. strives for excellence; focuses on the future
e. values doing things the way they've always been done
f. romantic; writes fluently; values integrity
g. values loyalty to career, success, and achievement

C Group work Discuss these questions. Then share your answers with the class.

1. How would you categorize your own values and temperament? Give examples.
2. Which category of people would you prefer to work with on a challenging project? Explain.

COMMUNICATION REVIEW

UNITS 10–12

1 SPEAKING
Speaking tips

A Pair work What would each person have to do to succeed? Think of several conditions that would work for each situation.

1. Mary has been asked to give a formal talk on a topic she knows little about.

2. Julia has been asked to give a short speech at a friend's wedding.

3. Hal is too timid to join in the group's conversation after class.

4. Tom had some bad experiences at job interviews, and now he gets really nervous before them.

B Group work Discuss your ideas with another pair. Do you have similar suggestions?

"Providing Mary spends time reading about the topic, she shouldn't have a problem."

"That's true, assuming she has time to do plenty of research and rehearse first."

2 LISTENING
Good language learners

 A Listen to a lecture about good language learning. Who is the lecture for? Choose the correct answer.

☐ a. people who are learning another language

☐ b. people who are going to travel abroad

☐ c. people who want to be language teachers

B Listen again. Choose the compound adjectives that are used to describe good language learners.

☐ 1. highly motivated   ☐ 4. pattern-seeking   ☐ 7. well-known

☐ 2. forward-thinking   ☐ 5. open-minded   ☐ 8. self-aware

☐ 3. risk-taking   ☐ 6. well-organized   ☐ 9. widely recognized

3 DISCUSSION
The most and the best

A Complete the sentences with your own information. Add reasons for your opinions, and compare with a partner.

1. One of the most open-minded people in my family is . . .
2. I imagine that a lot of the most hardworking people . . .
3. The most forward-thinking person I've ever met is . . .
4. The majority of my friends would agree that the best-dressed celebrities include . . .
5. The most easygoing person I've ever known is . . .
6. Some of the most well-informed people I can think of are . . .

"One of the most open-minded people in my family is my uncle John. He's always willing to go to new places and try new things."

B Pair work Who are some people you both admire? Use the superlative form of these compound adjectives to write sentences about them. Give reasons.

1. good-looking   2. thought-provoking   3. widely respected   4. kind-hearted

4 SPEAKING
Personal qualities

A Which of these people is most similar to you, and which is least similar?

Rita

"I've been told that I'm a charismatic person. The truth is that I'm a people person, and I'm not afraid to share my ideas with others."

Su Lyn

"I'm very optimistic. I try to look at the good side of things, and I'm always confident that even the worst situations will turn out to be fine."

Alberto

"I've lived in three different countries and have attended six different schools. Yet I've never had problems adapting to new situations."

B Pair work Which of these are your strongest qualities? Which do you feel are most necessary to realize your own personal and professional goals?

- adaptability
- charisma
- conscientiousness
- determination
- honesty
- initiative
- optimism
- self-confidence
- self-control

"I think I'm very adaptable. Since I'd like to be an actor, and the work is unpredictable, I think that's an important quality."

GRAMMAR PLUS

1A Phrasal verbs

Additional phrasal verbs
Separable: call off, count out, cut off, get across, hand over, pass up, take back
Inseparable: go over, hang around, live up to, look after, pick on, run out of, touch on
Intransitive: catch on, come along, come over, fall apart, show up, turn out

Certain intransitive two-word phrasal verbs, when followed by a preposition, can then take an object.

back down (from)	cut back (on)	drop out (of)	give in (to)
catch up (to)	cut down (on)	get along (with)	give up (on)
check out (of)	drop in (on)	get away (with)	look back (on)

When confronted with an argument, Mark never **backs down**.
Mark never **backs down from** an argument.

1 Underline the phrasal verb in each sentence. Is the verb separable (*S*) or inseparable (*I*)? Is it transitive (*T*) or intransitive (*NT*)? Write the correct letters.

S, T 1. The referees <u>called</u> the soccer match <u>off</u> due to heavy rain.

_____ 2. Jessica asked me to come over to her house for dinner.

_____ 3. Sometimes I find it hard to live up to my parents' expectations.

_____ 4. Sally insulted me yesterday, but today she took back her remark.

_____ 5. When entertaining, there's nothing worse than running out of food at your party.

_____ 6. When Jim gave me the chance to share his apartment, I couldn't pass up the opportunity.

2 Complete the sentences with intransitive phrasal verbs and a preposition from the grammar box. Be sure to use the correct form of the verb.

1. When my grandfather and I go jogging together, I sometimes need to stop and wait for him to _____*catch up to*_____ me.

2. I didn't want to try bungee jumping, but I finally _____ the pressure from my friends and tried it. It was fun!

3. Even when you fail, a true friend will never _____ you.

4. My friends and I are trying to _____ the money we spend, so on Fridays we just watch TV at my house.

5. Mia's father is successful, even though he _____ college.

6. There's a long line of people waiting to _____ the hotel.

7. I insist on honesty; I won't let anyone _____ lying to me.

1B Gerund and infinitive constructions

The verbs *forget*, *mean*, and *regret* can be followed by either an infinitive or a gerund. However, the meaning is significantly different in each case.

Forget followed by an infinitive refers to something you didn't actually do. *Forget* followed by a gerund refers to an action that you in fact did earlier.
Marcello **forgot to meet** his best friend at the train station.
Marcello never **forgot meeting** his favorite actor.

Mean followed by an infinitive means "intend." In this case, *mean* is usually used in the negative or in the past tense. *Mean* followed by a gerund means "involve or necessitate."
I **meant to visit** Sheila while I was in Hawaii, but I didn't have the chance.
Inviting Emile to the party **means inviting** Eva, too. She'd be so insulted if we didn't.

Regret followed by infinitives such as *inform*, *announce*, and *say* is a polite way of introducing bad news in official communication. *Regret* followed by a gerund means "be sorry for/about."
The corporation **regrets to inform** you that all job vacancies have been filled.
Donna really **regretted missing** her best friend's wedding.

Be + adjective expressions are often followed by an infinitive.

be amazed	be determined	be happy	be lucky
be ashamed	be eager	be hesitant	be ready

Be + adjective + preposition and verb + preposition expressions are often followed by a gerund.

be bored with	be convinced of	be good at	be used to	be worried about
apologize for	complain about	object to	participate in	take part in	think of

1 Choose the correct form of the verb.

1. Manny forgot *to do* / (*doing*) his homework for English class because he had completed it over a month ago.

2. Mina didn't mean *to frighten* / *frightening* the baby with the doll.

3. Though she didn't have much, Wendy never regretted *to spend* / *spending* money on her friends.

4. I always forget *to call* / *calling* my parents, and they get really mad at me.

5. Attending my high school reunion means *to see* / *seeing* old friends as well as people I didn't like very much.

6. We regret *to announce* / *announcing* that Flight 54 has been delayed.

2 Complete the sentences with the infinitive or gerund form of the verb in parentheses.

1. Gil is really eager ___*to rekindle*___ (rekindle) his relationship with Lana.

2. I've been worried about _____ (meet) my new college roommate.

3. I think you're really lucky _____ (have) so many close friends.

4. Have you thought of _____ (send) an e-card instead of mailing a card?

5. I'm ashamed _____ (say) that my college roommate and I never reconnected.

6. I would like to apologize for _____ (rehash) all these old issues.

Here are some verbs that are used with each pattern.

a. verb + infinitive
afford, fail, hasten, learn, prepare, proceed, seek, strive
I really **strive to wear** the latest styles and trends.

b. verb + object + infinitive
advise, allow, authorize, cause, convince, encourage, instruct, permit, persuade, urge
The salesperson **convinced me to buy** a dress I knew I didn't need.

c. verb + gerund
can't help, can't see, can't stand, enjoy, get through, keep on, (not) mind, miss, postpone, risk
I **can't see paying** high prices for clothes that will be out of style in a year.

d. verb + object + preposition + gerund/noun
blame (for), dissuade (from), forgive (for), interest (in), keep (from), suspect (of), thank (for)
Can I **interest you in going** on a shopping spree with me?

1 Label the words in boldface in the text below with the correct verb pattern above.

A famous saying goes, "Clothes make the man." My mother used to say that to me because I was a sloppy dresser, and she (1) __b__ **urged me to look** my best. She'd coax me to dress better, but nothing could (2) ____ **keep me from wearing** jeans. At my high school, students never (3) ____ **failed to wear** jeans to school, and my mother always sighed and tried to (4) ____ **dissuade me from leaving** the house in my old, torn jeans. On my graduation from high school, my parents gave me my first suit and (5) ____ **advised me to** "**dress** for success."

Since then, I've changed quite a bit. I really (6) ____ **enjoy dressing** fashionably. I can (7) ____ **afford to wear** stylish slacks and shirts, with well-polished shoes. It's funny, but I (8) ____ **don't miss wearing** jeans one bit.

2 Complete the sentences by putting the words in parentheses in the correct order and by choosing the correct verb form. Write the letter of the pattern from the grammar box next to each sentence.

__d__ 1. I _forgave my sister for giving away_ my old laptop. (my sister / forgive / give away / for)

____ 2. I never _____ more for quality clothes. (mind / pay)

____ 3. Harold _____ his jacket last week. (allow / wear / me)

____ 4. Shirley _____ her dry cleaning for another week. (pick up / postpone)

____ 5. Lydia's dad _____ him a necktie for Father's Day. (get / her / thank / for)

____ 6. The man stole the sneakers, and then _____ them in the mall. (wear / proceeded)

2B Cleft sentences with *what*

> To emphasize the whole sentence rather than just the part following the main verb, use a cleft sentence with *what* and a form of the verb *do*.
>
> I try to project a positive attitude.
> **What I try to project is** a positive attitude. *(emphasizes a positive attitude)*
> **What I do is** try to project a positive attitude. *(emphasizes the whole sentence)*
>
> She complained to the waiter about the quality of the food.
> **What she complained about to the waiter was** the quality of the food.
> **What she did was** complain to the waiter about the quality of the food.
>
> Cleft structures can include expressions like *the reason why, the thing that, the place where,* and *the person who.* These structures are typically used with the verb *be.*
> I'm wearing sunglasses to protect my eyes.
> **The reason why** I'm wearing sunglasses **is** to protect my eyes.
>
> I do all my shopping at the mall.
> **The place where** I do all my shopping **is** (at) the mall.

1 Rewrite these sentences as cleft sentences with *what* to emphasize the whole sentence.

1. The candidate showed the voters he was a trustworthy man.
   What the candidate did was show the voters he was a trustworthy man.

2. My mother shouldn't have made me wear my sister's old clothes.

3. I'm going to send all my shirts out to be dry-cleaned.

4. My friends call me at work all the time.

5. My father judges people too much by their appearance.

6. Employees should carry ID cards at all times.

7. Eleanor wore her mother's wedding dress at her own wedding.

8. Martin spilled spaghetti sauce on his shirt.

9. Sam bought a whole new wardrobe.

10. Mary is going to wear her diamond necklace to the party.

2 Rewrite these sentences as cleft sentences by starting them with the expressions in parentheses.

1. I'm wearing a tie to impress my boss. (the reason why)
   The reason why I'm wearing a tie is to impress my boss.

2. I lost my watch in the park. (the place where)

3. The office dress code changed last Friday. (the day when)

4. My dog wears a sweater because his fur is short. (the reason why)

5. I remember the intense expression on his face. (the thing that)

6. Lori keeps her jewelry under her bed. (the place where)

3A Indefinite and definite articles

In completely general statements with uncountable nouns, do not use an article before the noun. However, *the* is required when the noun is made more specific by a modifying phrase following it.
Ethics is becoming an important part of the field of genetics.
The ethics of cloning should be addressed by experts in the field.

Image is an important part of success.
The image she projected did not serve her well in court.

With certain exceptions, do not use *the* before:
countries (exceptions: *the Philippines, the United Arab Emirates, the United Kingdom, the United States*)
streets and cities (exception: *the Hague*)
individual lakes, bays, islands, continents, mountain peaks (exception: *the Matterhorn*)

Do use *the* before:
rivers, oceans, seas, gulfs, mountain ranges, peninsulas, deserts, forests

1 Do the nouns in these sentences require a definite article? Write *the*, or *X* if none is needed.

1. A large number of oil wells have been drilled in __*the*__ Gulf of Mexico.

2. There is no room for ____ frivolity when discussing ____ safety of nuclear power.

3. ____ United States utilizes more genetically modified food than ____ Europe does.

4. You shouldn't expect ____ confidentiality when you upload anything to the Internet.

5. In a moment, our experimental driverless vehicle will turn right on ____ Elm Street.

6. Many people do not believe that ____ rights of animals should be protected.

7. A global warming monitoring station is located on top of ____ Mount Rutherford.

8. I think ____ human error is to blame for the majority of aircraft accidents.

2 Review the rules for articles on page 19. Then fill in the blanks with a definite article, an indefinite article, or *X* if none is needed. Sometimes more than one answer is possible.

(1) __*X*__ Energy seems to be on everyone's mind these days. (2) ____ people are worried because they know that petroleum reserves are not infinite. It's also alarming that (3) ____ temperature of the earth seems to be rising year by year. Many scientists blame (4) ____ warming of the earth on (5) ____ burning of petroleum-based fuels.

However, there is no reason to give up (6) ____ hope, as (7) ____ alternatives are available. One example is (8) ____ wind farm, a collection of wind turbines that turn wind energy into electric power. Another example is (9) ____ hydroelectric facilities, which change (10) ____ energy created by moving water into electric power. (11) ____ hydroelectric facility on (12) ____ Paraná River in Brazil generates about 20 percent of the power used in the country. A final example is (13) ____ solar power. It is one of (14) ____ cleanest sources of energy and is attracting (15) ____ attention as well. Many countries, including (16) ____ United Arab Emirates, (17) ____ Spain, and (18) ____ India have built large solar power plants.

Lastly, it's important that we all conserve energy. Take (19) ____ moment to shut off and unplug any electrical items when you leave (20) ____ room.

3B -ing clauses

When -ing clauses begin a sentence, the agent of the -ing clause must be the subject of the main clause that follows.

Incorrect: Trying hard to fix my computer, ~~the dog~~ kept staring at me.
(The agent of the -ing clause seems to be the dog.)
Correct: Trying hard to fix my computer, **I** noticed the dog staring at me.
(The agent of the -ing clause and the subject of the main clause are the same.)

Incorrect: Doing yard work, ~~his clothes~~ got very dirty.
(The agent of the -ing clause seems to be his clothes.)
Correct: Doing yard work, **he** got dirt all over his clothes.
(The agent of the -ing clause and the subject of the main clause are the same.)

In addition to starting a sentence, -ing clauses can also follow these expressions:

have a good time	have an easy time	have fun	spend time
have a hard time	have difficulty	have problems	waste time

1 Choose the main clause that makes sense with the -ing clause.

1. Making strange noises, __b__
   a. I knew that my computer would crash.
   b. my computer stopped working.

2. Being technophiles, ____
   a. we're never afraid to try new gadgets.
   b. the latest gadgets always interest us.

3. Talking on her cell phone, ____
   a. the car went right through a red light.
   b. Pam didn't pay attention to her driving.

4. Quickly closing her laptop, ____
   a. Meg accidentally spilled her coffee.
   b. Meg's coffee was accidentally spilled.

5. Having studied robotics at school, ____
   a. they could explain how the robot worked.
   b. the robot was no mystery to them.

2 Combine these sentences using an expression from the grammar box to start the sentence.

1. I played video games all day Saturday. I had a good time.
   I had a good time playing video games all day Saturday.

2. My brother was shopping for cars. He had a hard time.

3. Fred constantly checks his social networking pages. He wastes a lot of time.

4. I'm attending the big technology expo next week. I'm going to have fun.

5. Nash is having difficulty. He's trying to comprehend the concept of DNA storage.

6. Norah was writing a genetic technology lecture. She spent a lot of time on it.

7. The guard used the video surveillance camera to identify the intruder. He had an easy time.

8. We were trying to follow what the scientist was saying. We were having problems.

> In reporting clauses, verbs such as *admit*, *agree*, *announce*, *comment*, *complain*, *confess*, *disclose*, *explain*, *inform*, and *reveal* are frequently followed by an indirect object. In this case, *that* should be retained for clarity.
>
> Several people **agreed with me that** logic, not superstition, is the best way to make decisions.
> Max **explained to the teacher that** a black cat never means bad luck in his country.
>
> The following nouns are also often used in reporting clauses. Here, too, *that* is helpful in making the meaning clear and should be retained.
>
> | | | | | |
> |---|---|---|---|---|
> | accusation | assertion | comment | explanation | response |
> | argument | claim | decision | remark | suggestion |
>
> Bill made the **assertion that** he'd have no luck at all if it weren't for bad luck.
> Liliana repeated her **argument that** only foolish people believe in magic.
> The class rejected Niran's **suggestion that** we cancel class on Friday the 13th.

1 Using the words in parentheses, rewrite these sentences with reporting clauses in the simple past.

1. He had an irrational fear of spiders. (Luis / admit / his friend)
   Luis admitted to his friend that he had an irrational fear of spiders.

2. Some people really are luckier than others. (Min / agree / me)

3. There are too many pigeons in the park. (many people / complain / park staff)

4. He had spent his father's lucky dollar on candy. (Marco / confess / his mother)

5. It's bad luck to step on a crack in the sidewalk. (Marcie / explain / her little sister)

6. The day he met his wife was the luckiest day of his life. (Felix / announce / his wedding guests)

2 Combine the sentences using a reporting clause with one of the nouns from the grammar box.

1. Kim accused Anna of being a superstitious person. Anna didn't agree.
   Anna didn't agree with Kim's accusation that she was a superstitious person.

2. Gianna argues that everything happens for a reason. Many people disagree.

3. Leslie asserted that superstition is based in fear. Carlos didn't understand.

4. Jae-woo decided that a trip to Las Vegas was what he needed. We were surprised.

5. Ernesto commented that hard work is more important than luck. Lily repeated what he said.

6. Hiroshi claimed he had won the chess game thanks to beginner's luck. Sandra didn't believe him.

7. Patrick remarked that Tanya probably shouldn't push her luck. Tanya ignored what he said.

8. Mr. Wang responded that actions speak louder than words. I understood him.

4B Reporting clauses in the passive

The following verbs can be used in reporting clauses in the passive.

announce   deny   maintain   reveal   suggest
confirm   estimate   observe   rumor   understand

Reporting clauses in the passive are commonly used with a variety of structures.
Simple present: It **is suggested** that passengers report anything suspicious to the driver.
Simple past: It **was** flatly **denied** that a nuclear submarine had been lost in the Arctic Ocean.
Present perfect: It **has been estimated** that the construction of Stonehenge took over 20 million hours.
Past perfect: It **had been rumored** that a monster was living in the lake.
With modals: It **couldn't be denied** that many mysteries elude scientific understanding.
With past modals: It **should have been confirmed** that the flight would be delayed.

Reporting clauses in the passive are used in written and formal English and are not common in conversation.

1 Add a reporting clause in the passive with *it* to these statements. Use the verb and the suggested structure in parentheses.

1. The lost city of Atlantis had been discovered on April Fool's Day, 1980. (announce, simple past)
   It was announced that the lost city of Atlantis had been discovered on April Fool's Day, 1980.

2. A fast-food restaurant discontinued a favorite hamburger as a publicity stunt. (reveal, present perfect)

3. Some people have a higher level of intuition than others. (understand, simple present)

4. Crop circles, patterns created by flattening crops, are a clever hoax. (can't deny, present modal)

5. The moon's pull on the earth affects the ocean tides. (maintain, simple present)

6. The politician was deceiving the nation. (should reveal, past modal)

7. A positive attitude was an important part of his cure. (observe, simple past)

8. One out of ten people falls for Internet scams every year. (estimate, past perfect)

2 Rewrite these statements with a reporting clause in the passive with *it*.

1. An unknown source maintains that the Loch Ness Monster has been sighted several times.
   It is maintained that the Loch Ness Monster has been sighted several times.

2. Archeologists have revealed that the ancient residents of Easter Island likely painted their statues.

3. Officials should have observed that there was a mysterious substance on the train floor.

4. People can't deny that ancient civilizations possessed knowledge lost to us today.

5. A newspaper has confirmed that a pack of 400 wolves was terrifying a town in Siberia.

6. The authorities have announced that 10 people on the ship got sick.

> To express the speaker's attitude about the entire sentence, sentence adverbs are most often located at the beginning of the sentence and set off by a comma.
> **Predictably**, the hero of the movie won the heart of the girl.
>
> Sentence adverbs can be used in place of longer clauses that modify a sentence.
> **People were amazed that** the movie sold 26 million tickets on its opening weekend.
> **Amazingly**, the movie sold 26 million tickets on its opening weekend.
>
> **Nobody was surprised that** the sequel was also extremely popular.
> **Not surprisingly**, the sequel was also extremely popular.
>
> The following conjunctive adverbs link a sentence with a preceding idea.
> accordingly   consequently   hence   indeed   meanwhile   otherwise   thus
>
> The coming attractions ended and the movie began; **accordingly**, the audience fell silent.

1 Rewrite the sentences using sentence adverbs to replace the boldfaced words.

1. **It's apparent to me that** movies with clichéd storylines are still very popular.
   Apparently, movies with clichéd storylines are still very popular.

2. **It's fortunate that** there were good movies available on the 13-hour plane ride.

3. **I'm being honest when I say that** I just don't care for love stories, no matter how moving they may be.

4. **Nobody can question the fact that** many historical movies present an incorrect view of history.

5. **It was bad luck that** Carol's computer froze while she was streaming that movie.

6. **In essence**, that movie is a tale of good versus evil.

7. **If it fulfills its potential**, the Internet could be the first place all new movies are shown.

8. **It's obvious to me that** you are only pretending to have seen the movie.

9. **I'm being serious when I say that** if a movie is based on a book, always read the book first.

2 Complete the sentences with a conjunctive adverb from the grammar box. Sometimes more than one answer is possible.

1. A growing number of students are watching the movie rather than reading the assigned book. _Consequently_ , there has been a decrease in the reading skills of graduating seniors.

2. At the Mainstreet Theater, you sit in front of a table to watch the movie. _____, you are served by waiters who take your order and walk between the rows.

3. Moviegoers are prohibited from texting and talking during the movie; _____, anyone who violates that policy will be asked to leave.

4. The most popular movie stars demand extremely high salaries; _____ the cost of producing movies with "big names" has risen.

5. It's recommended that you buy tickets in advance; _____, you might not get a seat.

5B Such . . . that and so . . . that

In written English, *so* and *such* are most often followed by a *that* clause. However, in conversation, *so* and *such* are frequently used alone to express emphatic stress.
The host on that game show is **so** funny!
That actress plays her role **so** convincingly!
The writers of that new sitcom show **such** originality!
That was **such** a great documentary!

So much, *so little*, *so many*, and *so few* can also be used without a *that* clause and for emphatic stress.
There are **so many** reality TV shows these days!
That game show gives away **so much** money!

In conversation, *much* and *little* can be used as adverbs following *so*.
Why do you watch TV **so much**? *(much = "frequently")*
That actor is featured **so little** that I sometimes forget he's on the show. *(little = "infrequently")*

Much, *little*, *many*, and *few* can also serve as pronouns for nouns.
TV can be bad for your health. I sometimes watch so **much** (TV) my eyes hurt.
He needs more free time. He has so **little** (free time) he can't keep up with the latest TV shows.
I don't watch soap operas anymore. I've seen so **many** (soap operas) that I'm tired of them.
TV news requires reporters, but there are so **few** (reporters) that many stories aren't covered.

1 Complete these sentences with *so*, *such*, *so much*, *so little*, *so many*, or *so few*.

1. You should see the Beyoncé documentary. It's _____*so*_____ interesting!

2. It's a good night for watching TV. There are _____ new shows on!

3. Ed spent _____ money on that TV that he can't afford a stand.

4. Turn off that program right now! I've never heard _____ language!

5. _____ TV shows interest Jon that he rarely watches TV.

6. Shelby works long hours. He has _____ time for TV.

2 Complete the text with *so*, *such*, *so much*, *so little*, *so many*, or *so few*.

I've spent (1) _____*such*_____ a lot of time watching reality TV that I guess I'm sort of an expert. There are (2) _____ genres of reality TV shows that it's confusing, and the list of individual shows is (3) _____ long nobody can remember them all.
A very popular one is about fishermen in Alaska. Those guys catch (4) _____ seafood they fill up the boat! They catch a lot of viewers, too, with consistently high ratings and more than a few important awards. One low-rated show is about home renovations. In fact, (5) _____ people watch it that it's going to be canceled.
My favorite is about pet cloning. It's quite popular. However, it's (6) _____ a strange show that I'm really surprised (7) _____ people like it.
I'm really glad there are channels dedicated entirely to reality TV. Honestly, I have (8) _____ interest in other TV genres that reality TV is all I watch!

6A Double comparatives

These structures are commonly used in double comparatives.

The + more / less + clause
The more I listen to classical music, the more I appreciate it.

The + comparative form of adjective + clause
The more romantic a song is, the less my brother wants to listen to it.

The + comparative form of adverb + clause
The louder Mario plays his stereo, the more his neighbors complain.

The + more / less / fewer + noun / gerund + clause
The more dancing you do, the more natural you'll feel on the dance floor.

Short double comparatives without verbs are common in conversation.
Many of them end in *the better*.
The more, the merrier!
The bigger, the better!
The sooner, the better!

1 Fill in the blanks to create appropriate double comparatives. For comparatives
with adjectives or adverbs, more than one answer is possible.

1. Ricky seems to play his music loud in his car in order to get attention.
   _____*The louder*_____ the music is, _____*the more*_____ people turn their heads.

2. This song is so catchy! _____ I listen to it, _____ I like it.

3. The price of concert tickets has really gone up. And, _____
   the performer is, _____ the ticket is.

4. I love soothing background music. _____ the music is,
   _____ stress I feel.

5. They play music at the baseball game to get the fans excited. _____
   the music plays, _____ the fans yell.

6. Practice makes perfect. _____ you practice, _____ you will become.

7. Even age won't slow that performer down. _____ she gets,
   _____ performances she gives.

2 Complete each conversation with one of the short double comparatives without
verbs from the grammar box.

1. A: When should we officially end this meeting?
   B: _____!

2. A: How many people do you think we should invite to the party?
   B: _____!

3. A: What would you like your new house to be like?
   B: _____!

6B   *Will* and *would* for habits and general truths

> *Used to* and *would* are both used to express habits in the past.
> Before he became a big star, Mark **used to** play music on the street for money.
> Before he became a big star, Mark **would** play music on the street for money.
>
> However, *would* cannot be used with stative verbs such as *be*, *have*, *like*, *live*, *love*, *mean*, and *own*.
> **Correct:** When I was young, I **used to** have a clarinet.
> **Incorrect:** When I was young, I ~~would~~ have a clarinet.

1 Complete the sentences using *would* wherever possible. If *would* is not possible, use *used to*.

1. Before Elvis made it big, he _____ *would* _____ sing with his family on the front porch of his house in Tupelo, Mississippi.

2. I _____ own a violin that my uncle gave me for my birthday. I don't know where it is now.

3. Since the young Beethoven loved nature, he _____ take long walks along the banks of the Rhine River.

4. That performer _____ be washed up, but he has since made a remarkable comeback.

5. Before he was discovered by a Hollywood talent scout, that singer _____ regularly announce local sports events on the radio.

6. Café La Fortuna in New York City, where John Lennon _____ like to have coffee and read the newspaper, closed down in 2008.

7. In the 1990s, Pavarotti _____ perform as part of The Three Tenors with José Carreras and Plácido Domingo.

8. In high school, Madonna _____ love to dance and _____ always get excellent grades.

9. Although my family wasn't wealthy, we _____ own a concert-quality grand piano.

2 Complete the paragraph using the correct form of the verb in parentheses. Use *would* or *will* for habits and general truths wherever possible.

Music has played an important role in my life since I was very young. When I was a boy, our family (1) _____ *would sit* _____ (sit) on the green lawn in the center of town on Saturday nights listening to the town band. Between songs, I (2) _____ (like) to talk to the musicians about their instruments, which fascinated me. I (3) _____ (ask) them if I could play their trumpets and clarinets, and they (4) _____ (say) no in as gentle a way as they could. Who could have imagined that I would become an instrument maker? I've got my own family now. On warm Saturdays, I (5) _____ (take) them down to the center of town to listen to the town band. And, every time we go, my own son (6) _____ (bother) the musicians with questions and requests. After all, like father, like son!

7A Optional and required relative pronouns

When the relative pronoun is the complement (or object) of a preposition, *whom* is required (not *who*).
No one can live on that land now except indigenous people **to whom** special permits have been given.

Similarly, *which* is required (not *that*) when the preposition precedes the relative pronoun.
My parents' generation stood for certain principles **against which** my generation has rebelled.

The relative pronoun *whose* is not only used for people. It can also represent animals or things.
This relative pronoun is required.
There are some new fitness classes **whose** purpose is to provide safe exercise for the elderly.

1 Complete the sentences with *whom*, *which*, or *whose*.

1. Junk food advertisements are particularly effective in influencing the buying patterns of the young people to _____*whom*_____ they are aimed.

2. "Where is society heading?" is a difficult question, the answer to _____ I don't think anybody really knows.

3. That insurance company currently offers low-cost health plans to people _____ workplace doesn't offer any.

4. I'd like to join the debate about the future of international travel, but I'm afraid it's a subject about _____ I know almost nothing.

5. Improper or insufficient education is the root of intolerance. The world would change for the better if we understood the people against _____ we have prejudices.

6. My parents owned a fully detached house with a big yard. Unfortunately, my friends and I are all apartment dwellers for _____ owning such a house just isn't possible.

2 Review the rules for pronouns on page 55. Complete the text with the appropriate relative pronouns. Sometimes more than one answer is possible.

I once read a story about a little boy (1) _____*who / that*_____ received an insect – a large beetle – for his birthday. Frustrated by the insect's frantic movements, the boy turned it over and over looking for a switch (2) _____ could turn it off. Clearly, this was a boy (3) _____ understanding of animals and the natural world was extremely limited. The result was a boy for (4) _____ a living thing was indistinguishable from a toy.

Parents should expose their children to nature from a young age. There is a farm not far from the city to (5) _____ hundreds of families go every weekend. There, city kids (6) _____ might not otherwise have had the chance are able to see, and even to touch, a wide variety of living things. By encountering animals (7) _____ are real, not just pictures, children learn the important lesson that these are living creatures (8) _____ are worthy of respect, just like us.

7B As if, as though, as, the way, and like

When *as* introduces a clause expressing a comparison, subject-verb inversion can occur in affirmative sentences.
With *do*: Marissa has a lot of trouble accepting change, **as does Trina**.
With auxiliary verbs: Mitt has coped well with changes at work, **as have his co-workers**.
With modals: Grandma would tell us stories of the old days, **as would Grandpa**.
With *be*: Marcel is wary of technology, **as is his whole family**.

When both clauses have the same subject, *as if* and *as though* clauses with adjectives or past participles are frequently shortened by removing the subject and *be*.
Bill is talking about quitting his job, **as though (he were)** single and carefree.
Marvin sat motionless in front of his new media center, **as if (he were)** glued to the chair.

Notice that we use a past form of a verb after *as if* and *as though* when these phrases are followed by a hypothetical or unreal situation.
Bill is talking about quitting his job **as though** he **were** carefree. *(He has responsibilities.)*
Some young people replace their gadgets every year **as if** they **had** all the money in the world.

1 Combine these sentences using a clause expressing comparison with *as*.
 Use subject-verb inversion.

 1. The students at my new school welcomed me warmly. The teachers welcomed me, too.
 The students at my new school welcomed me warmly, as did the teachers.

 2. Moving to Spain will bring about many changes in my life. Getting a new job will, too.

 3. Clarissa is enjoying retirement. Her husband is also enjoying it.

 4. Claudia went to a traditional Chinese opera last night. Jim went, too.

 5. The teachers' union is supporting a four-day workweek. The transit workers' union is supporting this as well.

 6. I've given up my car and am taking public transportation now. Several of my co-workers are taking public transportation, too.

 7. I can cope well with changes. My wife can cope well with changes, too.

 8. Amber believes that it is often foolish to resist change. Josh also believes that it is often foolish to do so.

2 Rewrite the sentences, shortening the longer clauses and lengthening the shorter clauses. Follow the model in the grammar box.

 1. Guests in the theater felt a strange sensation, as if transported back in time.
 Guests in the theater felt a strange sensation, as if they had been transported back in time.

 2. That family lives without electricity, as though they were trapped in the 1800s.

 3. The music sounded great on my new sound system, as if it were played by a live band.

 4. That kid's clothes looked too big for him, as though borrowed from an older brother.

 5. My grandmother looks odd in that photo, as if she were annoyed.

The following verbs are commonly used with both a direct and indirect object.

bring	hand	order	pay	serve
give	make	owe	promise	throw

When the direct object is a pronoun, it goes before the indirect object.
When the indirect object is a pronoun, it can go before or after the direct object.
The boss owes **it to Sid**. (it = *direct object*)
The boss owes **him a month's salary**. (him = *indirect object*)
The boss owes **a month's salary to him**. (him = *indirect object*)

When both objects are pronouns, only one pattern is possible:
direct object + *to* / *for* + indirect object.
The boss owes **it to him**.
The boss ordered **it for him**.

1 Complete the sentences using the words in parentheses. Write each sentence in two different ways.

1. Finally, the waiter brought . . . (our dinners / us)
   Finally, the waiter brought us our dinners.
   Finally, the waiter brought our dinners to us.

2. After an hour of searching, the clerk gave . . . (a suitable pair of shoes / me)

3. At that café, they won't serve . . . (your meal / you) unless you pay for it in advance.

4. I didn't have any cash, so I handed . . . (my credit card / the clerk)

5. The potter at that shop promised . . . (a beautiful vase / my mother)

6. While they were swimming, their father ordered . . . (lunch / them)

7. I don't have any more cash, but I can pay . . . (the rest / you) tomorrow.

8. At the baseball game, the vendor threw . . . (a bag of peanuts / him)

2 Rewrite the following sentences in as many ways as possible using pronouns in place of the nouns in boldface.

1. The clerk gave **Maria the wrong blouse**.
   The clerk gave her the wrong blouse. / The clerk gave the wrong blouse to her. /
   The clerk gave it to Maria. / The clerk gave it to her.

2. The salesman sold **his last vacuum** to **John**.

3. That company still owes **Michael one week's pay**.

4. The real estate agent didn't mention **the leaky roof** to **the customers**.

5. The travel guide found **two wonderful antique shops** for **the tourists**.

6. Thomas reminded Daniel that he had promised **a diamond ring** to **Liz**.

7. The hotel chef made **my mother an omelet**.

8. After the receipt was printed, the clerk handed **Eleanor a pen**.

8B Verbs in the subjunctive

The following verbs can be followed by a *that* clause with a subjunctive verb.

advise   beg   require   stipulate
ask   prefer   specify   vote

He **advised that** his students **be** on time.
Our store policy clearly **stipulates that** all sales associates **report** to work by 8:30 A.M.

The negative subjunctive is formed with *not* and the base form of the verb.
The advertising executive's contract required that he **not receive** a bonus that year.

The passive form of the subjunctive is formed by *be* + past participle.
The sponsors asked that their product **be featured** prominently in the movie.
The manufacturers preferred that their shaving cream **not be endorsed** by misbehaving stars.

1 Complete the sentences using an active or passive subjunctive form of the verbs in the box. Verbs may be used more than once.

broadcast   not contain   give   prevent   remove   not send

1. The return policy stipulated that customers ___*be given*___ cash refunds for returned items.

2. A new guideline advises that telemarketers _____ from calling after 8:00 P.M.

3. It is required that an advertisement _____ any false information.

4. Parents begged that companies _____ from advertising candy on children's TV shows.

5. The contract clearly specifies that the station _____ our ads 24 hours a day.

6. The customer repeatedly asked that she _____ a free sample of the perfume.

7. I would prefer that companies _____ me spam e-mail of any kind.

8. We voted that those billboards blocking the town's ocean view _____.

2 Complete the sentences with an appropriate form of the verb in parentheses. Use the subjunctive when possible.

1. It's clear that the time devoted to commercials on TV *has increased* (increase) over the past 10 years.

2. She advised that pressure _____ (apply) to companies that engage in false advertising.

3. I learned that my neighbor _____ (be) a stealth marketer.

4. The store required that each customer _____ (open) his or her bag for inspection.

5. He specified that this advertisement _____ (place) in this month's issue.

6. The actress begged that she _____ (not cast) in such a low-budget commercial.

7. I discovered that my sister _____ (be) addicted to shopping.

9A · Whenever and wherever contrasted with when and where

> If *whenever*, *wherever*, *when*, and *where* are followed by subject + *be* + adjective / past participle, the subject and *be* are often deleted. This occurs mainly in formal speech and writing.
> Pet owners must take their pets to the vet **whenever / when** ~~taking them is~~ **advisable**.
> Laws concerning the welfare of helper animals should be enforced **wherever / where applicable**.
>
> *Whenever* and *wherever* can have the meaning "no matter when / where."
> A: My dog doesn't like it when I give her a bath at night.
> B: Mine doesn't like it **whenever** I give him a bath!
>
> *Whenever* and *wherever* can also have the meaning "although I don't know when / where."
> We'll have to get together on his birthday, **whenever** that is!
> Their dog was found in a park outside of Hicksville, **wherever** that is!
>
> *Whenever* and *wherever* are rarely used following the focus adverbs *even*, *just*, *right*, and *only*.
> *When* and *where* are often used instead.
> My cats show me affection **even when** I'm in a bad mood.
> Elephants will survive in the wild **only where** they are protected from illegal hunting.

1 Shorten the sentences by crossing out the subject and the form of *be* in the adverbial clause.

1. Pets need to be given attention every day, not just when ~~giving them attention is~~ convenient.

2. Dog owners are expected to use leashes to walk their dogs where using those items is required by law.

3. My veterinarian suggested that I buy Barkies brand dog food when Barkies brand is available.

4. Whenever disciplining them is appropriate, owners of intelligent animals must be prepared to discipline their pets.

5. Exotic animals may not be kept as pets wherever keeping such pets is prohibited by law.

2 Review the grammar rules on page 71. Complete the sentences with *when*, *whenever*, *where*, or *wherever*. Sometimes more than one answer is possible.

1. *When* my dog ran out of the yard this morning, I called his name, but he kept on running.

2. _____ somebody walks past my house, my dog growls at him or her.

3. The insect looked so much like a leaf that I didn't notice it even _____ I looked right at it.

4. _____ we used to live, the landlord would let tenants have as many pets as they wanted.

5. The sign says that this parrot is from the Kakamega Forest, _____ that is!

6. Over the course of the year, _____ I visited her apartment, she seemed to have added another cat. By spring, she had at least five.

9B Noun clauses with *whoever* and *whatever*

In formal speech and writing, *whoever* is used for the subject and *whomever* is used for the object of a clause. *Whomever* is rare in conversation.
Whoever wants a unique experience should try scuba diving in a coral reef.
I'll take **whomever** the instructor chooses for my rock-climbing partner.

When referring to a known and limited group of items, *whichever* can be used to mean "whatever one" or "whatever ones."
For your birthday, I'll pay for kayaking or skydiving lessons. You can choose **whichever** you want.
I've packed three kinds of sandwiches for the picnic. Your friends can have **whichever** they want.

1 Complete the sentences with *whoever* or *whomever*.

1. I'm eating lunch outdoors today. ___*Whoever*___ wants to eat with me is welcome.

2. Access to this beach is strictly limited to residents and _____ they invite.

3. I believe urban environments without a significant presence of nature are unhealthy for _____ they surround.

4. _____ lives in that house must love the sun – it's made almost entirely of glass.

5. Some doctors say that spending more time in natural sunlight can be one source of relief for _____ winter depression afflicts.

6. _____ thinks that our city parks are just a waste of space has certainly lost touch with nature.

7. The manager position at the eco-resort will be filled by _____ the board of directors selects.

2 Fill in the blanks with *whoever*, *whatever*, or *whichever*.

Here's an idea for (1) ___*whoever*___ is feeling out of touch with nature. Why not enroll in a nature adventure program at a NaturVenture camp?

NaturVenture camps are convenient. Campers don't need to bring anything to our camps, because they can obtain (2) _____ they need from the camp stores. There's also a great selection of locations. There are four NaturVenture camps: on a river, in the forest, in the desert, and in the mountains.

In all four locations, we know how to get people in touch with nature! Our expert guides teach campers (3) _____ they want to know about kayaking, horseback riding, rock climbing, and many other outdoor activities. At our camps, we always keep safety in mind. Our trained medical staff is always on hand to assist (4) _____ might need help. The food is great, too. (5) _____ our chefs prepare always gets plenty of compliments.

Campers can choose (6) _____ of our four camps interests them. We offer one-week or two-week programs, so campers can choose (7) _____ suits their schedules and their budgets. And remember – there is a 10 percent discount for (8) _____ enrolls online. Sign up today!

10A Overview of passives

The passive voice with a modal can be used in short answers.
A: Why wasn't that author awarded the Nobel Prize for literature?
B: I don't know, but he **should have been**. *(He should have been awarded the Nobel Prize for literature.)*

The verb *get* can also serve as an auxiliary to form the passive voice. It is less formal and primarily used in spoken English. *Get* always indicates a change (with a meaning close to *become*), while *be* can indicate an unchanging state or a dynamic one.
Larry and Natalie **got married** in 2006. *(Their wedding occurred in 2006.)*
Larry and Natalie **were married** in 2006 when they went to Greece. *(Their wedding may have occurred before 2006.)*

The verb *get* is also commonly used in expressions such as *get acquainted, get arrested, get dressed, get excited, get married,* and *get scared.*

1 Complete the short answers with the appropriate modal in the passive voice. Sometimes more than one answer is possible.

1. A: Will that Shakespeare class be offered next semester, too?
   B: Oh, yes. I'm absolutely sure that it _____*will be*_____.

2. A: Should text speak be used in essays by some students?
   B: Actually, I think it _____.

3. A: Could English be overtaken as the main international language someday?
   B: Well, in my opinion, it _____.

4. A: Was the television turned off when we went to bed?
   B: No, it wasn't, but it _____.

5. A: Would our class have been canceled if the teacher had been sick?
   B: Yes, it _____. Thank goodness she's not sick!

6. A: Do you think fluency in English can be achieved in five years?
   B: I'm pretty sure it _____, but you'd have to study and practice diligently.

2 Complete the sentences with the correct form of *be* or *get.*

1. While I was reading a book in the bathtub, I heard someone knocking, so I quickly _____*got*_____ dressed and answered the door.

2. Sam and Al had never met, so I gave them a few minutes to _____ acquainted.

3. Martin Luther King Jr. _____ remembered for his contribution to advancing civil rights for African Americans in the United States.

4. When she saw my father carrying her birthday gift, all of a sudden, my little sister _____ really excited and started jumping up and down.

5. I've never tried that language-learning method myself, but I know that it _____ designed by a famous professor.

10B Subject-verb agreement with quantifiers

A (*large / small / great*) *number of* always modifies a plural noun. The resulting expression takes a plural verb.
A (**large**) **number of students** in my English class **were** absent on Friday.

When certain collective nouns, such as *majority* or *minority*, act as a whole unit or a single group, they take a singular verb.
All students can express their opinions, but **the majority rules**.
In the United States, **Spanish speakers** constitute a linguistic **minority** that **is** growing rapidly.

Majority and *minority* are followed by the plural form of *be* when the complement is a plural noun.
If you ask my father about young people today, he'll tell you that **the majority are slackers**.
Of people who are concerned with using language correctly, only **a small minority are linguists**.

1 Review the rules for quantifiers on page 85. Choose the correct form of the verb. If both forms are possible, choose both.

1. A minority of American English speakers (*understand*) / (*understands*) Australian slang.

2. A great number of my friends *has / have* sharp tongues.

3. My students can't write without spell check. The majority *isn't / aren't* great spellers.

4. In the parliament, the newly elected majority *is / are* ready to make some changes.

5. A number of hip-hop expressions *has / have* been added to dictionaries.

6. A majority of my friends *has / have* a way with words.

7. There are times when a minority *speak / speaks* louder than a majority.

8. A number of languages *is / are* spoken in India.

2 Complete these sentences with the singular or plural simple present form of the verb in parentheses.

1. Each person _____*finds*_____ (find) the level of formality he or she is comfortable with.

2. No one _____ (know) the exact number of words in the English language.

3. Most of my friends _____ (speak) English fluently.

4. None of the linking verbs _____ (be) normally used in the passive voice.

5. A lot of people _____ (go) abroad to practice English.

6. A recent report indicated that about one-fourth of American high school students _____ (not graduate).

7. Plenty of my friends _____ (like) to send each other text messages.

8. Every language _____ (have) formal and less formal registers.

9. Every one of my in-laws _____ (talk) my ear off on the phone.

10. All fluent speakers _____ (need) to have an understanding of idiomatic language.

The following compound adjectives follow the pattern: noun + past participle.

awestruck	frostbitten	handwritten	homemade	store-bought	waterlogged
bloodstained	handmade	heartbroken	moth-eaten	sunburned	windswept

The following compound adjectives are found written as one word in many dictionaries.

airborne	barefooted	downhearted	lightweight	painstaking
airsick	daylong	hardheaded	newfound	seaworthy

In the comparative form of compound adjectives, *more* and *less* are not followed by hyphens.
a more forward-looking plan   a less easygoing person   a more highly trained applicant

1 Use one-word adjectives from the grammar box to rewrite the sentences.

1. The flight attendant helped the passengers who felt sick on the airplane.
The flight attendant helped the airsick passengers.

2. We attended a meeting that lasted from 9:00 in the morning to 6:00 in the evening.

3. The passengers boarded the vessel that was worthy of making an ocean voyage.

4. The sailors stopped at an island that had only recently been discovered.

5. The star was overwhelmed by the fans who showed their admiration for her.

6. Jason caught a virus that was carried through the air.

2 Combine the words from both boxes to create compound adjectives and complete the sentences. Check a dictionary for meaning and hyphen use.

forward	hand	home	tender	broken	hearted	made	winded
frost	heart	long	widely	bitten	thinking	respected	written

1. The short __*handwritten*__ message on this photo of Marilyn Monroe makes it very valuable.

2. Because of his great experience in international affairs, the president is _____ in political circles.

3. The audience understood that they wouldn't be able to leave for a while; the speaker had a reputation for being _____.

4. Emma's boyfriend was exceptional. She was _____ when he moved away.

5. My grandmother would never serve anything store-bought. Her cakes and cookies were all _____.

6. Our country needs a more _____ leader, one who can prepare us for crises before they occur.

7. The _____ celebrity was well known for helping any needy person who contacted her.

8. The arctic explorers wore protective gear so that their hands and feet didn't get _____.

11B Superlative compound adjectives

The following adjectives and adverbs have irregular comparative and superlative forms. They are frequently used in comparative and superlative compound adjectives.

Adjective	Comparative	Superlative	Adverb	Comparative	Superlative
good	better	best	well	better	best
bad	worse	worst	badly	worse	worst
far	farther / further	farthest / furthest	little	less (lesser)	least
			much	more	most
			far	farther / further	farthest / furthest

As with other superlative adjectives, the article *the* is not used when the noun is preceded by a possessive.
Venezuela's **best-known** poet will be reading one of his works at the public library this week.

1 Write sentences as in the example using the information and the superlative form of the comparative adjective. Sometimes more than one answer is possible.

1. Charlize Theron is / good-looking actress / I've ever seen
   Charlize Theron is the best-looking actress I've ever seen.

2. My company president is / well-dressed executive / I've ever worked for

3. Last year, I went on one of / badly planned vacations / I've ever taken

4. Our chief of police is / little-appreciated public servant / our town has ever had

5. Mr. Fredericks is / well-loved teacher / our class has ever had

6. That player is / bad-tempered guy / our basketball team has ever hired

7. Professor Vargas is / much-honored academic / our college has ever invited to speak

8. That movie was filmed at / far-flung location / the studio has ever used

2 Write sentences using the superlative form of the compound adjective. Be careful to use hyphens and *the* correctly.

1. That company's (lightweight) camera is the Photoflash X25.
   That company's most lightweight camera is the Photoflash X25.
   That company's lightest-weight camera is the Photoflash X25.

2. My uncle's face looks (awestruck) in the photograph on the right.

3. Henry was (broad-minded) when it came to questions of cultural difference.

4. I take after my father, who is (hardheaded) man I know.

5. Joyce is quite smart, but she's not (well-read) person in the world.

6. To me, Japan's (awe-inspiring) sight is probably Mount Fuji.

7. Perhaps (widely recognized) actress from Malaysia is Michelle Yeoh.

8. One of the (low-lying) countries in Europe is Holland.

12A Subject-verb inversion in conditional sentences

When present or future real conditionals are expressed with *should* at the beginning of the sentence, the base form of the verb is used.

If you**'re** looking for a competent employee, Ted is your man.
Should you **be** looking for a competent employee, Ted is your man.

Subject-verb inversion in conditional sentences occurs rarely with *could* and *might*, usually in literary or archaic contexts, and often with adverbs such as *but* or *just*.

Could he **but** win her love, the world would be his.
Might I **just** see my country once more, my heart would find peace.

In formal situations, people sometimes replace *if* by putting the past subjunctive *were* at the beginning of unreal conditional sentences.

If she **found** enough investors, she could form a startup company.
Were she **to find** enough investors, she could form a startup company.

If she **had been** wealthy, she might not have gone into business.
Were she **to have been** wealthy, she might not have gone into business.

1 Rewrite these sentences using *should* at the beginning of the sentence and the base form of the verb.

1. If Sven goes into business for himself, I'm sure he'll do very well.
   Should Sven go into business for himself, I'm sure he'll do very well.

2. If Annie gets a raise, she'll be able to pay her college debts.

3. If Shin is sick tomorrow, would you be able to work in his place?

4. If you find yourself swamped by work, hire an assistant.

5. If a business is set up in a good location, customers will naturally come.

6. If a problem arises, you need to find a way to work around it.

7. If there's a chance of failure, I'd rather not take the risk.

8. If there's a lot of demand for a product, the price naturally rises.

2 Review the grammar rules on page 97 and in the grammar box. Then rewrite the sentences using subject-verb inversion.

1. If you asked him, he'd tell you the secret of his success.
   Were you to ask him, he'd tell you the secret of his success.

2. If the board approved the measure, the president would surely not veto it.

3. If his boss hadn't been working against him, Jake would have been promoted.

4. If I had looked at my calendar, I would have known about the meeting.

5. If I could just win the gold medal, I'd be happier than the richest man.

6. If we received adequate funding, our program could be a great success.

7. If they were aware of the risk, they would quickly patent their idea.

8. If Tamara hadn't spoken out, the boss would have ignored her.

12B Adverb clauses of condition

In the event (that) and *(just) in case* also introduce a condition on which another situation depends. *In the event (that)* is more formal.
In the event that a replacement cannot be found, you'll have to take on extra responsibilities.
Here's a number to call **just in case** the copy machine breaks down.

Whether or not is used instead of *if* to introduce a condition on which another situation depends. *Or not* is placed directly after *whether* or at the end of the clause.
Whether or not it involves travel, I'm going to have to take this job.
Whether it involves travel **or not**, I'm going to have to take this job.

Even if introduces a condition which, if it is true, doesn't affect the outcome of a situation. It is frequently used with *still*.
I'm (**still**) going to call in sick tomorrow **even if** I'm not actually sick.

If only introduces a condition that the speaker strongly wishes to be true.
If only I had known about that job opening, I would have applied for it immediately.

1 Match the clauses to make logical conditional sentences.

1. If only I hadn't insulted my boss, __*e*__
2. Whether you feel happy inside or not, ____
3. Even if you have great leadership skills, ____
4. Just in case you didn't get the memo, ____
5. If only I could wear casual clothes to work, ____
6. Whether or not the schedule is flexible, ____
7. Even if my company offers me a raise, ____
8. In the event that the manager retires, ____

a. here's a copy for your files.
b. I wouldn't have to spend so much money on suits.
c. you'll likely be promoted to fill her position.
d. I'm still going to take a job with another firm.
e. I'm sure he wouldn't have fired me.
f. the manager wants you to smile for the customers.
g. you can't be forced to work more than 40 hours a week.
h. you still have to earn the workers' respect.

2 Choose the expression that best completes the sentence.

1. (*Just in case*) / *If only* I have to go on a business trip this week, I've kept my schedule open.
2. *Even if / Assuming that* the weather is nice, this weekend's company picnic should be fun.
3. *In the event that / Whether or not* I receive training, I'm still not confident in my abilities.
4. *Even if / If only* I were in charge of hiring people, I'd give everybody a pay raise.
5. *Provided that / Just in case* employees do what is required, salaries are increased every year.

VOCABULARY PLUS

1A Adjectives and verbs to describe friendship

Use the verb or adjective form from each pair in the box to complete the conversations.

admire	clash	empathize	endure	harmonize
admirable	clashing	empathetic	enduring	harmonious

1. A: My dad has been friends with Ahmet since they were roommates in college, and they still get together once a month.

    B: I really _____ *admire* _____ that! They must get along really well!

2. A: Teresa listens to her friends when they have problems and makes a real effort to understand their feelings.

    B: It sounds like she's _____. In my opinion, that's an admirable quality.

3. A: Whenever I'm with Jake, we get into a fight about something ridiculous.

    B: It's too bad you two always _____. Some friends bring out the worst in us.

4. A: My parents get along really well. On the rare occasion they have an issue, they try to discuss it rationally and reach a fair compromise.

    B: It's good they have a _____ relationship. They must be great role models.

5. A: Some psychologists think that only people with similar personalities form strong, long-lasting friendships.

    B: I'm not sure I agree. I can think of lots of people with different personalities who have _____ friendships. Look at us! We've been friends for over 20 years.

1B re- verbs

Use the correct form of five more verbs from the box to replace the underlined mistakes.

rebuild	recall	reconnect	redefine	rehash	rekindle	replace	resurface

1. Emil and Lydia attended the same school many years ago. Recently, they found each other on a social networking site and <u>replaced</u> their friendship. _____ *rekindled* _____

2. We hadn't seen Ian in class for days and were getting worried. He finally <u>rehashed</u> this morning and said he'd been called away to a family emergency. _____

3. If I can't <u>reconnect</u> the last time I saw a friend, I can usually find that information by using the calendar function on my tablet. _____

4. It's annoying when Jack <u>resurfaces</u> the same old arguments. He repeats the same points over and over again, hoping that we'll finally agree with him. _____

5. Rachel and Yumi had a huge argument and stopped speaking to each other. Now, they've both apologized and are trying to <u>recall</u> their damaged friendship. _____

6. Smartphones let us send texts and photos, locate friends, and update our status on social networking sites. They've <u>rebuilt</u> how we communicate. _____

2A Adjectives to describe style

Cross out the word or phrase that does <u>not</u> fit the meaning of the sentence.

1. Fashion design students are up on the latest trends and always look so *chic / stylish / sloppy*.

2. The fashion photographer has a low opinion of people who always wear old jeans and T-shirts no matter the occasion. He thinks they're *frumpy / sloppy / elegant*.

3. The top women executives in that corporation favor beautifully tailored jackets and dresses. They all have *a classic / a quirky / an elegant* look.

4. On some airlines, the flight attendants wear well-designed uniforms that are functional yet *fashionable / retro / chic*.

5. The lawyers in my firm generally wear conservative suits to work, but on weekends, they often wear *functional / trendy / flashy* clothes to company parties.

6. The band members wear vintage jackets, ripped black jeans, and red sneakers. They're trying to achieve a look that's *stuffy / funky / quirky*.

2B Adjectives to describe outward appearance

Choose the correct words to complete the conversations.

1. A: I was watching that new British drama on TV last night. My favorite character is the college professor. He seems intelligent and looks *dignified / innocent* in his dark suit and neatly trimmed beard.

   B: I saw that show, too. I really like the psychologist. You can tell by his friendly, open personality that he's really *intense / trustworthy*.

   A: One character I dislike is the opera singer. She's always sneaking around and looks quite *sinister / sympathetic* in her dark sunglasses and black scarf.

2. A: Did you see the portraits at the exhibit? That general has a reputation as a great leader, but looked almost too confident in that photo. He seemed *arrogant / intellectual*.

   B: I agree. Did you see the photo of the fashion model? I think of her as being sophisticated, but in that photo, she looked sweet and *smug / innocent*.

   A: The photographer definitely has a knack for capturing personalities. I loved his shot of the artist who lives alone on a mountain. I thought she looked pretty *eccentric / sympathetic* hiking in that quirky hat and long dress.

3A Adjectives to discuss technology-related issues

Choose the best words to complete the text.

Technology does amazing things to improve our lives, but there are some things that we should keep in mind. We love all the cool things our smartphones can do, but do you think it's (1) *unethical / hazardous /*(prudent) to upgrade our phones every six months just to get a few more features? Aren't there more worthwhile ways to spend our money? Also, phones are made of plastic, metal, chemicals, and other potentially (2) *audacious / confidential / hazardous* materials, so we have to recycle or dispose of old devices carefully.

Another concern is electronic banking. It's certainly convenient to pay bills online, but many people worry about keeping financial information (3) *confidential / problematic / unethical*. It seems like no matter how complex our passwords are, (4) *frivolous / audacious / confidential* hackers are always able to break into our accounts – and they rarely get caught. We should track down these (5) *unethical / prudent / frivolous* tech wizards and hire them to be our security experts!

3B Collocations to express different attitudes

Combine words from the boxes to complete the sentences. Some of the prepositions are used more than once.

| aware | fed up | intimidated | knowledgeable | leery | reliant |

| about | by | of | on | with |

1. As a security expert, Mia is **knowledgeable about** using fingerprint and facial recognition systems instead of passwords.

2. Ryan is observant and notices things that most of us would miss. When he walks around our city, he's highly _____ surveillance cameras that record people's activities.

3. My father-in-law is skeptical about most things and is especially _____ people who offer get-rich-quick schemes. He prefers to make money by working hard and making prudent investments.

4. Jana is in her 80s now and has become increasingly _____ her daughters to help around the house and drive her to appointments.

5. The teenagers I know think most advertising is annoying and are becoming really _____ pop-up ads appearing on their smartphones all the time.

6. Our manager criticizes our work and often loses his temper. We sometimes feel _____ him, but we're not sure how to improve the situation.

4A   Expressions with *luck*

Use the phrases in the box to correct the underlined mistakes in the sentences.

bad luck	no such luck	the best of luck
beginner's luck	pushing his luck	the luck of the draw

1. As soon as Mei finished writing her paper, her computer crashed, and she lost all her work. That was <u>beginner's luck</u>! _____***bad luck***_____

2. It's dangerous for Todd to ride his motorcycle without a helmet. He hasn't had an accident yet, but he's <u>out of luck</u>. _____

3. Nico will start his new job at the engineering firm tomorrow. I wished him <u>the luck of the draw</u>. _____

4. Our favorite band was playing at the Village Jazz Club. I had hoped to get tickets, but <u>best of luck</u>. The performance was completely sold out. _____

5. Did you hear about the woman who bought a valuable antique vase for five cents at her first online auction? That was truly a case of <u>pushing her luck</u>! _____

6. Jeff had to move to a new apartment this month. By coincidence, there was an apartment available where his best friend lives. Talk about <u>no such luck</u>! _____

4B   Adjectives to describe truth and fabrication

Choose the correct words to complete the conversation.

Marla: Why are you reading that silly magazine? You know that most of those stories are (1) *conceivable /* (*dubious*) */ credible* at best.

Chad: But I enjoy making fun of the articles! Look at this crazy story about a man who saw an upside-down rainbow. Everyone knows that a rainbow's arc is at the top. It sounds pretty (2) *fishy / plausible / conceivable* to me.

Marla: Well, actually, I recently read in a science journal that an upside-down rainbow can occur. There's even a scientific name for it. So I think that story is (3) *iffy / misleading / well-founded* after all.

Chad: Really? Well, OK, here's a story about glowing green mushrooms. It's reported that if you put one on a newspaper in a dark room, it would give off so much light that you could read the words! This story sounds (4) *credible / phony / convincing* to me. I've never heard of anything like that.

Marla: But jellyfish and fireflies give off light, so why do you think it's (5) *far-fetched / convincing / misleading* for mushrooms to glow?

Chad: Well, I haven't see any (6) *fishy / convincing / dubious* evidence that glowing plants exist. But now that you say that, it does make me wonder.

Marla: Yeah, maybe that "silly magazine" isn't so silly!

5A Adjectives to describe movies

Cross out the word that does not fit the meaning of each sentence.

---

http://www.cup.org/bigcitycritic

Here are today's film reviews from our Big City Critic:

Mystery of the Purple Fox is set in a beautiful forest, and the actors are very talented. Unfortunately, it was easy to guess how the movie would end in the first five minutes because the story was (1) ~~riveting~~ / predictable / formulaic. This director's work in the past has been (2) clichéd / inspiring / engrossing, so I was disappointed to see such (3) predictable / touching / mediocre work in this film.

Glacier Meltdown is a documentary about how icebergs are melting at an alarming rate, causing the world's sea levels to rise. It was (4) engrossing / riveting / formulaic to see the gorgeous ice formations, but it was depressing to learn how quickly they are disappearing. It was (5) inspiring / mediocre / moving to watch the scientists endure dangerous conditions and severe weather as they examined the glaciers.

5B Types of TV programs

Choose the true statement for each sentence.

1. This season's most popular show has a complicated plot and characters that are always facing romantic problems and personal disasters.

    ☐ a. This season's most popular show is a sketch comedy show.
    ☐ b. This season's most popular show is a sports program.
    ☐ c. This season's most popular show is a soap opera.

2. This new program features fashion stylists who pick out clothing for celebrities for important events. Viewers get to see them in action as they work.

    ☐ a. The stylists are participants on a game show.
    ☐ b. The stylists are stars of a reality TV show.
    ☐ c. The stylists are hosts on a talk show.

3. The star of this show is a chef who demonstrates how to prepare exotic dishes from all over the world.

    ☐ a. The chef stars in a sitcom about a restaurant.
    ☐ b. The chef prepares unusual dishes on a cooking show.
    ☐ c. The chef gives reports about food on a news program.

4. This show features animated characters. Dee the Dinosaur is the smart one. Fritz the Frog is silly and funny.

    ☐ a. Dee and Fritz are characters in a cartoon.
    ☐ b. Dee and Fritz are reality TV stars.
    ☐ c. Dee and Fritz are the subjects of a documentary.

6A Collocations to describe music

Use the best two phrases from each box to complete the conversations.

| an exhilarating tempo | the mellow sounds | the monotonous beat |

Ann: I really enjoy listening to hip-hop music. I think it has
(1) _an exhilarating tempo_ .

Ben: Call me old-fashioned, but I actually prefer
(2) _____ of slow jazz.

| a catchy tune | a frenetic pace | a soothing rhythm |

Liz: When I work, I usually have classical music playing
in the background. It has (3) _____
that helps me stay calm.

Rob: I need to feel energized when I work, so I listen to rap.
It has (4) _____ that keeps me going.

| a catchy tune | a haunting melody | an exhilarating tempo |

Ted: I enjoy songs that are pleasant and easy to remember. There's something
very satisfying about singing along with (5) _____.

Jen: Oddly enough, I prefer evocative music that sounds sad. Folk music often
has (6) _____ that is hard to forget.

6B Idioms used in the entertainment industry

Match the correct words to complete the sentences.

1. Vanessa is a talented young actress who's auditioning to
   get her first part in a movie. She's trying to be _d_ .

2. My favorite band retired years ago, but I just heard it's
   making ____ . The band is playing at Music Hall next month.

3. If you're starting out as a comedian and want to get ____ ,
   you should try out your material in comedy clubs.

4. Maya's first song was at the top of the charts last year.
   She's working hard on new music because she doesn't
   want to be ____ .

5. That blues guitarist used to be a popular musician.
   Unfortunately, he's not getting any club dates, and he
   seems to be ____ .

6. To succeed as a dancer, you usually have to pay ____ in the
   chorus line and work hard for years before you're noticed.

7. That actor is ____ on the new television series. The network
   just signed him to a huge multi-year contract.

a. a one-hit wonder

b. a comeback

c. washed up

d. discovered

e. your foot in the door

f. your dues

g. a big hit

Cross out the word that does <u>not</u> fit the meaning of each sentence.

1. A: Today I saw a driver in a car at a stoplight. He was texting, talking on a cell phone, and had his laptop open – all at once!

   B: Unfortunately, that seems to be a common practice these days. It seems ~~indecisive~~ / illogical / irresponsible to me.

2. A: My sister really surprised me the other day. She actually picked up her clothes from the floor and cleaned our room!

   B: I used to think she was pretty irresponsible / immature / intolerant, but I guess she's changing.

3. A: My nephew hasn't even tried to get a job since he graduated. He lives with his parents, doesn't pay rent, and stays out all night.

   B: Wow, he sounds like an inconsiderate / immature / inconsistent person. It must be hard on your aunt and uncle. Maybe he'd be motivated if they made him pay rent.

4. A: A recent article said that it's becoming common for people to be expected to work extremely long hours in some professions.

   B: Yes, I've heard that lawyers often work past midnight to prepare for big trials. It's considered indecisive / irresponsible / improper to leave the office before being completely prepared.

7B Collocations with *change*

Correct the underlined mistake in each sentence. Write the correct form of a word or phrase from the box.

| anticipate | bring about | cope with | go through | welcome |

1. Some people get into financial trouble because they use their credit cards all the time and are unable to make their payments. Then they have to <u>anticipate</u> serious lifestyle changes to pay off their debt. ____*go through*____

2. The mayor is admired for consistently initiating action to improve the city. He is always looking for ways to <u>cope with</u> change.
   _____

3. A few longtime residents want everything in their neighborhood to stay the same. They're not the type of people to <u>resist</u> changes. _____

4. The company plans to provide more on-the-job training. The director <u>avoids</u> this change will lead to a more knowledgeable and productive staff. _____

5. During the last recession, some people were unemployed for several months. They <u>welcomed</u> some difficult changes by relying on their families for support.
   _____

8A Expressions to discuss shopping

Use the correct form of the expressions from the box to complete the text.

make an impulse buy	be a compulsive shopper	go over her credit limit
go window-shopping	have buyer's remorse	be a bargain hunter

Did you ever notice how people have different shopping styles? My mom has always been price conscious and (1) __*is a bargain hunter*__. Whenever there's a sale, she combs through everything, looking for the lowest prices. On the other hand, my friend Maggie doesn't even look at price tags and buys everything in sight. She just can't control her urge to shop. She definitely (2) _____. She often spends more than the bank allows on her charge cards, but doesn't worry about (3) _____. Now, my sister Shelly has a totally different shopping style. She drives me insane because she never buys anything. She prefers to (4) _____, just peering at the displays of the latest fashions. Crazy, right? As for me, I have to admit that at times, I have the urge to go on a shopping spree. Shopping is all about having fun. I certainly don't plan to buy three pairs of shoes, but all of a sudden, there they are in my shopping bag! OK, I admit to (5) _____ every once in a while. But I confess that I (6) _____ on occasion and end up returning things. There's only so much room in my closets!

8B Marketing strategies

Read the situations. Then choose the correct ending to make a true sentence.

1. That actress made a commercial for a new floral perfume. She makes a point of saying that she wears it in real life. The perfume maker . . .
   - ☐ a. is offering a comparative-marketing program.
   - ☐ b. must think a celebrity endorsement will increase sales.

2. Every time the main character on that sitcom has breakfast, viewers can clearly see the product name on the box of cereal on the table. That cereal company . . .
   - ☐ a. is using a product-placement strategy.
   - ☐ b. is offering free samples.

3. The credit card company gives points every time shoppers use their card. Many customers keep the card for a long time to earn points. The credit card company retains its customers by using . . .
   - ☐ a. a loyalty program.
   - ☐ b. coupon codes.

4. When consumers searched for smartphone features and prices, one brand kept popping up. As part of its marketing strategy, the smartphone company is using . . .
   - ☐ a. word-of-mouth marketing.
   - ☐ b. search-engine marketing.

9A Physical features of animals

Choose the correct words to complete the conversation.

Ahn: I've been studying how animals defend themselves. It's fascinating how a bird can use its (1) *feathers / fangs / beak* to fight off predators.

Phil: Birds can be fierce, especially if they're protecting their nests.

Ahn: Speaking of fierce, when I was hiking last week, I ran across a herd of wild mountain goats. Two male goats were in a battle, using their (2) *horns / scales / gills* and (3) *claws / hooves / tusks*.

Phil: Goats are considered to be smart, and they are amazing climbers. What other animals have you studied?

Ahn: Last year, I spent time at an ocean research facility to study dolphins.

Phil: Oh, my eight-year-old son has been fascinated by them lately. Someone told him that dolphins didn't have (4) *fins / scales / tails* and didn't breathe through (5) *gills / paws / wings*, and he was really puzzled – "Why not, if they live in the ocean?" When I explained that dolphins are mammals, and not fish, he was amazed. Now he reads every dolphin book he can find.

Ahn: Hey, maybe he'll want to study animals someday, like I do!

9B Nature-related idioms

Replace the underlined phrases with the correct idioms from the list.

a breath of fresh air	as clear as mud	set in stone	under the weather
a drop in the ocean	a walk in the park	the tip of the iceberg	up in the air

1. They're going to open the new nature preserve to the public sometime soon, though the exact date is still <u>not decided on</u>. ____*up in the air*____

2. I know my own effort to reduce carbon pollution by driving an electric car is just <u>a small thing</u>, but I like to know I'm doing something to help. _____

3. I've been feeling <u>unwell</u> for days now. I should really see my doctor. _____

4. A politician helping clean up the park is <u>something new and exciting</u>! I wish more public officials would help the community. _____

5. His explanation of the new environmental law was <u>extremely confusing</u>. I still have no idea of what it's about! _____

6. People are cutting down trees illegally, but I'm sure that's just <u>a small part of the problem</u>. There are bound to be more problems than that. _____

7. I was nervous about presenting my research to the Conservation Board, but in the end it was <u>really easy</u>. They were such good listeners! _____

8. The timetable for the conference is <u>unchangeable</u>. There's no way we can reschedule. _____

10A Discourse markers

Cross out the discourse marker that does not fit the meaning of the sentence.

Greetings, jobseekers!

Do job interviews make you nervous? I used to feel that way, too, but not anymore. My advice is to be prepared for the interview. (1) *Furthermore* / *To begin* / *First of all*, do some research on the company you will interview with, so you can talk about the company in an informed way during the interview. Learn about its business goals, products and services, and financial health. (2) *Next* / *Nevertheless* / *Second*, anticipate the questions the interviewer may ask you – and think of good answers! (3) *Yet* / *In addition* / *Furthermore*, it's a good idea to jot down your own questions about job responsibilities and opportunities for growth. At this point, you may feel totally ready for your interview. (4) *Likewise* / *Yet* / *Nevertheless*, there's one more step you should take: role-play an interview with a trusted friend or relative. That will increase your ability to communicate with self-assurance. (5) *In conclusion* / *To sum up* / *Similarly*, it may feel like all this preparation is a lot of work, but it'll be worth it when you walk confidently into that interview room.

10B Idioms related to the use of language

Complete the sentence about each situation using an expression from the box.
Use the correct form of the verbs and pronouns.

have a sharp tongue	stick to the point	talk behind someone's back
have a way with words	talk around a point	talk someone's ear off

1. Last night, Jessica called Mei Ling and discussed her personal problems for three hours. Mei Ling didn't know how to get her friend off the phone!

   Mei Ling thought that Jessica was *talking her ear off* .

2. Tom began his presentation by talking about oil drilling in Alaska. Then suddenly, he changed the subject to farming methods in China. The audience seemed a little confused.

   Tom needed to _____.

3. My uncle often criticizes my cousin about his grades, his choice of friends, and how little he helps around the house. I think sometimes my uncle is a little harsh.

   My uncle can sometimes _____.

4. Ron is one of those salespeople who can talk his customers into buying anything! I once saw him convince a guy to spend half his salary on a ring for his girlfriend.

   Ron certainly _____.

5. When Pat has to discuss a thorny issue with a friend, she never addresses the problem directly. People get frustrated because she won't say what's really bothering her.

   Pat has to stop _____.

6. After we left the party, Josh started complaining about how unfriendly Anna was. I told him that it was unfair to talk about someone who wasn't there to defend herself.

   I wanted Josh to stop _____.

11A Compound adjectives related to the body

Choose the true statement for each sentence.

1. To be effective during a crisis, it's a good idea not to get overly emotional.
   - ☐ a. You should remain coolheaded even during a crisis.
   - ☐ b. You should be cold-hearted even during a crisis.

2. People should be willing to consider different points of view, no matter how extreme.
   - ☐ a. People should be absent-minded about different points of view.
   - ☐ b. People should be open-minded about different points of view.

3. Some people can be stubborn about doing things their own way and rarely compromise.
   - ☐ a. People who can't make compromises are hard-hearted and poor team players.
   - ☐ b. People who can't make compromises are hard-headed and poor team players.

4. Mammals maintain a fairly constant body temperature, regardless of their environment.
   - ☐ a. Mammals are warm-blooded creatures.
   - ☐ b. Mammals are warm-hearted creatures.

5. Some folks have little tolerance for people who have different beliefs or ideas.
   - ☐ a. It's unfortunate that some folks are so empty-headed about others.
   - ☐ b. It's unfortunate that some folks are so narrow-minded about others.

11B Phrasal verbs

Choose the correct words to complete the conversation.

Amy: I have to fly home this weekend to (1) *take after /* check on my grandparents. They don't like to admit it, but they can use a little help around the house these days.

Luke: You go home a lot, don't you? That's great that you (2) *look after / look to* your grandparents!

Amy: Well, I feel compelled to (3) *get through / live up to* my responsibilities. Besides, my grandparents took such good care of me as a child. Now it's my turn!

Luke: It sounds like you (4) *take after / side with* your grandparents! They must be excellent role models for you and your brothers.

Amy: Unfortunately, my younger brother Ethan is having a hard time at school. I'm going to talk with him this weekend. He needs to (5) *face up to / live up to* his problems. I think I'll remind him about the challenges our grandparents faced when they were young, and how they were still able to finish college.

Luke: I'm sure that you'll help him (6) *get through / look to* this difficult period.

12A Prepositions following *work*

Complete the conversations with the words from the box. Use the correct form of the verbs.

work against   work around   work for   work off   work toward

1. A: We've been discussing this issue with the manufacturer for months. The engineers are getting close to figuring out a way to make the batteries last longer.

   B: That's great! Sounds like you're ___*working toward*___ a solution.

2. A: We don't have enough staff to finish the analysis on time. We've asked management for help, but they can't hire any new people right now.

   B: That's too bad! It seems like your bosses are _____ you.

3. A: My parents lent me a lot of money, and I don't know how to pay them back.

   B: Do they need help around their house? Maybe you could _____ some of your debt by doing yard work, cleaning the garage, and things like that.

4. A: Our firm has offices in Beijing and New York. Sometimes it's tricky to juggle the time zones, especially when we're trying to schedule meetings.

   B: Having colleagues in different locations can be a challenge, but hopefully you'll find a way to _____ that problem.

5. A: My last boss was extremely demanding. I learned a lot from her, but it was tough working 80 hours a week! If she was in the office, we had to be there, too.

   B: Sounds like a valuable learning experience. In the future, I hope you get to _____ a manager with a more balanced approach to life!

12B Expressions related to success in the workplace

Choose the best words to complete the email.

Hello Mark,

Thank you for agreeing to write the job description for our new position. Here are my thoughts on what to include when you write it. Since this is an entrepreneurial company, we should put a high priority on finding someone who has original ideas and (1)(*is innovative*)/ *has charisma* / *has influence*. We need a person who (2) *has specialized training* / *has initiative* / *has influence* and doesn't wait to be told what to do. In addition, since our company works in close-knit teams, the new hire should (3) *have good communication skills* / *have self-discipline* / *be optimistic* and be good at explaining ideas. We also want a candidate who (4) *has specialized training* / *is conscientious* / *has leadership ability* and can inspire others to do their best work. Finally, since we deal with a lot of internal and external change, the person we hire must (5) *be adaptable* / *be trustworthy* / *be conscientious* and able to cope with some degree of uncertainty.

I look forward to reading the job description.

Regards,

Laura

Credits

Illustration credits

Jo Goodberry: 12, 103
Paul Hostetler: 22, 23, 64, 101

Kim Johnson: 3, 26, 36, 65
Dan McGeehan: 41, 56, 84

Rob Schuster: 72, 87
Koren Shadmi: 9, 17, 53, 83

James Yamasaki: 28, 86

Photography credits

Back cover: (*clockwise from top center*) ©Leszek Bogdewicz/Shutterstock, ©Wavebreak Media/Thinkstock, ©Blend Images/Alamy, ©limpido/Shutterstock; **2** ©George Doyle/Thinkstock; **5** ©Davide Mazzoran/Thinkstock; **6** (*left to right*) ©Corbis/SupersStock, ©Jeff Greenberg/Alamy, ©Blend Images/Alamy; **8** ©Corbis/SuperStock; **10** (*top to bottom*) ©Coprid/Shutterstock, ©Neamov/Shutterstock, ©Barghest/Shutterstock, ©robert_s/Shutterstock, ©mama_mia/Shutterstock; **11** ©Ira Berger/Alamy; **13** ©alexnika/Thinkstock; **14** ©Fuse/Thinkstock; **15** ©Cultura Limited/SuperStock; **16** (*clockwise from top left*) ©Dimitrios Kambouris/Getty Images, ©Alberto E. Rodriguez/Getty Images, ©Jeffrey Mayer/WireImage/Getty Images, ©Vittorio Zunino Celotto/Getty Images; **18** (*left to right*) ©Krzysztof Gawor/Getty Images, ©Science Photo Library – SCIEPRO/Getty Images, ©Eric Isselée/Thinkstock; **19** ©EVERETT KENNEDY BROWN/epa/Corbis; **20** ©Beyond/SuperStock; **21** ©Gilles Podevins/Science Photo Library/Corbis; **24** ©Europics/Newscom; **25** ©Newspix/Getty Images; **27** (*clockwise from top left*) ©Christin Gilbert/agefotostock/SuperStock, ©al_ter/Thinkstock, ©Franck Boston/Thinkstock, ©GregC/Thinkstock, ©Nathan Allred/Thinkstock, ©Comstock/Thinkstock; **29** ©Photimageon/Alamy; **31** (*top to bottom*) ©Stockbyte/Thinkstock, ©Mykola Velychko/Thinkstock, ©Jupiterimages/Thinkstock, ©Valeriy Lebedev/Thinkstock; **32** (*clockwise from top left*) ©Jupiterimages/Thinkstock, ©Maksim Kabakou/Thinkstock, ©Elnur Amikishiyev/Thinkstock, ©Paul Poplis/Getty Images, ©guy harrop/Alamy; **33** ©Eric Staller/Splash News/Newscom; **34** ©GERARD CERLES/Getty Images; **35** ©MANAN VATSYAYANA/Getty Images; **38** ©I love images/SuperStock; **39** ©AF archive/Alamy; **42** ©Digital Vision/Thinkstock; **43** (*top to bottom*) ©courtesy of One Day on Earth, ©courtesy of One Day on Earth, ©courtesy of One Day on Earth; **44** ©OJO Images/SuperStock; **45** ©RichardBaker/Alamy; **46** ©Fernando Garcia-Murga/AgeFotostock; **47** (*left to right*) ©Fox Photos/Getty Images, ©Dave J Hogan/Getty Images; **48** (*left to right*) ©Kevin Winter/Getty Images, ©John Shearer/Getty Images, ©Chris McGrath/Getty Images; **49** ©Stanislav Tiplyashin/Thinkstock; **50** ©Jack Hollingsworth/Thinkstock; **51** ©Red Box Films/ZUMA Press/Newscom; **52** ©CBS/Getty Images; **54** ©Exactostock/SuperStock; **57** ©Wavebreakmedia Ltd/Thinkstock; **58** (*left to right*) ©Jose Luis Pelaez Inc/Blend Images/Alamy, ©Image Source/Alamy, ©David Litschel/Alamy; **59** ©Sergey Mikhailov/Thinkstock; **62** (*clockwise from top left*) ©Iryna Rasko/Shutterstock, ©Nastco/Thinkstock, ©Jupiterimages/Thinkstock, ©Ilya Shapovalov/Shutterstock; **63** ©james turner/Alamy; **66** (*left to right*) ©Art Directors & TRIP/Alamy, ©Raine Vara/Alamy, ©Raymond Boyd/Getty Images; **67** ©John Wynn/Thinkstock; **69** ©Photos 12/Alamy; **70** (*clockwise from top left*) ©Presselect/Alamy, ©Jean-Louis Atlan/Corbis, ©Rick Friedman/Corbis, ©Paris Match/Getty Images; **71** ©Photo by Adam Scull/Newscom; **73** ©Image Source/Getty Images; **74** ©Brad Perks Lightscapes/Alamy; **75** ©Getty Images/Agefotostock; **76** ©David De Lossy/Thinkstock; **77** ©STAN HONDA/Getty Images; **78** (*left to right*) ©Purestock/Thinkstock, ©Flirt/SuperStock, ©iStock/Thinkstock; **79** (*left to right*) ©iStock Collection/Thinkstock, ©Mitchell Kranz/Shutterstock, ©Fuse/Thinkstock; **80** (*left to right*) ©Tim Mosenfelder/Getty Image News/Getty Images, ©AFP/Getty Images; **82** ©Khakimullin Aleksandr/Shutterstock; **85** ©Tom Briglia/Getty Images; **88** (*left to right*) ©Elliot & Fry/Getty Images, ©Nick Harvey/WireImage/Getty Images, ©Michael Tran/FilmMagic/Getty Images; **90** (*clockwise from top left*) ©Christian Alminana/WireImage/Getty Images, ©L. Busacca/WireImage/Getty Images, ©Valerie Macon/Getty Images, ©Michael Kovac/WireImage/Getty Images, ©John Parra/WireImage/Getty Images; **91** ©Ian Gavan/Getty Images; **92** (*top to bottom*) ©iStock Collection/Thinkstock, ©iStock Collection/Thinkstock, ©iStock Collection/Thinkstock, ©Blend Images/Shutterstock, ©Siri Stafford/Thinkstock, ©gulfimages/SuperStock; **93** ©Jacek Sopotnicki/Thinkstock; **94** ©itanistock/Alamy; **95** ©VMAA/ZOB WENN Photos/Newscom; **96** (*clockwise from top right*) ©Bryan Smith/ZUMAPRESS/Newscom, ©YOSHIKAZU TSUNO/AFP/Getty Images/Newscom, ©Andrew Hasson/Photoshot/Getty Images; **100** ©Comstock Images/Thinkstock; **102** ©mediaphotos/Thinkstock; **105** (*left to right*) ©Jacob Wackerhausen/Thinkstock, ©Suprijono Suharjoto/Thinkstock, ©Chace & Smith Photography/Fuse Collection/Thinkstock; **131** ©mangostock/Thinkstock; **133** ©Mark A Schneider/Getty Images; **135** ©Blend Images/SuperStock; **136** ©George Doyle/Thinkstock; **138** ©William Curch – Summit42.com/Getty Images; **140** ©Agefotostock/SuperStock

Text credits

The authors and publishers acknowledge the following sources of copyright material and are grateful for the permissions granted. While every effort has been made, it has not always been possible to identify the sources of all the material used, or to trace all copyright holders. If any omissions are brought to our notice, we will be happy to include the appropriate acknowledgments on reprinting.

9 Adapted from "How Social Media 'Friends' Translate Into Real-Life Friendships" by Terri Thornton, *Mediashift*, July 13, 2011. Reproduced with permission of Mediashift, PBS; **16** Adapted from "Judging Faces Comes Naturally" by Jules Crittenden, *Boston Herald*, September 7, 1997. Reproduced with permission of the Boston Herald; **17** Adapted from "Overcoming a Bad First Impression" by Susan Fee, Professional Clinical Counselor, www.susanfee.com. Reproduced with permission of Susan Fee; **25** Adapted from "Family: I Unplugged My Kids" by Melissa McClements, *The Guardian*, January 1, 2011. Copyright © Guardian News & Media Ltd 2011; **35** Adapted from "Do Good-luck Charms Really Work in Competitions?" by Alex Hutchinson, *The Globe and Mail*, October 18, 2010. Reproduced with permission of Alex Hutchinson; **43** Adapted from "'One Day On Earth' Debuts Worldwide, Offers Time Capsule Of Our Lives" by Mark Johanson, *International Business Times*, April 21, 2012. Reproduced with permission of International Business Times; **51** Adapted from "Sixto Rodriguez: On the Trail of the Dylan of Detroit" by David Gritten, *The Telegraph*, June 14, 2012. Copyright © Telegraph Media Group Limited 2012; **61** Adapted from "Living the Simple Life – and Loving It" by Julia Duin, *The Washington Times*, January 5, 1996. Copyright © 1996 The Washington Times LLC. This reprint does not constitute or imply any endorsement or sponsorship of any product, service, company or organization. License # 37237; **69** Adapted from "Word-of-Mouth Marketing: We All Want to Keep Up with the Joneses" by Martin Lindstrom, www.martinlindstrom.com, September 21, 2011. Reproduced with permission of Martin Lindstrom; **77** From "A Summer Job That Promises Nature Walks for Pay" by Cara Buckley, *The New York Times*, August 13, 2008. Copyright © 2008 The New York Times. All rights reserved. Used by permission and protected by the Copyright Laws of the United States. The printing, copying, redistribution, or retransmission of this Content without express written permission is prohibited; **80** Adapted from *Schaum's Quick Guide to Great Presentation Skills* by Melody Templeton and Suzanne Sparks Fitzgerald, published by McGraw-Hill, 1999. Copyright © 1999 by the McGraw-Hill Companies, Inc.; **87** Adapted from "Slang Abroad" by Ben Falk, *The Daily Colonial*, April 1, 2006. Reproduced with permission; **95** Adapted from "Leading Questions" by Alison Benjamin, *The Guardian*, March 28, 2007. Copyright © Guardian News & Media Ltd 2007; **103** Adapted from *Job Savvy: How to Be a Success at Work Fifth Edition* by LaVerne L. Ludden, published by JIST Publishing, 2012. Reproduced with permission of JIST Publishing.

Answers

Page 32, Exercise 1B: Story 2 is false.
Page 34, Exercise 5B: They are all hoaxes.
Page 84, Exercise 2A: before, Are you OK?, See you later, excellent, great, tonight

Jack C. Richards & Chuck Sandy

Passages
Third Edition

CAMBRIDGE
UNIVERSITY PRESS

Video Activity Worksheets **2**

1 DO OPPOSITES ATTRACT?

Before you watch

A What do people need to have in common for a harmonious relationship? Choose the three most important things partners should share in your opinion.

☐ cultural background ☐ past experiences ☐ religion

☐ hobbies/interests ☐ personality type ☐ tastes in books and movies

☐ outlook on life ☐ political views ☐ values

B **Pair work** Compare and discuss your choices in part A. Then decide upon the most important thing people should have in common. Share your choice with the class. Give reasons and examples to support your opinion.

A: We think the most important thing people should have in common is their values. If your values are different, it can affect a lot of areas in your life, like your future plans or how you raise your family.

While you watch

A Take notes to answer the questions in your own words.

1. What do experts think people need to look for in friendships and love relationships?

_____

2. What may the differences that are attractive at first cause a couple to do later on?

_____

3. Why is it harder for people with opposite personalities to form a relationship?

_____

B Write the letter of the correct video character to complete each sentence. Use each letter twice.

a. The good girl   b. The laid-back artist   c. The outgoing boyfriend   d. The type-A businesswoman

1. ____ should find someone with relaxed energy.
2. ____ is not a good match for a shy partner.
3. ____ may be better off dating a businessperson.
4. ____ would enjoy being with a highly social person.
5. ____ is preferred by the laid-back artist but is not a good match for one.
6. ____ may tend to fall for the rebel.
7. ____ may feel a businessperson has traits that are helpful.
8. ____ will have a harmonious relationship with a nice person.

C Choose the correct answer according to information in the video.

1. Research shows that people may admire _____ .
   - a. people like them
   - b. expert opinions
   - c. people who have skills they lack

2. We need to date people whose _____ are similar to our own.
   - a. experiences and values
   - b. personality and attitudes
   - c. religious and political beliefs

3. People on dating websites usually decide to go out with people who _____ them.
   - a. complement
   - b. are similar to
   - c. are the opposite of

4. If you end up dating someone who is your opposite, you should _____ .
   - a. remember to reconnect after arguments
   - b. say good-bye
   - c. examine the differences in attitude and personality

5. Differences in views on things like politics and movies are usually differences in _____ .
   - a. attitude
   - b. personality
   - c. values

6. Once opposite personalities clash, it may be harder for them to _____ .
   - a. reconnect with each other
   - b. rehash old times
   - c. share relaxed energy

After you watch

A Pair work The video states that there is a big difference between opposite attitudes and opposite personalities in relationships. Look at the personal aspects in *Before you watch* part A. Write *A* next to those related to attitude and *P* next to those related to personality. Discuss your choices.

B Pair work List the 10 most important things for you in a mate. Exchange lists and classify your partner's choices into traits relating to attitude, appearance, or personality. Then discuss the questions below.

1. Do you agree or disagree on the classifications?
2. Do you feel either list should be adjusted? If so, how and why?

A: The trait "likes sports" is an attitude, so it may not be very important.

B: I have to disagree. For me, sports are everything! If my partner didn't go to sporting events with me, he'd be very lonely!

Before you watch

A **Pair work** Match the adjectives with the pictures. Then compare your answers. Did you choose the same images? Discuss your choices.

conservative	flashy	futuristic	quirky
dignified	functional	over-the-top	sloppy

1. _____

2. _____

3. _____

4. _____

5. _____

6. _____

7. _____

8. _____

B **Pair work** Look at the styles in part A. Talk about your impression of each person based on what he or she is wearing.

A: I think number two looks elegant, but she may be a bit stuffy.

B: I agree. She looks like a person who might be nice but phony.

While you watch

A Choose the main topics discussed in the video.

☐ 1. self-expression

☐ 2. royalty

☐ 3. very large hats

☐ 4. youth culture

☐ 5. large necklaces

☐ 6. very high shoes

☐ 7. Egyptian eye makeup

☐ 8. bikinis

☐ 9. shopping

☐ 10. sweatshirts

☐ 11. retro looks

☐ 12. quirky combinations

B Write *T* (true) or *F* (false). Then correct the false statements with a partner.

____ 1. Clothing has only recently become important to people.

____ 2. People dress for self-expression and are often inspired to dress like famous people.

____ 3. When we think of over-the-top seventeenth-century fashions, we tend to think of Queen Elizabeth.

____ 4. One of the biggest influences on fashion since the 1960s has been comfort.

____ 5. High shoes were invented to make people feel taller.

____ 6. The heavy eye makeup Egyptians wore served a functional purpose.

____ 7. In the future, we probably won't be permitted to choose what to wear.

C Choose the correct answers according to the information in the video.

1. Our clothing tends to tell the world _____ .
   a. how we think   b. what our job is like   c. who we think we are

2. Fashion has been about self-expression _____ .
   a. for about 3,000 years   b. since King Louis XIV   c. since the 1960s

3. Men were encouraged to wear powdered wigs _____ .
   a. because the king did   b. because they wanted to be king   c. to cover their bald spots

4. An aspect of 1960s youth culture is that people decided to _____ .
   a. dress more like celebrities   b. be comfortable   c. create their own styles

5. Usually the latest trend is a look that rebels against _____ .
   a. revealing the body   b. the established look   c. sloppy looks

6. After a frumpy style has been around a while, the next look will probably be _____ .
   a. quirky   b. futuristic   c. dignified

After you watch

A The video points out that the following things have been behind creating fashions. Give an example of a fashion item created for each reason.

1. People we look up to: _____

   _____

2. Comfort: _____

   _____

3. Necessity: _____

   _____

B **Group work** Discuss your answers to part A. What are the group's best examples? Share them with the class.

C **Writing** What is the biggest influence on your fashion choices? Why is it important to you? Write a paragraph explaining your view.

3 PAST AND FUTURE PREDICTIONS

Before you watch

Pair work What will the world be like 100 years from now? What new things will we have? What will we do differently? What will stay the same? Discuss the questions for each category. Then write your predictions.

1. Travel

_____
_____
_____

2. Technology

_____
_____
_____

3. Health

_____
_____
_____

4. Education

_____
_____
_____

5. (Other area / Your choice) _____

_____
_____
_____

While you watch

A Write *T* (true) or *F* (false). Then correct the false statements with a partner.

_____ 1. Very few predictions for the future that were made 100 years ago were accurate.

_____ 2. Predictions that came true included the invention of certain types of communication and travel.

_____ 3. Predictions that didn't come true included certain changes to education and special medical advancements.

_____ 4. Two of the predictions that were somewhat true were about travel and communication.

_____ 5. The modern-day people in the video make very different predictions for the future than the people of 100 years ago.

_____ 6. Four of the modern-day people make predictions about transportation.

B Complete the predictions made in the past that were mentioned in the video.

1. People thought telephones would be _____.
2. They predicted that we would be able to communicate worldwide using _____.
3. They thought we would tour the country driving _____.
4. They suggested that we would clean our homes automatically using _____.
5. They thought that a college education would be _____.
6. They believed we would have killed all the _____.
7. They were certain we would have put an end to _____.
8. They thought we would get our shopping delivered by _____.
9. They thought students would learn because of _____ connected to their heads.

C Write the letter of the correct phrase to complete each sentence.

a. cars will drive themselves
b. people will choose their dreams
c. there won't be any cars

d. robots will do all the work
e. people won't get sick anymore
f. we will have flying cars

1. Joshua predicts that in the future ____.
2. Bao thinks that ____.
3. Yasmin expects that ____.
4. Mike thinks that ____.
5. Patricia believes ____.
6. Shane predicts that ____.

After you watch

A Pair work Look at your partner's predictions from *Before you watch*. How are they the same or different from the ones at the end of the video? How likely do you think they are to come true? Rate the predictions from 0 (very unlikely) to 10 (very likely).

B Group work Compare your predictions from part A. Choose a favorite prediction for each category and present it to the class. Do they think it will come true? Why or why not?

C Writing Write a paragraph about the three technological advances made in the last 100 years that you consider the most important. Give facts, reasons, and examples to support your opinion.

4 SUPERSTITIONS AROUND THE WORLD

Before you watch

A Pair work Answer the questions about common superstitions. Then interview a partner about his or her beliefs. Discuss your answers.

Do you . . .	Me		My partner	
	Yes	No	Yes	No
1. believe the number 4 is unlucky?	☐	☐	☐	☐
2. believe the number 13 is unlucky?	☐	☐	☐	☐
3. assume black cats are good or bad luck?	☐	☐	☐	☐
4. carry a rabbit's foot for luck?	☐	☐	☐	☐
5. avoid walking under ladders?	☐	☐	☐	☐
6. avoid writing your name with red pen?	☐	☐	☐	☐
7. cross your fingers for good luck?	☐	☐	☐	☐
8. think breaking a mirror is unlucky?	☐	☐	☐	☐
9. think that an itchy palm means you will lose or gain money?	☐	☐	☐	☐

B Pair work Can you think of any other superstitions? Make a list and share it with the class.

While you watch

A Choose the superstitions that you hear mentioned in the video.

☐ 1. wearing red for good luck
☐ 2. crossing fingers for luck
☐ 3. the thirteenth floor of tall buildings
☐ 4. Loki the Norse god of evil
☐ 5. the number 7 being lucky
☐ 6. tossing a coin in a fountain
☐ 7. leaving chopsticks in a bowl of rice
☐ 8. dumping coconuts off a boat
☐ 9. leaving shoes overturned
☐ 10. walking under ladders

B Choose the correct answers according to the information in the video.

1. Most cultures have _____ ideas about luck.
   a. very different   b. very similar   c. several

2. The origin of number 13 as being unlucky may originate from _____.
   a. historians   b. the ancient Persians   c. tall buildings

3. Many superstitions are related to a fear of _____.
   a. ladders   b. death   c. rats

4. In some places, _____ is considered bad luck.
   a. how you eat   b. serving rice   c. placing certain eating utensils incorrectly

5. Some superstitions are based upon _____.
   a. real situations   b. travel restrictions   c. the style of objects

6. In Hawaii, there is a practice of dumping bananas off a boat as it is _____.
   a. arriving at the shore   b. sailing at sea   c. leaving the shore

C Take notes to answer the questions in your own words. Then compare answers with a partner.

1. Name three superstitions that are considered lucky.

_____

_____

_____

2. What are three possible origins for the fear of the number 13?

_____

_____

_____

3. Why is the number 4 considered unlucky in some places?

_____

4. What is the reason for the Hawaiian superstition of dumping bananas off a boat?

_____

After you watch

A **Pair work** The video mentions some reasons behind superstitions. List three superstitions and possible reasons behind them. You can make the reasons up, but try to make them believable.

1. Superstition: _____

   Reason: _____

2. Superstition: _____

   Reason: _____

3. Superstition: _____

   Reason: _____

B **Group work** Which reasons from part A seem the most convincing? The most unbelievable? Share your most believable reasons for the superstitions with the class. Which group's reasons are the best?

C **Writing** Do you think superstitions and good luck charms actually influence outcomes in life? Write a paragraph about your opinion. Give reasons and examples to support your view.

5 MEET THE DIRECTOR

Before you watch

A Which of these steps involved in making a movie do you think would be difficult to do? Which would be easier to do? Which do you think you might enjoy doing? Complete the chart.

	Difficult	Easier	I might enjoy doing
1. coming up with a good idea for the movie	☐	☐	☐
2. writing the script	☐	☐	☐
3. finding actors	☐	☐	☐
4. financing the movie	☐	☐	☐
5. shooting the movie	☐	☐	☐
6. directing the movie	☐	☐	☐
7. getting the movie into theaters	☐	☐	☐

B **Pair work** Compare your answers in part A. How similar or different are your choices? What are the reasons behind them?

While you watch

A Number the steps for making the movie *Rot* from 1 to 7 in the order the director mentions them.

____ using crowdfunding to get money for the movie

____ trying to raise money for the movie by showing people the unfinished script

____ more and more people connecting with the film idea

____ scouting locations and talking to people

____ paying for part of the movie with his own money

____ having small ideas that connected with a number of other ideas

____ putting the movie in film festivals

B Choose the correct answers according to the information in the video.

1. The director knew he had to make the movie when _____ .

   a. the ideas connected
   b. he realized it had a great metaphor
   c. everyone said it was a strong, moving idea

2. The director was _____ as he was writing the first draft of the script.

   a. scouting locations and trying to raise money
   b. asking studios for money
   c. living in a cabin

3. One challenge a new director faces is getting _____ .

   a. support from family and friends
   b. funding for a movie
   c. good ideas to connect

4. The director found it surprising that so many people _____ .

   a. thought the movie sounded cool
   b. helped pay for an unknown movie
   c. were making inexpensive movies

5. By putting his movie in as many film festivals as possible, the director hopes to
   _____ .

   a. encourage studios to make his next movie
   b. get his message across
   c. win lots of awards

6. One problem for new filmmakers nowadays is that _____ .

   a. there are not a lot of good ideas left
   b. people donate smaller amounts of money
   c. it is harder to get noticed

C Match the underlined words with the items to which they are referring.

   a. the movie
   b. get a movie noticed
   c. the first draft of the script
   d. the first ideas for the movie
   e. the main character
   f. universal themes

   ____ 1. "I wanted it to be touching."
   ____ 2. ". . . but I wanted to do them in a more original way . . ."
   ____ 3. ". . . some of them go back over a year ago . . ."
   ____ 4. ". . . I thought that was a great metaphor for just what's going on with him . . ."
   ____ 5. "So I would give it to people, and at this point it probably wasn't that good . . ."
   ____ 6. "But I feel that with the right idea and the right story, there's no reason why you can't do it."

After you watch

A Pair work Answer the questions and discuss the video. Then share your discussion with the class.

1. What things did you learn about making a movie as a new director?
2. What information from the video did you find the most interesting or surprising? Why?

B Pair work The video shows a few clips from the movie. Based on those clips, how do you think the story goes? Take turns summarizing your ideas about the story.

C Writing Crowdfunding is now being used to fund movies, art projects, travel plans, and special products. What would you like to raise money to do? Write a paragraph explaining your idea and why people might connect with it.

Before you watch

Pair work What do you think life is like for a new band that has not signed with a record label? Discuss the questions.

1. What kinds of tasks would a band have to do themselves if they have no agent or manager?
2. Where are the best venues for a new band to play?
3. What kinds of songs should a band play to catch people's attention?
4. How important are social media and the Internet in becoming successful today?

A: Without a manager or agent, there would be a lot of things a band would have to do.

B: Yeah, like book their own shows, talk to music producers, and maybe even manage the money.

While you watch

A Choose the best answers according to the information in the video.

1. What is one way the Hillary Reynolds Band describes their music?
   a. acoustic folk
   b. pop acoustic
   c. indie-folk

2. What is one challenge the band faces right now?
   a. They cannot get enough studio time.
   b. They have to book everything themselves.
   c. Their upcoming tour was canceled.

3. How does the band write and arrange songs?
   a. Hillary writes all their songs.
   b. The band collaborates on all their songs.
   c. Their songwriting processes are varied.

4. How does the band get people to listen to their music?
   a. They make sure a lot of people hear them.
   b. They do cold calls to make contacts.
   c. They play cover songs to get people's attention.

5. What does the band enjoy hearing most from their fans?
   a. that they were able to find them on social media
   b. that a song has made them feel good
   c. that they heard them on the radio somewhere

6. What does the band think it takes to be successful in the music business?
   a. hard work and passion
   b. passion and a good agent
   c. a good agent and love for the business

7. What are the band's hopes for the future?
   a. to get their songs on mainstream radio
   b. to meet more people in the music industry
   c. to continue playing music for people

B Write *T* (true) or *F* (false). Then correct the false statements with a partner.

_____ 1. The Hillary Reynolds Band met at the Berklee College of Music.

_____ 2. The band combines catchy pop melodies with electric instruments.

_____ 3. Trevor plays the mandolin, Jeff plays the ukulele, Hillary plays the cello, and Chris plays the upright bass.

_____ 4. Sometimes Hillary and the band write an entire song in one session.

_____ 5. According to the band, a big résumé makes it easier to get more high-profile gigs.

_____ 6. The band enjoys making music but also hopes that they will sign with a major label and become really famous.

C Who says it? Write *H* for Hillary, *T* for Trevor, or *J* for Jeff.

Hillary

Trevor

Jeff

_____ 1. ". . . so we try to use those kinds of instruments and those kinds of sounds and textures to get across pop songwriting."

_____ 2. "Most signed artists have a whole team of people that are dedicated to making the 'machine' work."

_____ 3. "And that is what makes our songwriting so complex and so . . . so great."

_____ 4. "And I think the more we play covers, the more they are willing to give our original songs a chance."

_____ 5. "In the past, we would make a lot of cold calls because we wouldn't have a lot of contacts around the country . . ."

_____ 6. ". . . bands would define success, by signing with a major label, becoming really famous . . . "

After you watch

A In the video, the band gives their opinions about what bands can do to be successful. What is your opinion on the following points related to this topic?

1. Does playing cover songs make a band more popular? Why or why not?

2. What does it take to be successful in the music business?

3. How would you define a successful band?

B **Pair work** Discuss your answers to part A. Then compare and contrast the Hillary Reynolds Band with a band that you think is successful. How are they the same? How are they different?

C **Group work** What does *success* mean in the entertainment industry in general? Choose a successful entertainer and describe why he or she has done well.

7 CHANGING GENDER ROLES

Before you watch

A Look at the jobs. Which are for men? Which are for women? Think of your first reaction and write *M* for men, *W* for women, or *B* for both.

____ 1. business leader	____ 5. hairstylist	____ 9. police officer
____ 2. doctor	____ 6. homemaker	____ 10. secretary
____ 3. engineer	____ 7. lawyer	____ 11. soldier
____ 4. farmer	____ 8. nurse	____ 12. teacher

B **Pair work** Do you agree or disagree on your choices? Discuss your answers and explain your opinions.

While you watch

A Choose the statement that best summarizes the main idea presented at these points in the video.

1.
   a. The gender roles of men and women in the past were not that diverse.
   b. For many centuries, gender roles in the home business were separated.
   c. Men and children worked on the farm and women worked in the home for many centuries.

2.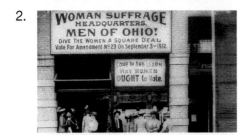
   a. The Industrial Revolution made people behave as though gender roles would not change.
   b. During the 200 years after the Industrial Revolution, gender roles went through a big change.
   c. In the twentieth century, gender roles went through a big change.

3.
   a. With further education, many women entered fields dominated by men.
   b. With women entering new fields, most men welcomed them.
   c. Some men welcome women in the workplace, but there are still some who resist them.

4.
   a. Children growing up today may not be able to decide what to do.
   b. Children who are growing up today may be able to choose any career they want.
   c. Attitudes and roles are likely to reverse for the new generation of children.

B Number the events from 1 to 8 in the order they are mentioned in the video.

_____ Men left to fight in wars.

_____ Men went to work in factories while women stayed home with the kids.

_____ Women started to become doctors and business leaders.

_____ Gender roles were similar, sharing work and having businesses at home.

_____ Women started working in factories, offices, and stores.

_____ More men started becoming teachers, nurses, and stay-at-home dads.

_____ The Industrial Revolution created many jobs away from home.

_____ Women sought further education.

C Take notes to answer the questions in your own words. Then compare answers with a partner.

1. How did many women feel after filling in for men during World Wars I and II?

_____

_____

_____

2. What issues exist today for women who are in the same jobs as men?

_____

_____

_____

3. What issues exist today for men whose jobs are considered feminine?

_____

_____

_____

After you watch

A Pair work Ask and answer the questions about the video. Then share a summary of your discussion with the class.

1. What new things did you learn about gender roles?
2. What information did you find the most interesting or surprising? Why?

B Writing Do you think the jobs in *Before you watch* part A will always be associated with a gender, or might they change as the video infers? Write a paragraph explaining your opinion. Support your ideas with reasons and examples.

8 THE HISTORY OF ADVERTISING

Before you watch

A How many different ways to advertise can you think of? Write as many different types of advertising as you can (e.g., television commercials, magazine ads, mail, etc.).

_____

_____

_____

_____

B **Pair work** Compare your answers. Did your partner have any advertising media you didn't think of? Work together to think of other ways to advertise.

While you watch

A Watch the video and check your answers from *Before you watch* part A. How many of your answers are mentioned in the video? Watch again and write any types of advertising that you missed.

_____

_____

_____

B Choose the correct answers according to the information in the video.

1. Including online ads, it is estimated we see _____ of ads per day.
   a. hundreds   b. thousands   c. millions

2. Egyptian stone tablets may be considered a type of advertising because they
   _____ .
   a. sold things from time to time   b. communicated messages   c. were a new medium

3. The first magazine was _____ .
   a. a magazine for hairstylists   b. published in 1631   c. started in England

4. With direct marketing, advertising took the form of _____ .
   a. recommending products in articles   b. sending postcards and catalogs   c. speaking to people individually

5. Billboards were useful to _____ .
   a. advertise gas   b. promote radio ads   c. introduce television to the world

6. The invention of television _____ the most effective form of advertising.
   a. provided advertisers with   b. created infomercials as   c. entertained viewers with

7. The infomercial was created _____ .
   a. in the 90s   b. 30 years after the first television commercial   c. when cell phones became popular

8. A possible future advertising medium mentioned is _____ .
   a. dream commercials   b. infomercials on the moon   c. ads on glasses

C Choose the correct answers according to the information in the video.

	Newspaper	Mail	Television
1. This got a lot cheaper over time.	☐	☐	☐
2. This is one of the most effective forms of advertising.	☐	☐	☐
3. Advertising as we know it started with this.	☐	☐	☐
4. Magazine ads came after these ads.	☐	☐	☐
5. An ad for a watch is given as an example for this medium.	☐	☐	☐
6. Direct marketing was born in this medium.	☐	☐	☐

After you watch

A Think about the types of advertising you saw in the video. Which (if any) do you find enjoyable? Which (if any) do you find annoying? Make lists.

Enjoyable	Annoying

B **Pair work** Compare your lists from part A. Give reasons for your classifications. How similar or different are your views?

C **Group work** Discuss these questions. Then share your opinions with the class.

1. What are the positive and negative aspects of advertising? How does advertising help us? How might it be problematic?

2. What are some changes that could be made to improve advertising in general?

3. What are some other ways people might advertise in the future?

9 HUMANS AND ANIMALS

Before you watch

A Pair work At times, people compare human traits with animals, for example: *as quiet as a mouse*. Look at the adjectives and write the animal(s) you think are associated with them. Then add your own ideas.

1. courageous _____
2. hairy _____
3. slow _____

4. evil _____
5. busy _____
6. wise _____

7. my idea: _____
8. my idea: _____
9. my idea: _____

B Group work Compare your answers. Why might these comparisons be made? What characteristics tie these animals and human traits together?

While you watch

A Choose the statement that best summarizes the main idea presented at these points in the video.

1.
   a. When we have wanted animal companions, we have domesticated them.
   b. Wherever humans have wanted to go, animals have provided transportation.
   c. When we need help pulling things, animals are there.

2.
   a. When the earliest humans depicted their gods, it was usually an animal or part human and part animal.
   b. Whenever early humans depicted animals, they were really depicting humans.
   c. The earliest humans saw their gods when they looked to the skies.

3.
   a. Thousands of years ago, when humans described animals, they compared them to people.
   b. When different cultures describe humans, they usually compare humans to bears.
   c. Different cultures may use different descriptions, but we all compare humans to animals.

4.
   a. When we look at owls, we compare them to humans, too.
   b. When we tell stories, we often attribute human qualities to animals.
   c. Animal-like humans are common in entertainment media.

B Choose the correct answers according to the information in the video.

1. Through domestication, transportation, and survival, _____.

   a. humans have depicted animals as useful
   b. animals have become dependent on humans
   c. humans and animals have become strongly linked

2. The tradition of depicting gods as animals shows _____.

   a. that people saw gods all around them
   b. that all cultures are the same
   c. man's deep connection to animals

3. Early humans thought they saw _____.

   a. humans in animals
   b. animals in humans
   c. gods in some people

4. We use many phrases that _____.

   a. contrast human and animal behavior
   b. make fun of people by comparing them to animals
   c. use animals to describe the essence of a person

5. Cartoons and movies often show _____.

   a. animal attributes in humans
   b. interesting animal behavior
   c. animals with human qualities

C Match the animals with their associated human traits.

1. snake ____
2. lion ____
3. peacock ____
4. chicken ____
5. owl ____
6. bee ____
7. lamb ____
8. fox ____
9. gorilla ____
10. horse ____
11. kitten ____
12. snail ____

a. vain
b. wise
c. slow
d. sly
e. playful
f. courageous
g. scared
h. hungry
i. hairy
j. evil
k. busy
l. gentle

After you watch

A Compare your list of human–animal comparisons from *Before you watch* part A with the comparisons in the video. How similar or different are they?

B **Pair work** Review your comparisons from part A. Then think of famous people or characters with those traits. Share your choices with the class.

C **Group work** Discuss possible reasons why some animal comparisons may be different around the world. Consider the influences of culture, geography, and literature in shaping our perceptions of animals. Share your discussions with the class.

10 TIPS FOR BETTER PRESENTATIONS

Before you watch

A What do you know about making a good slide presentation? Take the quiz.
Write *T* (true) or *F* (false).

_____ 1. It is better to stick only to the facts in a presentation and not tell stories,
as they may divert listeners' attention.

_____ 2. It is better to read your slides to make sure you get your information correct.

_____ 3. If you are reading from a presentation, do not look at the screen the whole time.
It can be distracting.

_____ 4. It is best to put complete sentences and paragraphs on the screen to ensure
you present all needed information.

_____ 5. It is best to use a large dark font on a light background so that everyone
can read your slides.

_____ 6. Hand out any notes and presentation materials before you begin your talk
so that people can follow along.

B **Pair work** Discuss your answers. Were most of your answers the same or different?
Would you like to change any answers?

While you watch

A Who does each action while giving their presentation? Write *M* for the man or *W* for the woman.
Then check your answers to *Before you watch* part A.

_____ 1. uses storytelling to present information

_____ 2. reads the presentation word for word

_____ 3. talks in a conversational manner

_____ 4. watches the slides during the presentation

_____ 5. does not use bullet points

_____ 6. does not put everything on the slides

_____ 7. uses a small font

_____ 8. does not give a handout until after the presentation ends

B Write the letter of the correct phrase to complete each sentence.

a. use bullet points
b. try to tell a story
c. post slide points one at a time
d. watch the presenter
e. look at the screen the whole time
f. talk as if you were having a conversation
g. give handouts at the end of the presentation
h. use a large, dark font on a light background

1. The audience will find it more interesting if you _____ .
2. No one wants to hear you read, so _____ .
3. You take the focus off yourself if you _____ .
4. A successful presentation is when people _____ .
5. Because paragraphs on slides are hard to read, you need to _____ .
6. People who sit in the back will be able to read if you _____ .
7. The audience will get ahead of you if you don't _____ .
8. To encourage people to pay attention and not write while you are speaking, _____ .

C Choose the correct expressions to complete the statements according to the information in the video.

1. *Poor slideshows / Boring subjects* are the reason audiences dread watching presentations.
2. It is tedious for people to sit there while someone *talks as if having a conversation / reads exactly what is on the screen*.
3. A common problem during presentations is *looking only at the screen / talking too long about a subject*.
4. It is not necessary to *look at your slides at all / put your entire speech on the screen*.
5. In choosing to write the text for the slides, you should include *no more than three words / only the key words*.
6. It is a good idea to view your slides from the back of the room to check if *everyone can see you / your font is too small*.
7. Letting people know they will get a copy of the presentation discourages them from *taking their own notes / reading ahead on the slides*.

After you watch

A **Pair work** Which problems mentioned in the video have you or your partner seen or done in a presentation? How did it affect the presentation? Share your experiences with the class.

_____
_____
_____

B **Pair work** Think of three additional tips that could improve a presentation. Prepare a presentation about your tips.

1. _____
2. _____
3. _____

C **Group work** Take turns giving your presentation with another pair. Give each other tips to improve your presentation styles. Choose the best presenters and have them present the best ideas to the class.

11 ROLE MODELS

Before you watch

A Choose the top five qualities that first occur to you when you think of people who are role models.

☐ awe-inspiring   ☐ highly acclaimed   ☐ outspoken

☐ coolheaded   ☐ kind-hearted   ☐ positive-thinking

☐ easygoing   ☐ near-perfect   ☐ well-known

☐ hard-driving   ☐ open-minded   ☐ widely respected

B Pair work Select three qualities you both agree are typical of most role models. Share your opinions with the class and give reasons for your choices.

While you watch

Rachel

Edgar

Sierra

Tim

A Write *T* (true) or *F* (false). Then correct the false statements with a partner.

____ 1. People are signing a pledge to share information about their role models.

____ 2. At first, Edgar does not see the connection between being a coach and being a role model.

____ 3. Rachel believes only celebrities can make good role models.

____ 4. At first, Sierra thinks nurses make better role models than pediatricians.

____ 5 Tim thinks Nelson Mandela was a great role model because he had an impact on a whole country.

____ 6. Rachel thinks a role model should try to affect everyone in the world.

B Choose the correct names to make the statements true.

1. *Rachel / Edgar / Sierra / Tim* thinks you can't feel better if you feel sad.

2. *Rachel / Edgar / Sierra / Tim* is popular with the children that live near him.

3. *Rachel / Edgar / Sierra / Tim* points out that a positive attitude is a great thing to model.

4. *Rachel / Edgar / Sierra / Tim* makes entertainment products for children.

5. *Rachel / Edgar / Sierra / Tim* has a class project and talks to people on Saturdays.

6. *Rachel / Edgar / Sierra / Tim* is too self-critical and claims to be too hotheaded.

7. *Rachel / Edgar / Sierra / Tim* takes care of people for a living.

8. *Rachel / Edgar / Sierra / Tim* is eventually convinced that role models can be online, too.

C Who says it? Write *R* for Rachel, *E* for Edgar, *S* for Sierra, or *T* for Tim.

_____ 1. "He made you want to work harder to live up to his expectations, you know."

_____ 2. "It's not about being the most awe-inspiring person or even a near-perfect person."

_____ 3. "Who's going to want to take after me?"

_____ 4. "That's very thought provoking."

_____ 5. "But I'll bet the way you interact with them could have far-reaching effects on their lives."

_____ 6. "I try to always be the most positive-thinking person in the room."

_____ 7. "You might be onto something."

_____ 8. "But don't you actually have to meet people to be a role model?"

After you watch

A **Pair work** List five qualities Rachel demonstrates that make her a good role model. Then compare your list with a partner and give reasons for your choices.

1. _____
2. _____
3. _____
4. _____
5. _____

B Think about your own role model. List five qualities that make this person a good role model. Give reasons why these qualities are important.

1. _____
2. _____
3. _____
4. _____
5. _____

C **Writing** Write a paragraph about your own role model. Describe the person and write about at least three qualities that make him or her a good role model and why they are important.

JOB INTERVIEW
DOS AND DON'TS

Before you watch

A What are some dos and don'ts for a job interview? List two or three items for each category.

Should do	Should not do
wear appropriate clothing	*chew gum*

B **Pair work** Compare your lists. Are your ideas the same or different? Discuss your thoughts and think of additional suggestions.

Additional DOs	Additional DON'Ts

While you watch

A Take notes to label each picture with the tips presented at or around these points in the video.

1. _____
_____
_____

2. _____
_____
_____

3. ACME DESIGN _____
_____
_____

4. _____
_____
_____

B Choose the correct answers according to the information in the video.

1. It's good to _____ and go over your notes to prepare for the interview.
   a. practice   b. arrive early   c. study the company

2. Staying calm and still helps you to _____ .
   a. have good posture   b. seem confident   c. maintain good eye contact

3. Had Steve not _____ , it might not have looked like he was interested in the job.
   a. asked intelligent questions   b. mentioned the salary   c. talked about the marketing director

4. One way Steve _____ was by mentioning the company's marketing region.
   a. acted confident   b. did research   c. demonstrated initiative

5. One reason Steve mentions he wants the job is because of _____ .
   a. his interest in the hardware industry   b. the opportunities for advancement   c. his feeling he is the right person for the job

C Take notes to answer the questions in your own words. Then compare your answers with a partner.

1. What three tips for keeping still and calm are mentioned in the video?

   _____
   _____
   _____

2. What three tips for "doing your homework" are mentioned in the video?

   _____
   _____
   _____

3. What is an example of a standard interview question in the video?

   _____
   _____

After you watch

A Pair work Which three suggestions from the video do you think are most important? Why? Discuss your opinions.

B Pair work Choose a job and think of details about a fictional or real company that offers the job. Prepare three questions and possible answers for a job interview with that company. Include at least one standard question.

	Question	Possible answer
1.		
2.		
3.		

C Pair work Use the questions and answers from part B to take turns role-playing a job interview. Offer helpful feedback about the interviewee's answers and performance.

Video Activity Worksheets Credits

Video credits

Video screen grabs courtesy of Steadman Productions, Boston, MA: 198, 201, 208, 210, 211, 212

Photography credits

190 (*left to right*) ©YuriyZhuravov/Shutterstock, Inc., ©pav197lin/Shutterstock, Inc., ©Inna Astakhova/Shutterstock, Inc., ©Hasloo Group Production Studio/Shutterstock, Inc.; **191** ©altafulla/Shutterstock, Inc.; **192** (*top left to right*) ©Africa Studio/Shutterstock, Inc., ©S_L/Shutterstock, Inc., ©gpointstudio/Shutterstock, Inc., ©3355m/Shutterstock, Inc., (*bottom left to right*) ©elvistudio/Shutterstock, Inc., ©Geo Martinez/Shutterstock, Inc., ©AlexAnnaButs/Shutterstock, Inc., ©Elisanth/Shutterstock, Inc.; **193** ©PHOTOCREO Michal Bednarek/Shutterstock, Inc.; **195** ©Jean Marc Cote/Wikipedia Commons; **197** ©Everett Collection/Shutterstock, Inc.; **202** (*top to bottom*) ©Adriaen van Ostade/Wikipedia Commons, ©Library of Congress/Wikipedia Commons, ©Unknown/Wikipedia Commons, ©Williams/Wikipedia Commons, ©benjikat/Shutterstock, Inc.; **203** ©Hotelfoxtrot/Shutterstock, Inc.; **205** (*top left to right*) ©eFOOTAGE.com, ©Oleg Znamenskiy/Shutterstock, Inc., ©James Steidl/Shutterstock, Inc., (*bottom*) ©Boguc/Shutterstock, Inc.; **206** (*top to bottom*) ©alex83/Shutterstock, Inc., ©iofoto/Shutterstock, Inc., ©Vishnevskiy Vasily/Shutterstock, Inc., ©OlegD/Shutterstock, Inc., ©Matthew Cole/Shutterstock, Inc.; **207** ©Mykhaylo Palinchak/Shutterstock, Inc.

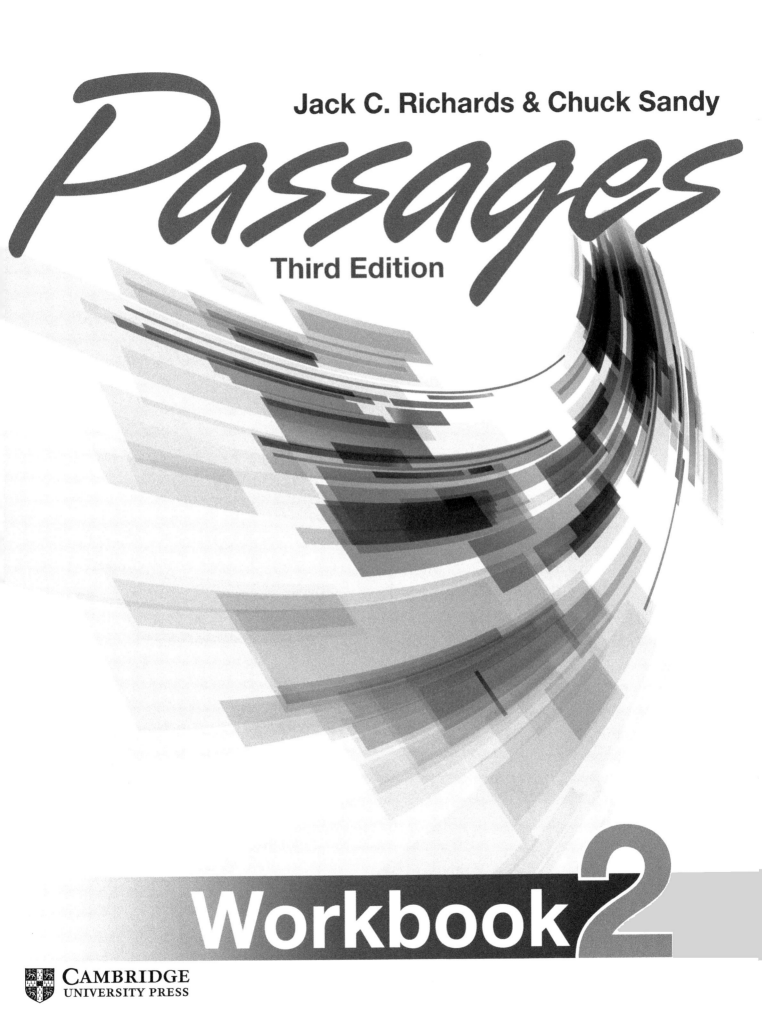

Jack C. Richards & Chuck Sandy

Passages

Third Edition

Workbook **2**

CAMBRIDGE
UNIVERSITY PRESS

Contents

Credits

Illustration credits

Jo Goodberry: 12
Paul Hostetler: 19, 26, 38, 49
Kim Johnson: 10, 31, 36, 55, 64
Dan McGeehan: 17, 18, 48
Koren Shadmi: 3, 20, 34, 43, 61
James Yamasaki: 41, 68

Photography credits

1 ©Photodisc/Thinkstock; **4** (*left to right*) ©Blend Images/Alamy, ©arek_malang/Shutterstock, ©Suprijono Suharjoto/Thinkstock; **5** (*clockwise from center left*) ©Fuse/Thinkstock, ©Michael Simons/Alamy, ©pcruciatti /Shutterstock, ©Dmitriy Shironosov/Thinkstock; **6** ©Catherine Yeulet/Thinkstock; **7** ©Fuse/Thinkstock; **8** ©crystalfoto/Shutterstock; **13** ©ID1974/Shutterstock; **14** (*top to bottom*) ©Olena Mykhaylova/iStock/Thinkstock, ©Oleksiy Mark/Thinkstock; **15** ©Stocktrek Images/Getty Images; **21** ©Flirt/SuperStock; **22** ©Photononstop/SuperStock; **23** ©BananaStock/Thinkstock; **24** ©ollyy/Shutterstock; **25** ©Khakimullin Aleksandr/Shutterstock; **27** (*top to bottom*) ©Vuk Vukmirovic/iStock/Thinkstock, ©Moviestore Collection Ltd/Alamy; **28** ©NBC/Getty Images; **30** ©CBS Photo Archive/Getty Images; **32** ©Larry Busacca/TAS/Getty Images; **35** ©Creatas/Getty Images/Thinkstock; **39** ©Cusp/SuperStock; **40** ©Tammy Hanratty/MediaBakery; **42** ©Photoshot/Hulton/Getty Images; **45** (*top to bottom*) ©Sergey Nivens/Shutterstock, ©iStock/franckreporter, ©iStock/MachineHeadz; **47** (*left to right, top to bottom*) ©Dean Bertoncelj/iStock/Thinkstock, ©Universal/Courtesy: Everett Collection, ©Kylie McLaughlin/Lonely Planet Images/Getty Images, ©MariusdeGraf/Shutterstock, ©Blend Images/Masterfile, ©Gao lin hk/Imaginechina/AP Images; **50** (*left to right, top to bottom*) ©MustafaNC/Shutterstock, ©Dmitry Zinovyev/Shutterstock, ©e2dan/Shutterstock, ©Reinhold Leitner/Shutterstock, ©Reddogs/Shutterstock, ©Nailia Schwarz/Shutterstock, ©Sergey Goruppa/Shutterstock, ©Wendy Kaveney Photography/Shutterstock, ©Donovan van Staden/Shutterstock, ©Nantawat Chotsuwan/Shutterstock, ©Steve Byland/istock/Thinkstock, ©iStock/Sergey Goruppa; **52** ©KidStock/Blend Images/Corbis; **53** (*top to bottom*) ©Gary Crabbe/Enlightened Images/Alamy, ©Falk Kienas/istock/Thinkstock; **54** ©Eric Isselée/Thinkstock; **57** ©E+/MachineHeadz/Getty Images; **59** ©Assembly/Media Bakery; **62** (*left to right, top to bottom*) ©Pressmaster/Shutterstock, ©Olga Danylenko/Shutterstock, ©iStock/btrenkel, ©Stockbyte/Thinkstock, ©Graham Oliver/Media Bakery, ©Andrey Yurlov/Shutterstock; **63** © INTERFOTO/Alamy; **65** ©Jon Kopaloff/FilmMagic/Getty Images; **66** ©ZUMA Press, Inc./Alamy; **71** ©Goodluz/Shutterstock; **Back cover:** (*clockwise from top center*) ©Leszek Bogdewicz/Shutterstock, ©Wavebreak Media/Thinkstock, ©Blend Images/Alamy, ©limpido/Shutterstock

Text credits

The authors and publishers acknowledge the following sources of copyright material and are grateful for the permissions granted. While every effort has been made, it has not always been possible to identify the sources of all the material used, or to trace all copyright holders. If any omissions are brought to our notice, we will be happy to include the appropriate acknowledgments on reprinting.

12 Adapted from "Decoding Body Language," by John Mole, 1999, http://www.johnmole.com. Reproduced with permission; **18** Adapted from "How Artificial Intelligence is Changing Our Lives," by Gregory M. Lamb. Adapted with permission from the September 16, 2012 issue of *The Christian Science Monitor*. Copyright © 2012 The Christian Science Monitor, www.CSMonitor.com; **24** Adapted from "Rumor Detectives: True Story or Online Hoax?" by David Hochman, *Reader's Digest*, April 2009. Reprinted with permission from Reader's Digest. Copyright © 2009 by The Reader's Digest Association, Inc.; **30** Adapted from an NPR news report titled "Is The 'CSI Effect' Influencing Courtrooms?" by Arun Rath, originally published on NPR.org on February 5, 2011 and used with the permission of NPR. Copyright © 2011 National Public Radio, Inc. Any unauthorized duplication is strictly prohibited; **36** Adapted from "Study Suggests Music May Someday Help Repair Brain," by Robert Lee Hotz, *Los Angeles Times*, November 9, 1998. Copyright © 1998 Los Angeles Times. Reprinted with permission; **42** Adapted from "What's the Tipping Point?" by Malcolm Gladwell. Copyright © by Malcolm Gladwell. Reprinted by permission of the author; **48** Adapted from "Sensory Ploys and the Scent of Marketing," by Robert Budden, *Financial Times*, June 3, 2013. Copyright © The Financial Times Limited 2013. All Rights Reserved; **54** Adapted from "Fairy Tale Comes True," by Alexandar S. Dragicevic, *The Toronto Star*, July 23, 1998. Copyright © Associated Press; **60** Adapted from "Does the Language you Speak Change the Way You Think?" by Kevin Hartnett, *The Boston Globe*, February 27, 2013. Reproduced with permission of Kevin Hartnett; **66** Adapted from "Tiny Grants Keep 'Awesome' Ideas Coming," by Billy Baker, *The Boston Globe*, October 10, 2011. Copyright © 2011 Boston Globe. All rights reserved. Used by permission and protected by the Copyright Laws of the United States. The printing, copying, redistribution, or retransmission of this Content without express written permission is prohibited; **72** Adapted from "The Twelve Attributes of a Truly Great Place to Work," by Tony Schwartz, *Harvard Business Review*, September 19, 2011. Reproduced with permission.

RELATIONSHIPS

LESSON A ▶ *The best of friends*

1 GRAMMAR

Read this paragraph from a blog post about friendship. Find the phrasal verbs and write them in the correct columns in the chart.

I have a lot of friends, but my best friend is Anna. She is one of those great friends you come by only once in a while. Anna knows how to cheer me up when I'm feeling bad, and she brings out the best in me when I'm feeling happy. Whenever I run into a problem, she always has great advice, and she usually helps me solve it. She never puts me down when I do something silly or embarrassing. I guess the thing I like best about Anna is that I can open up to her and talk about anything, like bad grades in school or family problems. I would never turn her down if she needed my help. I would stand up for her in just about any situation. I really hope that we don't drift apart in the future. I don't think I could do without her friendship!

Separable	Inseparable	Three-word verbs	Intransitive
	come by		

2 VOCABULARY

Choose the words that best complete the sentences.

1. When Mike's and Ed's ideas about art (clash) / *admire*, they argue.

2. My sister is a truly *admirable* / *beneficial* person. She works two jobs, goes to school at night, and still has time to help me with my problems.

3. Jon and Scott *empathize* / *harmonize* well as a team since they have similar working styles.

4. Kim and Emily have a truly *clashing* / *enduring* relationship. They have been best friends for more than 10 years.

5. Catherine has *benefited* / *endured* a lot from living with her grandmother, who is very understanding and a great listener.

6. Lara is good with teenagers. She is very *empathetic* / *harmonious*, really listening to their problems and helping them find their own solutions.

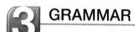

3 GRAMMAR

Complete these conversations with the correct form of the phrasal verbs in the box.
Use an object pronoun where needed.

| cheer (someone) up | drift apart | stand up for |
| do without | run into | turn (someone) down |

1. A: I'm surprised that Tom didn't support what you said in the meeting.
   I thought he agreed with you.
   B: He does agree with me, but he was afraid of what our boss would say.
   I can't believe he didn't _____**stand up for**_____ me!

2. A: What's wrong with Carmen? She looks so sad.
   B: I'm not sure. Let's ask her to go to lunch with us. Maybe we can
   _____.

3. A: Did Eric ask you to present your work at the conference next week?
   B: Yes, he did, but I _____ because I have other
   things to take care of at work.

4. A: Sam isn't serious about anything. I think we could really
   _____ him on our team.
   B: I agree. Let's talk to the others about it and make a decision.

5. A: Have you seen Yuki lately?
   B: Actually, I _____ her when I was downtown today.

6. A: Is it true that you and Roger aren't in touch anymore?
   B: Yes, it is. We kind of _____ when I moved to Los Angeles.

4 GRAMMAR

Complete these sentences to make them true for you.

1. Nothing cheers me up as much as _going out to dinner with a few of my_
   good friends!

2. I like to hang on to friends who _____
   _____

3. When someone puts me down, I _____
   _____

4. I will stand up for anyone who _____
   _____

5. I can do without people who _____
   _____

6. I open up around people who _____
   _____

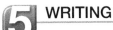

WRITING

A Read the thesis statements. Find the three best paragraph topics to support each one. Write the topics below the thesis statements.

Paragraph Topics

- ✔ Keep in touch through social media, video calls, and email.
- ✔ Be a person that your friend can trust.
- ✔ Join clubs and other organizations related to your interests or hobbies.
- ✔ Know when to give advice and when to keep silent.
- ✔ Sign up for a class, such as painting or cooking.
- ✔ Participate in community service activities, such as working with the elderly.
- ✔ Pay attention to what your friend thinks and feels.
- ✔ Get together and travel whenever possible.
- ✔ Send cards and presents for special occasions such as birthdays and holidays.

Thesis statements

1. Developing a friendship requires attention and work.

   Be a person that your friend can trust.

   _____

   _____

2. People living in big cities often have trouble making friends, but there are ways to solve this problem.

   _____

   _____

   _____

3. Maintaining a long-distance friendship is difficult, but it can be done.

   _____

   _____

   _____

B Write one additional topic for each thesis statement in part A.

1. _____

2. _____

3. _____

C Choose one of the thesis statements and write a composition. Use three paragraph topics that best support your thesis.

1 GRAMMAR

Read these online profiles. Underline the verb + gerund constructions, and circle the verb + infinitive constructions.

1 Naomi

My name is Naomi. I'm 30 years old, and I'm a teacher. I tend to be on the shy side, so I'm considering starting a book club so I can meet some new people. I plan to start this club as soon as possible, so email me if you're interested!

Naomi247@cup.org

2 Renee

I just moved here, and I'm looking for some new friends. I appreciate spending evenings at home cooking and listening to music. People say I tend to be kind of quiet, but I'm fun once you know more about me. If you enjoy sharing recipes, email me.

Renee8334@cup.org

3 Alex

I'm Alex Ramirez, an engineering student at National University. I really enjoy biking. Can I suggest starting a bikers' meet-up group? I'm considering entering a race, and therefore, I intend to start riding my bike every day. I hope others will join me!

alex.ramirez@cup.org

2 GRAMMAR

Complete the questions using the gerund or infinitive form of the verbs. Note that one of the constructions uses the passive voice. Then answer the questions and give reasons.

1. Do you get annoyed when friends ask _____*to borrow*_____ (borrow) your clothes?
   No, I don't get annoyed because I know my friends will return the clothes.

2. Would you give up _____ (practice) an instrument or sport if you got to spend more time with friends?
   _____

3. Would you refuse _____ (go out) with a friend if he or she wanted to see a movie you weren't interested in seeing?
   _____

4. Do you expect _____ (invite) every time your best friend goes out?
   _____

5. Which friend do you prefer _____ (hang out) with the most?
   _____

6. When a friend treats you to lunch, do you enjoy _____ (go) to a casual restaurant or a more formal one?
   _____

7. Would you continue _____ (talk) to a friend if he or she never answered your texts or emails?
   _____

3 VOCABULARY

Choose the words that best complete the sentences.

1. Maria and Emma (rekindled) / *resurfaced* their friendship after drifting apart from each other for many years.

2. Good friends are impossible to *replace* / *resurface*. They share so many of our memories.

3. Too much damage has been done to Al and Sam's friendship to *redefine* / *rebuild* it.

4. I can't *rehash* / *recall* the name of my tenth-grade English teacher.

5. Tim has *reconnected* / *redefined* his outlook on life. He's more optimistic now.

6. Don't bring that subject up again. I don't want to *rehash* / *rebuild* it with you.

7. After studying for the exam for two days, Cara *redefined* / *resurfaced* to eat dinner with her family.

8. I'm glad I came home for spring break. I've been *recalling* / *reconnecting* with friends that I haven't seen since last summer.

4 GRAMMAR

Imagine your friend is coming to visit you for the weekend. Write sentences describing some possible activities you can do together. Use the cues and the gerund or infinitive form of the verbs.

1. plan / take a walk somewhere nice

   We should plan to take a walk
   somewhere nice.

2. suggest / relax at a cozy café

   _____

   _____

3. consider / go to a club

   _____

   _____

4. prefer / get tickets to a concert

   _____

   _____

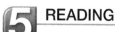

A Read the article. Find the words in boldface that match the definitions.

1. causes _____*spurs*_____
2. thin _____
3. annoying reminders _____
4. a good indication of _____
5. more commonly affected by _____
6. take care of and engage socially _____

Your FRIENDS & Your HEALTH «

"You're not what you eat – you're who you eat with," wrote *Scientific American*'s Christie Nicholson, reporting on research examining why our friends' weight influences our own. The study found that overweight students were more likely to lose weight if they hung out with **lean** friends – **a clear nod to** the influence of our social networks on our waistlines. But helping you lose weight isn't the only way your friends can affect you. Here are some other ways friends are good for our health:

FRIENDS GET YOU MOVING Research has found that something you might expect from your family – **nagging** – can actually work when it's coming from a pal pushing you to move more. Also, working out with a friend has the added benefit of keeping you committed to your workout plan. There's no rolling over to hit the snooze button on that early morning run if someone's waiting for you to show up!

FRIENDS KEEP YOU RELAXED Talking with friends really can help you get through troublesome times. Women in particular may be **predisposed to** the calming benefits of friendship. Researchers found that women release the hormone oxytocin when stressed, which encourages **"tend and befriend"** behavior, the *San Francisco Chronicle* reported. Chatting with friends when stressed **spurs** the release of more oxytocin, which can have a calming effect.

FRIENDS KEEP YOUR HEART HEALTHY Perhaps because they help us relax, friends are also good for the heart. Stronger social ties in general seem to lower blood pressure, which helps the heart. Married men, for example, seem to experience a particular boost in heart health, WebMD reported.

FRIENDS HELP YOU LIVE LONGER In an analysis of 148 studies, researchers found that people with stronger relationships had a 50 percent greater chance of long-term survival than those with weaker social networks. It's not quite as simple as connecting with friends and, poof, you're guaranteed to live to 100, but there is a significant body of research linking strong social ties to a longer lifespan.

B Choose the statements that are supported by information in the article.

☐ 1. Men don't seem to benefit from the relaxing effects of friendship.

☐ 2. The eating habits and lifestyle of our friends can have an influence on our own health.

☐ 3. Making plans to exercise with a friend increases the likelihood that you will.

☐ 4. Having strong social ties does not seem to have an effect on women's blood pressure.

☐ 5. Evidence suggests that strong social ties can lead to a longer life.

2 CLOTHES AND APPEARANCE

LESSON A ▶ *The way we dress*

 GRAMMAR

Match the two parts of each sentence to tell the story of Mimi, a fashion designer.

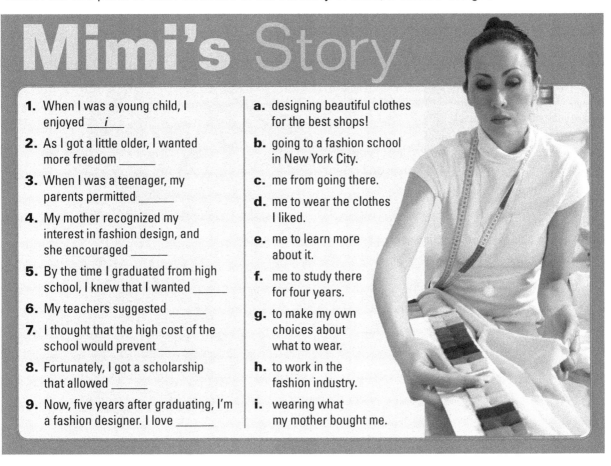

Mimi's Story

1. When I was a young child, I enjoyed ___i___

2. As I got a little older, I wanted more freedom _____

3. When I was a teenager, my parents permitted _____

4. My mother recognized my interest in fashion design, and she encouraged _____

5. By the time I graduated from high school, I knew that I wanted _____

6. My teachers suggested _____

7. I thought that the high cost of the school would prevent _____

8. Fortunately, I got a scholarship that allowed _____

9. Now, five years after graduating, I'm a fashion designer. I love _____

a. designing beautiful clothes for the best shops!

b. going to a fashion school in New York City.

c. me from going there.

d. me to wear the clothes I liked.

e. me to learn more about it.

f. me to study there for four years.

g. to make my own choices about what to wear.

h. to work in the fashion industry.

i. wearing what my mother bought me.

 VOCABULARY

Choose the words that best complete the sentences.

1. People read fashion magazines to learn about the *sloppy* / *stylish* new clothing for each season.

2. If you are planning to go to a fancy club, wear something *chic* / *functional*.

3. Marco's *conservative* / *quirky* suit was appropriate for his interview at the bank.

4. Many teenagers think adults wear unimaginative, *fashionable* / *stuffy* clothing.

5. When I'm alone at home, I can wear *formal* / *sloppy* clothes if I want.

6. I can't understand why some people wear *retro* / *trendy* clothes from decades ago – they're so old-fashioned!

7. When I'm gardening, I wear *flashy* / *functional* jeans and a T-shirt.

8. Pop stars often wear *trendy* / *frumpy* clothes on stage.

3 GRAMMAR

Read the blog post about clothes and fashion. Use the gerund or the infinitive form of the verbs in parentheses.

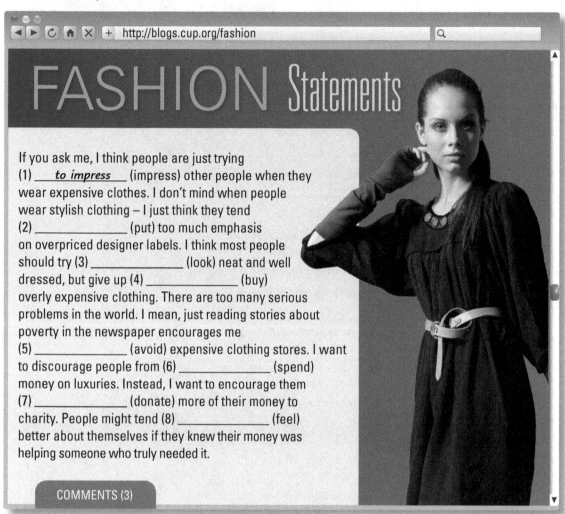

http://blogs.cup.org/fashion

FASHION Statements

If you ask me, I think people are just trying (1) __to impress__ (impress) other people when they wear expensive clothes. I don't mind when people wear stylish clothing – I just think they tend (2) _____ (put) too much emphasis on overpriced designer labels. I think most people should try (3) _____ (look) neat and well dressed, but give up (4) _____ (buy) overly expensive clothing. There are too many serious problems in the world. I mean, just reading stories about poverty in the newspaper encourages me (5) _____ (avoid) expensive clothing stores. I want to discourage people from (6) _____ (spend) money on luxuries. Instead, I want to encourage them (7) _____ (donate) more of their money to charity. People might tend (8) _____ (feel) better about themselves if they knew their money was helping someone who truly needed it.

COMMENTS (3)

4 GRAMMAR

Complete these sentences to make them true for you.

1. I don't mind wearing clothes that __are handed down to me from my brothers__ __or cousins.__

2. I hate to wear clothes that _____

   _____

3. I love to wear clothes that _____

   _____

4. When I'm shopping for clothes, I enjoy _____

   _____

5. When getting dressed for a night out, I tend _____

   _____

WRITING

A Underline the thesis statements in these introductory paragraphs. Then complete each paragraph that follows with examples supporting each thesis statement.

There are many reasons for getting dressed up. Yet many of my friends seem to despise wearing anything but jeans and T-shirts. Personally, I look forward to opportunities to put on my best clothes and like to dress nicely for many different types of occasions.

There are many advantages to dressing nicely. For example, _____

_____

_____

_____

_____

Young people spend a significant portion of their income on the "right clothes." Following the newest trends in an effort to fit in can become an obsession, and keeping up with the latest fashions can be an expensive pursuit. I feel that young people need to reject the pressure to dress stylishly.

Young people should be aware that fashion magazines and blogs do not always set a good example. That is, _____

_____

_____

_____

B Choose one of these topics to write about. Then choose one of the verbs to make the thesis statement express your point of view.

1. There *are / aren't* many advantages to dressing casually at work.

2. Students *should / shouldn't* be required to wear school uniforms.

3. People *should / shouldn't* be judged by what they wear.

C Make a list of examples that support your thesis statement.

_____

_____

_____

D Use your thesis statement and examples to write a composition containing an introductory paragraph and at least two supporting paragraphs.

GRAMMAR

Read the email and underline the cleft sentences.

To:	beth234@mail.cup.org
Subject:	Kyle's visit

Dear Beth,

Guess what! My brother Kyle visited me yesterday. I hadn't seen him in a year. What I noticed first was the three inches he grew. He looks so tall now!

He wanted to go out for lunch, so we went to my favorite café. We talked for a while. What struck me most about him was how grown up he sounded. He told me that he's doing well in school and that he has a part-time job at a supermarket – and he's even been saving money for college.

After lunch, we walked through the park. Then he had to leave, but before he did, he gave me a big hug and promised to visit me again. What I realized at the end of the visit was that I have a really terrific brother!

Love, Erica

 GRAMMAR

Read what each person thought about Gina Riccardi, a model who visited an advertising agency. Then complete the conversation using cleft sentences with *admired, liked, noticed,* or *struck me*.

Jin: She's as beautiful in person as she is in her ads.

Brian: She is gorgeous, but (1) *what I noticed first was how relaxed and friendly she seems* .

Dolores: That's true, but (2) _____.

How about you, Jin?

Jin: Yes, her eyes are stunning, but (3) _____.

Ted: As for me, (4) _____.

Brian: You're right. Her voice is very expressive. Actually, I hear she's about to act in her first movie.

3 VOCABULARY

Choose the words in the box that best complete the sentences.

| arrogant | eccentric | intense | sympathetic |
| dignified | intellectual | sinister | trustworthy |

1. People think Ryan is strange and _____*eccentric*_____ because he lives with 12 cats.

2. The villain was so _____ that I shivered with fear.

3. Jonathan is so _____. He thinks he's better than everyone in the office.

4. If you need a _____ person to talk to, try Maya. She's very understanding.

5. Don't count on David to keep any secrets. He's not very _____.

6. Jiro was very _____ during the debate. He clearly has strong opinions about the topic!

7. Keri is so _____. She could be a college professor!

8. Despite all the reporters shouting questions at her, the politician remained calm and _____, not showing that she was upset at all.

4 GRAMMAR

Imagine you are moving to a town where you don't know anyone. What personal characteristics do you look for in potential friends? Use your own ideas to complete these sentences.

1. What I look for in a friend is *a sincere interest in other people and*
   *a sympathetic personality.*_____

2. What I think is most important is _____

   _____

3. What I probably notice first is _____

   _____

4. What I pay attention to is _____

   _____

5. What I try to find out about a new friend first is _____

   _____

6. What I think is least important is _____

   _____

A Read the article quickly. Which of these behaviors apply to each body language type?

	Willing to listen	Not willing to listen	Engaged in conversation	Not engaged in conversation
1. responsive	☐	☐	☐	☐
2. reflective	☐	☐	☐	☐
3. combative	☐	☐	☐	☐
4. fugitive	☐	☐	☐	☐

Understanding BODY LANGUAGE

In European and North American cultures, body language behaviors can be divided into two groups: open/closed and forward/back.

Open/closed postures are the easiest to recognize. People are open to messages when they show open hands, face you fully, and have both feet on the ground. This indicates that they are willing to listen to what you have to say, even if they are disagreeing with you. When people are closed to messages, they have their arms folded or their legs crossed, and they may turn their bodies away. What this body language usually means is that people are rejecting your message.

Forward/back behavior reveals an active or a passive reaction to what is being said. If people lean forward with their bodies toward you, they are actively engaged in your message. They may be accepting or rejecting it, but their minds are on what you are saying. On the other hand, if people lean back in their chairs or look away from you, or perform activities such as drawing or cleaning their eyeglasses, you know that they are either passively taking in your message or that they are ignoring it. In either case, they are not very engaged in the conversation.

The chart below shows how these types of body language can suggest the general mental state of the listener.

OPEN

RESPONSIVE:
The person is willing to listen to you (open) and wants to participate in the conversation (forward).

REFLECTIVE:
The person is willing to listen (open) but not to share his or her opinion (back). He or she wants more time to think.

FORWARD ← → BACK

COMBATIVE:
There is risk of an argument. The person is engaged in the conversation (forward) but rejects your message (closed).

FUGITIVE:
The person is trying to avoid the conversation. He or she does not want to be a part of the conversation (back) and is rejecting your message (closed).

CLOSED

B Write the body language type under each picture.

responsive
reflective
combative
fugitive

1. _____ 2. _____ 3. _____ 4. _____

3 SCIENCE AND TECHNOLOGY

LESSON A ▶ *Good science, bad science*

1 GRAMMAR

Choose the sentences that use articles incorrectly, and then rewrite them.

☑ 1. For some people, using an abacus is an alternative to using calculator.

For some people, using an abacus is an
alternative to using a calculator.

☐ 2. Abacus is the earliest form of mechanical computing.

_____

☐ 3. The abacus was invented more than 4,000 years ago.

_____

☐ 4. It consists of wires strung across wooden frame.

_____

☐ 5. An abacus can have up to 13 wires. On wires are beads, which represent units.

_____

☐ 6. Calculations are made by moving the beads up and down the wires.

_____

☐ 7. Skilled operator can make calculations on it very quickly.

_____

2 VOCABULARY

Choose the words in the box that best complete the sentences.

audacious	frivolous	problematic	unethical
confidential	hazardous	prudent	

1. Some people consider cosmetic surgery harmful and a/an _____frivolous_____ waste of money when not done for serious health reasons.

2. Curing cancer is still a/an _____ issue for scientists.

3. In some countries, doctors must keep medical records _____. They are forbidden to share information, even with family members.

4. Some people get sick due to improper storage or disposal of _____ materials like chemicals and poisons.

5. It's illegal and _____ to download music without permission.

6. It would take _____ actions to go against our boss's plans.

7. It would be _____ to review the contract with a lawyer before signing it. Don't put yourself at risk by making a bad deal.

3 GRAMMAR

Complete the text with *a*, *an*, or *the*. Write an *X* where an article is not required.

Digital Cameras

Since the early 1990s, (1) ___*the*___ digital camera has changed the way we take (2) _____ pictures.

Traditional film cameras worked by focusing (3) _____ image onto light-sensitive film in the camera. To see the pictures, you had to send (4) _____ film to (5) _____ company that processed it. This was (6) _____ process that could take several hours.

Of course, digital cameras don't use film. Rather, they convert light entering the camera into (7) _____ information that can be read by (8) _____ computer. One advantage of this process is that you can see (9) _____ images immediately.

Another advantage is that you can delete (10) _____ pictures you don't like, and you can improve (11) _____ image by using special software. Of course, this can be (12) _____ disadvantage, too, since it's nearly impossible to tell just from looking whether a photo is real or not.

4 GRAMMAR

Write a sentence about each topic.

- the most helpful kind of technology
- the trendiest product on the market
- the silliest invention
- a medical cure I'd like to see discovered
- the most interesting website

1. *I think the most helpful kind of technology is the solar panel, which can provide electricity without producing much harmful waste.*

2. _____
   _____

3. _____
   _____

4. _____
   _____

5. _____
   _____

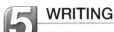

WRITING

A Read the article. Underline the main information in each paragraph that would belong in a summary.

ASTEROID MINING

One day in the not-so-distant future, small robotic spaceships will search the inner solar system mapping asteroids and determining which to harvest. Those asteroids containing valuable resources like iron, nickel, hydrogen, and reusable water will then be mined by larger robotic spacecrafts or turned into space-based manufacturing centers.

Robotically controlled factories built on asteroids will turn space rock water into rocket fuel and asteroid metals into everything needed for space-based manufacturing. Given the possibly endless supply of resource-rich asteroids, the pioneers of asteroid mining will become incredibly wealthy as they lead us into a new age of space development. At least, that's the plan.

Although it may sound like science fiction, big investors are already taking such ideas seriously enough to put substantial money into asteroid mining and space exploration companies. NASA, the U.S. space agency, is enthusiastic. In fact,

NASA sees these plans as the first step toward colonizing space. By locating manufacturing facilities and rocket fueling stations on asteroids already in space, costs will be reduced and long journeys into space will become possible. This will make human colonization of other parts of the solar system a real possibility.

Before we get too excited, though, it's important to remember that most of the technology needed to mine asteroids and build orbital factories doesn't exist yet. Still, early investors and the companies they're investing in believe they will be successful and that along the way the asteroid-mining technologies they develop will help bring about a new age.

B Choose the sentence in each pair that could belong in a summary of the article.

1. ☐ There is a great deal of serious interest in mining asteroids for their valuable resources.

☐ Many asteroids contain valuable resources such as iron and nickel.

2. ☐ NASA feels asteroid mining could make space colonization possible.

☐ Asteroid mining could lead to a new era of space exploration and colonization.

C Now, write a summary of the article by rewriting the main points in your own words.

_____

_____

_____

_____

_____

_____

_____

_____

_____

_____

GRAMMAR

Read the sentences. Choose whether the *-ing* clause implies actions that happened at the same time, at a different time, or for a reason. Sometimes more than one answer is possible.

	Same time	Different time	Reason
1. Having recently learned how to text, my grandmother now sends me several messages a day!	☐	☑	☑
2. Being a prudent consumer, I did some research before I bought my laptop.	☐	☐	☐
3. While going to the birthday party, I got lost.	☐	☐	☐
4. Having lost my ATM card, I can't withdraw money from an ATM.	☐	☐	☐
5. Having downloaded a new video calling app, I can call friends anywhere in the world for free.	☐	☐	☐
6. Zoe is in her room watching movies on her tablet.	☐	☐	☐
7. Having had trouble programming my home security system, I now ask my wife to program it for us.	☐	☐	☐

② GRAMMAR

Write sentences using the cues and an *-ing* clause.

1. *Same time:* Lily / break her digital camera / take a picture

   Lily broke her digital camera taking a picture.

   Taking a picture, Lily broke her digital camera.

2. *Different time:* Diego / watch a show about alternative energy / buy an electric car

   _____

3. *Reason:* Bella / be a resourceful person / build her own computer

   _____

4. *Different time:* Dan / injure his arm / receive a bone scan

   _____

5. *Same time:* Celia / be in her car / listen to satellite radio

   _____

6. *Reason:* Ken / be an eco-conscious person / always recycles his old electronics

   _____

VOCABULARY

Match the clauses to make logical sentences.

1. Anita is fed up with Tyler __c__
2. Children are reliant on their parents ____
3. Julia is grateful for all the help ____
4. Make sure you are familiar with ____
5. I'm curious about ____
6. People are intimidated by George, ____
7. Gwen is so crazy about cooking ____
8. I've been suspicious of Ryan ____

a. she got from friends while she was ill.
b. ever since I saw him holding my phone.
c. because he asks too many questions.
d. that she opened her own restaurant.
e. but he's actually nicer than he looks!
f. to feed, shelter, and clothe them until they're grown.
g. what happens next on my favorite TV show.
h. the program before using it in your next presentation.

GRAMMAR

Have you had good or bad experiences doing the activities in the box or similar activities using technology? Write sentences about your experience using -ing clauses.

> using a video streaming service
> learning how to use a new cell phone
> creating a social networking profile
> shopping online

1. *Having signed up for a new video streaming service, I realized it didn't offer all the movies I wanted to see.*

2. _____

3. _____

4. _____

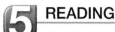

A What does *mundanely ubiquitous* mean? Read the article and choose the answer.

☐ unsurprisingly common ☐ amazingly rare

ARTIFICIAL INTELLIGENCE
IN OUR LIVES

From the Curiosity space probe that landed on Mars without human help, to the cars whose dashboards we can now talk to, to smartphones that talk back to us, so-called artificial intelligence (AI) is changing our lives – sometimes in ways that are obvious and visible, but often in subtle and invisible forms.

AI is making Internet searches quicker, translating texts from one language to another, and recommending a better route through traffic. It helps detect fraudulent patterns in credit-card searches and tells us when we've crossed over the center line while driving. Even your toaster is about to join the AI revolution. You'll put a bagel in it, take a picture with your smartphone, and the phone will send the toaster all the information it needs to brown the bread perfectly.

In a sense, AI has become almost **mundanely ubiquitous,** from the intelligent sensors that adjust the settings in digital cameras, to the heat and humidity probes in dryers, to the automatic parking feature in cars. And more applications for AI are coming out of labs and laptops by the hour. "It's an exciting world," says Colin Angle, cofounder of a company that has created a robotic vacuum cleaner that uses AI to navigate its way around furniture.

What may be most surprising about AI today, in fact, is how little amazement it creates. Perhaps science-fiction stories with humanlike androids – from the charming Data in *Star Trek*, to the obedient C-3PO in *Star Wars*, to the sinister Terminator in the similarly named series of movies – have raised unrealistic expectations. Or maybe human nature just doesn't stay amazed for long.

"Today's mind-popping, eye-popping technology in 18 months will be as blasé and old as a 1980s pair of double-knit trousers," says Paul Saffo, who analyzes trends to predict the future. "Our expectations are a moving target." If voice-recognition programs in smartphones had come out in 1980, "it would have been the most astonishing, breathtaking thing," he says. But by the time they arrived, "we were so used to other things going on we said, 'Oh, yeah, no big deal.' Technology goes from magic to invisible-and-taken-for-granted in about two nanoseconds."

B For each pair of sentences, choose the one the author would agree with.

1. ☐ a. AI has become so integrated into technology that most people are unaware of it.

   ☐ b. AI is making some aspects of daily life more complicated than necessary.

2. ☐ a. People are surprised that AI is even better than their expectations from movies.

   ☐ b. People aren't amazed by AI because of their high expectations from movies.

3. ☐ a. Technology advances so quickly that it creates astonishment.

   ☐ b. Technology advances so rapidly that people don't stay impressed by it for long.

4. ☐ a. It's likely we'll quickly see an increasing number of new applications for AI.

   ☐ b. It's unlikely that there will be many new developments in AI.

LESSON A ▶ *Superstitions*

1 VOCABULARY

Match the phrases to make logical sentences.

1. I got into the best dorm on campus due to the __*e*__
2. Muriel had never bowled before, so her high score was _____
3. I tried to get tickets to the play, but I couldn't. I was _____
4. Before Max went off to college, I wished him the _____
5. Celia drives too fast. One day she's going to have an accident. I wish she wouldn't _____
6. I was hoping to get more information about the job, but _____
7. Jim's car was broken into twice in one week. He's had some really _____

a. push her luck.
b. bad luck.
c. best of luck.
d. out of luck.
e. luck of the draw.
f. beginner's luck.
g. no such luck.

2 GRAMMAR

Underline the reporting clauses in this passage.

Fact OR Fiction?

Some ideas have been repeated so often that we just accept them as facts. <u>When someone asserts that</u> you can see the Great Wall of China from outer space, do we ask for proof? Probably not. But if you speak to anyone who's looked closely at photos of the earth taken from the moon, they'll sometimes admit that they can't find a trace of the Great Wall. And if people argue that you can badly hurt someone with a coin dropped from a very tall structure, we assume it must be true. Others have claimed that it's true many times before, right? However, experts agree that there's really no need to worry, and they report that a dropped coin could not reach a high enough speed to cause any real damage. One more case: Do you ever doubt that we, as humans, have only five senses? Not likely. Yet, apart from sight, smell, taste, and so on, some scientists explain that many other senses are in play: balance, movement, time, and hunger among them. However, there isn't much agreement about the total number, so maybe we should accept that there are five basic senses and leave the rest open to Continue . . .

3 GRAMMAR

Combine each pair of sentences using the words in parentheses.

1. As a child, I believed some strange things. A monster was living under my bed. (believe)

   As a child, I ____*believed (that)*____ a monster _*was living under my bed*_ .

2. To keep the monster away, I had to do certain things. I had to adjust the covers over me. (feel)

   To keep the monster away, I _____ I _____ .

3. I needed extra protection. My teddy bear would help me. (assume)

   I _____ my teddy bear

   _____ .

4. I was fairly sure of one thing. My parents wouldn't believe me. (doubt)

   I _____ my parents

   _____ .

4 GRAMMAR

Use the verbs in parentheses to explain what you think these people would do in the following situations.

1. Anna's friend won't travel on Friday the 13th because he considers it to be an unlucky day. Anna disagrees. How do you think Anna would reassure him? (explain)

   Anna would explain that Friday the 13th is just like any other day.

2. Luke's soccer teammate saw him rubbing a charm for good luck. How would Luke explain this? (admit)

   _____

3. Farah isn't superstitious, but her friend claims that following some superstitions brings good luck. How do you think Farah would respond? (argue)

   _____

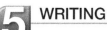

A Read the text and answer the questions. Write the letter of the appropriate sentence.

1. Which sentence is the thesis statement? _____
2. Which sentence gives general examples? _____
3. Which sentence reflects the author's personal opinion about traditional beliefs? _____
4. Which sentence restates the thesis statement? _____

Traditional Beliefs

a Traditional beliefs are not the same as superstitions. They differ in that they supposedly transmit useful information from one generation to another. **b** For example, I'm sure most of us can remember our parents telling us to eat certain foods or to avoid specific behaviors. Is there wisdom in these teachings, or are they without value? **c** Some beliefs passed down through generations reflect current medical thinking, whereas others have not passed the test of time.

Did your mother ever tell you to eat your carrots because they're good for your eyes? Well, the truth is carrots contain high levels of vitamin A. Research has linked vitamin A deficiencies to vision problems in low light, so in this sense, eating plenty of carrots actually is good for your eyes. And is garlic really good for you? It turns out that it is. Eating garlic on a regular basis can reduce the risk of serious illness and detoxify the body. How about chicken soup? We now understand that chicken contains an amino acid that is similar to a drug often prescribed for people with respiratory infections.

Unfortunately, not all of mom's advice has withstood medical inquiry. For example, generations of children have been told not to go swimming for an hour after eating. But research suggests that there is no danger in having lunch and then diving back into the ocean. Is chocolate really bad for you? Well, no, not if it's dark chocolate. Researchers now understand that dark chocolate contains enough antioxidants to make small amounts of it a healthy choice. Are fresh fruit juices really better for you than sodas? Well, yes and no. Fruit juices can contain as much sugar as soda, and both can contribute to weight gain and tooth decay. The best drink of all is simply water.

d Even though science can persuade us that some of our traditional beliefs don't hold water, there is still a lot of wisdom in the beliefs that have been handed down from generation to generation. **e** After all, much of this lore has been accumulated from thousands of years of trial-and-error experience in family healthcare. **f** We should respect this informal body of knowledge even as we search for clear scientific evidence to prove it to be true or false.

B Write a composition about traditional beliefs in your own culture. Include some you think are true and some you think are not true. Be sure to restate the thesis statement from your first paragraph in the last paragraph.

1 GRAMMAR

Read the article and underline the reporting verbs that are in the passive voice.

A Famous HOAX

On October 30, 1938, perhaps the most famous broadcast in the history of radio took place. Heard all over the United States, the broadcast reported that a spacecraft from Mars had landed in a small town in New Jersey. It <u>was said</u> that the Martians were attacking the surrounding area with a deadly "heat ray." Radio reporters also claimed that huge war machines had emerged from the spacecraft. After much destruction, it was announced that the Martians were dying. Specialists suggested that the Martians had no resistance to earth's infectious diseases.

Of course, this story was just a radio play, based on the novel *War of the Worlds* by H. G. Wells and directed and performed by Orson Welles. However, it is generally claimed that many people believed it, and it was reported that there was widespread panic throughout the country, especially in New Jersey. While it was not the intention of the broadcast to frighten people, its effects were widespread and dramatic. It has been suggested that Welles's broadcast offers many lessons about how the mass media can affect people in their daily lives.

Orson Welles

2 VOCABULARY

Cross out the word that does not fit the meaning of the sentence.

1. It is *conceivable* / ~~*misleading*~~ / *plausible* that many lowland areas will be under water if the current trend in climate change continues.

2. Fad diets that promise you'll lose 10 pounds the first day sound *convincing* / *fishy* / *far-fetched* to me. There's no way you can lose 10 pounds in one day!

3. Beware of *dubious* / *phony* / *well-founded* emails that ask you to supply personal information like your credit card number or your salary.

4. Greta gave such a(n) *believable* / *convincing* / *iffy* performance in the play that I almost forgot she was acting!

5. Stephanie's blog is *misleading* / *fishy* / *believable*. Her profile says she's 24, but I know for a fact she's only 18.

6. That Carl is a chef seems *far-fetched* / *dubious* / *conceivable* to me. The food he cooked for dinner was awful.

7. I don't believe that "all-natural" foods are better for you. Show me a *plausible* / *dubious* / *well-founded* article that proves it, and then maybe I'll believe it.

8. When Kay told me she found a great used car online, it sounded *iffy* / *far-fetched* / *credible* to me. But the car is actually pretty nice!

3 GRAMMAR

Rewrite these sentences with the words in parentheses. Use a reporting clause
in the passive with *it*.

1. More than two billion people use the Internet. (estimate)
   It is estimated (that) more than two billion people use the Internet.

2. Fingernails grow faster on the hand that you use the most. (report)

   _____

3. The oldest living tree on earth is nearly 5,000 years old. (say)

   _____

4. In a baby's first year of life, parents lose between 400 and 750 hours
   of sleep. (believe)

   _____

5. Items like plastic cups and bags take between 500 and 1,000 years
   to break down. (explain)

   _____

6. About 100 hairs fall from a person's head each day. (claim)

   _____

4 GRAMMAR

Use the cues to write sentences with a reporting clause in the passive.

1. say / 15 minutes of exercise per day / may extend your
   life by three years
   It is said (that) 15 minutes of exercise per
   day may extend your life by three years.

2. report / the average American child / watches 20,000
   commercials each year

   _____

   _____

3. suggest / traditional treatments such as acupuncture / are effective

   _____

   _____

4. claim / a cure for certain types of cancer / will be found soon

   _____

   _____

5. believe / some animals / can predict earthquakes

   _____

   _____

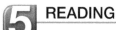

5 READING

A Read the article quickly to find the answers to these questions.

1. When did the Mikkelsons begin Snopes.com? _____

2. How many people visit the website each month? _____

3. What is the mission of Snopes.com? _____

RUMOR DETECTIVES

A few years ago, a woman and her husband were coming home from a ski trip when they spotted a disabled car on the side of the road. It was raining, and the driver looked distressed, so they stopped and helped him fix his flat tire. The man was extremely grateful but didn't have any cash to reward them, so he took down their personal information. A week later, the couple got a call from their bank saying their mortgage had been paid and $10,000 deposited into their account by an appreciative Bill Gates.

"Ah, the grateful millionaire," says Barbara Mikkelson with a satisfied grin.

Barbara and her husband, David, run Snopes.com, the Internet's preeminent resource for verifying and debunking rumors, ridiculous claims, and email chain letters. Whether it's an urban legend like the Gates story, an overblown warning about the latest computer virus, or that bizarre photo circulating of "Hercules, the world's biggest dog," chances are Snopes has checked it out and rated it as "true," "false," or "undetermined."

What began in 1995 as a hobby for a pair of amateur folklorists has grown into one of the Internet's most trusted authorities – and a full-time profession for the Mikkelsons. Each month, millions of people visit Snopes.com. Even the word *Snopes* has gone viral – as in, "Why didn't you Snopes that junk before forwarding it to your entire email list?"

"It's not easy to find out if these things are true or not, so people turn to us," David says.

A passion for nosing around is what brought the Mikkelsons together, and it's still their prime motivation, though their work is more than just a labor of love. The couple now earns a "very healthy" income, David says, from advertising on the site.

Though the Mikkelsons are established figures on the Web, they still prefer old-fashioned research – scouring vintage catalogs, thumbing through four newspapers a day – over finding quick answers online. David admits, however, that he might use Google or Wikipedia as a starting point.

B Are these statements true (*T*), false (*F*), or is the information not given (*NG*) in the article? Write the correct letters.

_____ 1. The Mikkelsons are now millionaires because of their work on Snopes.com.

_____ 2. Snopes.com gets hundreds of stories a day that are as far-fetched as "the grateful millionaire" one.

_____ 3. The Mikkelsons never resort to using online sources to check dubious facts.

_____ 4. The word *Snopes* is sometimes used as a verb by people familiar with the site.

_____ 5. Snopes receives income from ads placed by major international corporations.

5 MOVIES AND TELEVISION

LESSON A ▶ *Movies*

1 VOCABULARY

Choose the words that best complete the sentences.

1. I love movies that are so *predictable* /(*riveting*) that you completely lose track of the time.

2. The last movie I saw wasn't original at all. In fact, it seemed pretty *formulaic* / *touching* to me.

3. The critics were disappointed with the director's new film. They said his work was unoriginal and *moving* / *mediocre*.

4. The heartbreaking relationship between the two main characters in this movie is beautiful and *predictable* / *touching*.

5. That movie was so *clichéd* / *engrossing* that I honestly forgot I was in my living room.

6. After seeing the *inspiring* / *predictable* story of a woman who set up an elephant rescue organization, I decided to volunteer at an animal shelter.

2 GRAMMAR

Underline the sentence adverbs in these conversations. Then write them in the chart below.

1. Jack: I don't trust all the facts in this documentary about Coco Chanel.
    Lisa: I don't agree. The writer <u>clearly</u> did his research and interviewed many people who knew her.

2. Jill: When is your new film coming <u>out</u>?
    Fei: <u>Apparently</u> in May, but there will <u>be</u> a private viewing in April.

3. Aaron: I wanted to see the new documentary about a homeless family, but it isn't playing <u>anywhere</u>.
    Emma: Haven't you <u>heard</u>? It was removed from the theaters. <u>Supposedly</u>, the director used footage of certain people without <u>asking permission</u>, and now there's a lawsuit.

4. Kurt: I'm surprised. That new action movie <u>was</u> so dull! → boring
    Teresa: I know. The director probably thinks he doesn't need to try <u>very</u> hard after so many successful movies.

5. Josh: This is the third science fiction movie I've seen this month!
    Tara: <u>Obviously</u>, you <u>really</u> like that kind of movie.

6. Kazuo: This director's films are <u>so</u> funny!
    Julie: Yes, but <u>unquestionably</u>, there's a lot of deep emotion in them <u>as well</u>.

Certainty	Less certainty	Possibility and probability
clearly		

GRAMMAR

Rewrite these sentences using the sentence adverbs in parentheses.

1. That famous Dutch actor is going to direct a movie. (apparently)

   Apparently, that famous Dutch actor is going to direct a movie.

   That famous Dutch actor is apparently going to direct a movie.

2. Some movie studios are not interested in good acting as much as extreme action. (frankly)

   _____

3. This is a magazine for anyone with a very strong interest in cinema. (definitely)

   This is a magazine for anyone definitely with a very strong interest in cinema.

4. There would be more interest in historical movies if they received more publicity. (probably)

   Probably there would be more interest

5. Because of a lack of funding, fewer independent films will be made this year. (potentially)

   _____

GRAMMAR

How does watching movies in theaters compare with watching movies at home?
Write sentences using the adverbs provided.

1. _Watching a movie at home_ is clearly _more comfortable than watching a movie_
   in a theater.

2. _____ is potentially _____

   _____

3. Overall, _____

   _____

4. _____ unquestionably the most _____

   _____

5. Unfortunately, _____

   _____

5 WRITING

A Choose either a comedy or a documentary that you are familiar with, and write a review of the movie you have chosen. Your review should answer the following questions.

Documentary

1. What is the title of the documentary?
2. What is the documentary mainly about?
3. What is the primary purpose of the documentary? Does it try to explain, persuade, or something else?
4. How successful is the documentary at achieving its purpose? Explain.
5. Which aspects of the documentary are especially memorable?
6. Would you recommend it to others? Why or why not?

Comedy

1. What is the title of the comedy?
2. Who are the actors, and what characters do they play?
3. What is the basic plot of the movie?
4. What are the best aspects of the movie? Explain.
5. Is the movie successful as a comedy? Why or why not?
6. Would you recommend it to others? Why or why not?

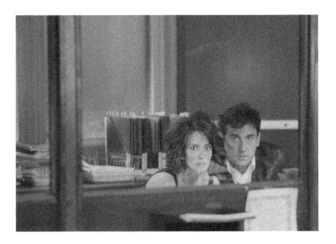

_____

_____

_____

_____

_____

_____

_____

_____

_____

_____

_____

_____

B Read your review again. Are there places where adding more details would make your writing better? If so, go back and add these details.

LESSON B ▶ *Television*

GRAMMAR

Complete the email with *so, such, so many, so few, so much,* or *so little.*

To: nataliem3@cup.com
Subject: House

Hey Natalie,

Have you ever seen the TV show *House*? The series ended a while ago, but it's
1 _____such_____ a good show that I can't stop watching the reruns! It's about a cranky doctor
and his medical team who save the lives of patients with mysterious diseases. I usually
have **2** _____ time for TV that I skip most medical dramas. But this show isn't a typical
medical drama where doctors are compassionate and
caring. Dr. House is rude. In fact, he's **3** _____ rude
that his patients are often afraid of him. But he's also
4 _____ a brilliant doctor that everybody admires
him. He knows **5** _____ about rare diseases that
he's usually the only person who can cure these patients.
I had no idea there were **6** _____ different kinds
of illnesses. I think you'd like this show. There are
7 _____ good shows on TV these days that you'll
really appreciate this one.

Marcus

VOCABULARY

Write the type of TV show next to its description.

| cartoon | documentary | news program | sketch comedy show | sports program |
| cooking show | game show | sitcom | soap opera | talk show |

game show 1. Participants compete for money and prizes by answering
              questions that an average fifth grade student would know.

_____ 2. The complicated lives of the wealthy Ramirez family are
              dramatized daily.

_____ 3. Ann Brady reports on the top news stories of the day.

_____ 4. The Lakers take on the Suns in game three of the playoffs.

_____ 5. Ty Ott interviews actor Ash Lake and chef Ami Tran.

_____ 6. Astronaut Neil Armstrong's life is reviewed in this program.

_____ 7. A boy and his ladybug friend star in this animated kids' show.

_____ 8. Alice Lee stars in this funny half-hour show about high school.

_____ 9. To win, chefs live together and prepare dishes for celebrity judges.

_____ 10. Weekly guests star with the regular cast in a series of ridiculous
              situations.

3 GRAMMAR

Write six logical sentences by choosing one word or phrase from each column.
Sometimes more than one answer is possible.

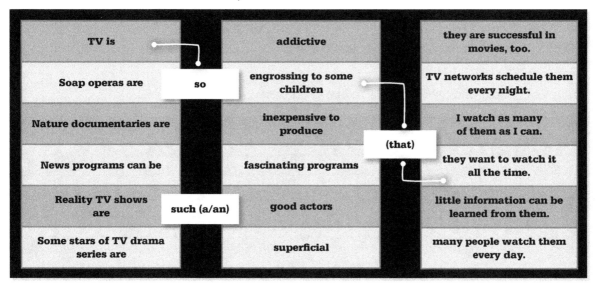

TV is		addictive		they are successful in movies, too.
Soap operas are	**so**	engrossing to some children		TV networks schedule them every night.
Nature documentaries are		inexpensive to produce	**(that)**	I watch as many of them as I can.
News programs can be		fascinating programs		they want to watch it all the time.
Reality TV shows are	**such (a/an)**	good actors		little information can be learned from them.
Some stars of TV drama series are		superficial		many people watch them every day.

1. *TV is so engrossing to some children (that) they want to watch it all the time.*
2. _____
3. _____
4. _____
5. _____
6. _____

4 GRAMMAR

Complete these sentences with your own ideas.

1. Some crime drama series can be so *violent* that *I don't think children should*
   watch them.

2. There are so many _____ to watch this season that I
   _____

3. _____ is such a great actor that I _____
   _____

4. _____ night is such a good night to watch TV that _____
   _____

5. There are so few really funny shows on TV that I _____
   _____

6. Reality shows can be so _____ that I _____
   _____

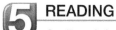

A Read the article. Find the words in boldface that match these definitions.

1. legal officials who accuse someone of a crime __*prosecutors*__
2. disqualify _____
3. scientific techniques used to investigate a crime _____
4. based on data rather than theory _____
5. groups of people who make a decision in a court case _____

IS THE "CSI EFFECT" INFLUENCING COURTROOMS?

The fictional forensic investigators in shows like *CSI: Crime Scene Investigation* put old-time detectives like Sherlock Holmes to shame. They can read a crime scene like it's a glossy magazine. But many **prosecutors** complain that shows like *CSI* make their job harder by creating the expectation that every trial must feature high-tech **forensic tests**. Some fear that when they don't show off *CSI*-style technology, **juries** might let criminals get away. It's termed the "*CSI* effect."

"I think that *CSI* has done some great things," says Mike Murphy, the coroner for Clark County, Nevada, whose office was the model for the original *CSI* show. "It's also caused some problems. And some of those problems are [that] people expect us to have DNA back in 20 minutes or that we're supposed to solve a crime in 60 minutes with three commercials. It doesn't happen that way," he says. Legal experts are concerned that juries may well be confusing fact with fiction.

However, Donald Shelton, the chief judge of Washtenaw County, Michigan, is skeptical. After realizing no **empirical** research on the *CSI* effect had been done, Shelton conducted a study showing that while jurors do expect to see scientific evidence in murder cases, their expectations have nothing to do with the TV shows they watch. They're more likely to be affected by the technology in their own pocket. "The more sophisticated [the] technological devices that jurors had, the higher their expectations for the prosecutors to present evidence," Shelton says.

Despite the lack of empirical evidence, lawyers, judges, and investigators act as if the *CSI* effect is real. In the U.S., some states now allow lawyers to **strike** potential jurors based on their TV habits. Judges are issuing instructions that warn juries about expecting too much scientific evidence based on what they see on TV. And in the field, Shelton says, investigators sometimes run useless tests just to show they went the extra *CSI* mile.

B Read these statements. Are they supported by the information in the article? Choose yes or no.

	Yes	No
1. Real or not, the *CSI* effect is clearly having an influence on courtrooms.	☐	☐
2. Shows like *CSI* definitely raise the expectations of jurors.	☐	☐
3. *CSI* realistically depicts how criminal investigations are conducted.	☐	☐
4. Some investigators now conduct tests only to impress juries.	☐	☐

6 MUSICIANS AND MUSIC

LESSON A ▶ *A world of music*

 GRAMMAR

Choose the words that best complete the sentences.

1. Generally, the more well known a singer is, the (more) / less money he or she makes.

2. The less publicity a musician gets, the *easier / harder* it is to make a living.

3. Some say the earlier you expose children to classical music, the *more / fewer* likely they are to excel in school.

4. The more relaxing the music, the *faster / slower* I fall asleep.

5. In my opinion, the more you listen to some song lyrics, the *fewer / less* you are able to understand them.

6. For some musicians, the more people gossip about their private lives, the *better / sooner*!

 GRAMMAR

Complete the interview with the words from the box.

better	less	longer	more	sooner

Lily: When did you realize you wanted to be a guitarist?

Shane: I was 10 years old. My brother was taking guitar lessons, and the more I heard him practice, the (1) _____**more**_____ I wanted to play guitar just as well.

Lily: Who were your biggest musical influences?

Shane: My biggest influence was Jack White. The more I listened to his music, the (2) _____ it got.

Lily: Jack White is great, but your music doesn't sound like his.

Shane: Yeah, I know. I realized that the more I listened to Jack White's music, the (3) _____ I wanted to sound like him. I wanted my own sound – something that made me unique.

Lily: You've certainly succeeded! What's next for you?

Shane: I'm moving to New York City. The (4) _____ I stay in Los Angeles, the more I realize I need a change.

Lily: Why is that?

Shane: I'd like to be part of a growing music scene, and apparently a lot is happening in New York.

Lily: When will you leave?

Shane: I'm not sure yet, but I think the (5) _____ I leave, the better.

3 VOCABULARY

Choose the adjectives that best describe your opinion of each kind of music. Then write a sentence explaining why.

1. pop (catchy / frenetic / monotonous)

   Successful pop music is catchy. The best pop songs are
   hard to forget — even years later.

2. classical (exhilarating / haunting / soothing)

   _____

   _____

3. jazz (evocative / mellow / frenetic)

   _____

   _____

4. hip-hop (catchy / evocative / monotonous)

   _____

   _____

5. folk (haunting / soothing / catchy)

   _____

   _____

6. rock (monotonous / exhilarating / frenetic)

   _____

   _____

4 GRAMMAR

Complete the sentences with double comparatives and your own ideas to make them true for you.

1. The _____*louder*_____ the music, the _____*more*_____ I like it.

2. The _____ the lyrics of a song, the more likely I am to

   _____.

3. The _____ the music, the _____ I find it.

4. The _____ a musician's reputation, the _____
   I am to go to his or her concerts.

5. The _____ a piece of music, the more difficult it is to

   _____.

6. The _____ musicians use _____ in their songs,
   the less I enjoy them.

WRITING

A Read the characteristics of listening to live music and listening to recorded music. Then put them under the correct heading below.

> You listen with many other people.
> Sometimes you hear music you don't like.
> You can't see the musicians while you listen.
> You can sing along with your favorite songs.
> You can adjust the volume.
> You can hear music by well-known artists.
>
> You can't adjust the volume.
> You can listen to a song over and over.
> You can listen to any kind of music you're in the mood for.
> You can listen to music in any order you'd like.
> You can turn off or skip songs you don't like.
> You can listen only when musicians are playing on stage.

Live music

_____
_____
_____
_____
_____
_____

Recorded music

_____
_____
_____
_____
_____
_____

Live music and recorded music

_____
_____
_____
_____
_____
_____

B What is your opinion of listening to live music versus listening to recorded music? Write a thesis statement expressing your opinion on the subject.

_____
_____
_____

C Now write a compare-and-contrast essay. Include your thesis statement in the introduction, two paragraphs describing the similarities and differences, and a conclusion restating your point of view.

VOCABULARY

Correct the underlined mistake in each sentence with one of the words in the box. Some words will be used more than once.

| be | break | get | make | pay |

1. Most musicians must <u>break</u> their dues before they become successful. _____*pay*_____
2. After retiring in 2012, my favorite band is planning to <u>get</u> a comeback. _____
3. Gotye's latest song is going to <u>pay</u> a big hit. _____
4. I want to be a singer. What advice do you have to <u>make</u> into the business? _____
5. Many famous singers <u>be</u> their big break as contestants on *American Idol*. _____
6. It was so difficult for Jay-Z to <u>break</u> his foot in the door that he started his own record label. _____
7. The first time I heard Madonna, I knew she wouldn't <u>pay</u> a one-hit wonder. _____
8. While some musicians may be talented and work hard, they might never <u>get</u> a name for themselves in the music industry. _____

GRAMMAR

Complete these conversations. Use the verbs in parentheses and *would* or *will*.

1. Kim: I used to listen to all kinds of music when I was younger.
   Ron: Not me! When I was young, I _____*would listen*_____ (listen) only to rock music.

2. Dan: You play the guitar so well. How often do you practice?
   Sally: I practice all the time. In fact, I _____ (practice) four to five hours a day, depending on my schedule.

3. Mario: What do you like to do in your spare time?
   Kate: I don't have much spare time, but when I do, I _____ (go) to jazz clubs and concerts. Music helps me relax.

4. Fay: I can't believe the lead singer of the band we saw spent so much time after the show talking with his fans and signing autographs.
   Amy: I know. Most singers these days _____ (not spend) any time with their fans, let alone sign autographs!

5. Paula: When I was a teenager, I loved to listen to music that was really loud.
   Diana: Me, too. In fact, I _____ (turn up) my stereo as loud as I could. Unfortunately, now I have hearing problems.

6. Rob: I just heard my favorite Beatles song on the radio.
   Lori: I love the Beatles. In college I _____ (listen) to them every day.

3 GRAMMAR

Read the sentences about a band. Then choose the sentences that incorrectly use *will* or *would* and correct them.

☑ 1. When the band comes onstage, the crowd would scream.
When the band comes onstage, the crowd will scream.

☐ 2. Before the band got so popular, it will never sell out a concert in such a short time.

☐ 3. Years ago, only bands with great musicianship would make it big.

☐ 4. When the guitarist was young, he would practice in front of a mirror.

☐ 5. In the past, the band will play only hard rock songs.

☐ 6. Although the band used to sign autographs after a show, these days, security guards would not let fans backstage.

4 GRAMMAR

Which music habits were or were not true for you in the past?
Which are or are not true now? Write sentences with *would* or *will*.

1. listen to a song over and over again
When I find a song I really love, I will listen to it over and over again.

2. listen to very loud music

3. spend a lot of money downloading music

4. take music lessons

5. travel long distances to see live concerts of favorite bands

6. argue with family members about musical tastes

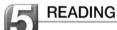

READING

A Read the article quickly. What do you think the root *neuro-* in words such as *neurobiologist* means?

Music May Someday
Help Repair the Brain

The music that makes the foot tap, the fingers snap, and the pulse quicken stirs the brain at its most fundamental levels, suggesting that scientists one day may be able to retune damaged minds by exploiting rhythm, harmony, and melody, according to some research.

"Undeniably, there is a biology of music," said neurobiologist Mark Jude Tramo. "Music is biologically part of human life, just as music is aesthetically part of human life."

Researchers found that the brain:

■ Responds directly to harmony. Neuroscientists discovered that different parts of the brain involved in emotion are activated depending on whether the music is pleasant or unpleasant.

■ Interprets written music in an area on its right side. That region corresponds to an area on the opposite side of the brain known to handle written words and letters. So, researchers uncovered an anatomical link between music and language.

■ Grows in response to musical training. In a study of classically trained musicians, researchers discovered that male musicians have significantly larger brains than men who have not had extensive musical training. Although no similar increase has been found in female musicians, this might be explained by insufficient and inconclusive research.

Overall, music seems to involve the brain at almost every level, and researchers are already looking for ways to harness the power of music to change the brain. Research also suggests that music may play some role in enhancing intelligence. Indeed, so seductive is the possibility that music can boost a child's IQ that some politicians have lobbied for children to be exposed regularly to Mozart sonatas, although such research has yet to be confirmed.

The scientists said the research could help the clinical practice of neurology, including cognitive rehabilitation. As a therapeutic tool, for example, some doctors already use music to help rehabilitate stroke patients. Surprisingly, some stroke patients who have lost their ability to speak retain their ability to sing, and that opens an avenue for therapists to retrain the brain's speech centers.

B Read the statements. Are they supported by the information in the article? Choose yes or no.

	Yes	No
1. Different areas of the brain respond to music.	☐	☐
2. The brains of classically trained male musicians grow larger than the brains of nonmusical males.	☐	☐
3. Different pieces of classical music affect the brain in different ways.	☐	☐
4. Children who listen to Mozart sonatas develop higher intelligence than those who do not have exposure to this music.	☐	☐
5. Some stroke victims who are unable to speak are able to sing.	☐	☐

7 CHANGING TIMES

LESSON **A** ▶ *Lifestyles in transition*

GRAMMAR

Underline the relative pronouns in this announcement.

If these statements describe your situation, then telecommuting may be right for you.

1. You have a job <u>that</u> you can do independently of your co-workers.
2. You can work productively without the pressure that you may get from supervisors.
3. Your home has a quiet room which you can use as your office.
4. You have the technology that you will need to do your job at home.
5. There are no family members who will require your attention while you are trying to work.
6. You won't miss the social interaction that many people enjoy in the workplace.
7. You don't get distracted by household chores which interfere with your work.
8. You can effectively use remote communication tools to keep in touch with those co-workers whose help you may need while you are working from home.

See your Human Resources representative for details about our telecommuting policy.

GRAMMAR

Combine these sentences using a relative pronoun. Then write *O* if the relative pronoun is optional and *R* if the relative pronoun is required.

___O___ 1. Physical fitness is an important goal. A lot of people try to achieve this goal.

       Physical fitness is an important goal that a lot of people try to achieve.

_____ 2. Many people stay fit. These people find the time to work out regularly at a gym.

_____ 3. For the best results, it's important to find a gym. You like this gym.

_____ 4. It may be a good idea to hire a trainer. A trainer can work with you privately.

_____ 5. Your trainer can give you advice. The advice can help you avoid injuries.

_____ 6. If you get bored at the gym, try bringing some music. You can listen to the music while you exercise.

3 VOCABULARY

Use the words in the box to complete these conversations.

| consistent | illogical | immature | inconsiderate | indecisive | responsible |

1. A: I can't make up my mind. Which tie looks better?

   B: Don't be so _____*indecisive*_____. Just choose one.

2. A: Jim is 40 years old, and he still depends on his mother to clean his apartment.

   B: I know. He really is _____ in some ways.

3. A: Why did Meredith buy such a large car with gas prices so high?

   B: I know it seems _____, but she needs a big car for her job.

4. A: Doesn't Allison look great? What is she doing?

   B: She's been eating better and exercising on a _____ basis.

5. A: Why does Nate play his music so loudly when he knows we have to study?

   B: I don't know. He's so _____ of our needs. He just doesn't care.

6. A: I really like the new waiter you hired. He's very dependable.

   B: Yes, he is. Even though he's young, he's quite _____.

4 GRAMMAR

Use relative clauses and your own ideas to complete these sentences.

1. I have always admired people _*who are good at organizing their time.*_

2. I've always thought that I would enjoy a lifestyle _____

3. Parents _____ should be greatly admired.

4. These days many people want jobs _____

5. Finding enough time to spend with family and friends is a problem _____

_____

A Read this composition about a personal experience and answer the questions.

The family that eats together, stays together

I feel it is very important for families to have regular meals together. One of my most positive childhood memories was dinner with my parents and two sisters. As a result, last year I decided that my family would have dinner together three days a week. Because my husband and I both work, and our kids are busy with school activities, we found that we rarely had a chance to get together as a family. But we thought it would be possible for everyone to set aside three evenings a week for a sit-down dinner.

First, we tried setting three fixed days for our experiment – Mondays, Wednesdays, and Fridays. After a couple of weeks of trying this plan, almost everyone was unhappy. Then my son had the idea of having everyone post his or her schedule for the week on the refrigerator every Sunday. I would choose the three best days, and those with scheduling conflicts . . .

For a while, the kids continued to resist the idea. They said they would rather spend the time with their friends or participate in sports or other activities. Gradually, though, they began to see these evenings together in a very positive way. We laughed a lot. We made vacation plans. We discussed each other's problems. After a couple of months, anyone who had to miss a family meal felt . . .

We all feel that we have been able to build much stronger relationships within the family than we had before. Of course, there are still disagreements, but we communicate better with each other now. The idea of having regular family meals together, which seemed difficult at first, has brought about many positive changes in our lives.

1. What is the thesis statement?

   _____

2. What is the focus of the second paragraph?

   _____

3. What is the focus of the third paragraph?

   _____

4. What sentence in the conclusion restates the thesis statement?

   _____

B Write a thesis statement for a composition about an important decision you have made recently.

   _____

   _____

C Now write your composition. Include an introduction, two paragraphs providing background information and details, and a conclusion.

GRAMMAR

Choose the expressions that best complete the sentences.

1. Cathy has decided to give up her high-powered job and do something more personally satisfying *like* / *as though* several of her friends have done.

2. Doesn't it seem *the way* / *as if* more people are trying to live a simpler life?

3. Elena feels *as* / *as though* she spends too much of her time commuting, so she is looking for work that she can do from home.

4. Today's kids don't have a lot of free time, *as* / *as if* we did when we were growing up, but they have many more opportunities.

5. Schools should offer music and art *as if* / *the way* they did when I was a student.

6. *As* / *As though* my aunt always says, "Make new friends, but keep your old ones."

7. Some days I feel *as if* / *the way* time passes too quickly.

8. *Like* / *As though* my mother before me, I serve a traditional dinner on special holidays for my family to enjoy.

VOCABULARY

Choose the expressions that are best exemplified by each situation.

a. anticipate a change	c. cope with change	e. resist change
b. bring about a change	d. go through a change	f. welcome a change

__e__ 1. Sherri's friends want her to move to Los Angeles with them, but she keeps coming up with reasons why she shouldn't go.

_____ 2. Mr. Viera's ideas encouraged our company to find ways for employees to work more closely with other departments.

_____ 3. After being on a plane for eight hours, Eun-ju was happy to finally land in Hawaii and begin her vacation.

_____ 4. When Mark retired from his job, he started playing golf and volunteering at the food bank.

_____ 5. Our school is in the process of moving to a new building and revising the schedule, so it's a challenging time for everyone.

_____ 6. We've realized it's time to move to a bigger house. We plan to start looking for a new place next month.

3 GRAMMAR

Read each situation and answer the questions using *as if*, *as though*, *as*, or *the way*.
Sometimes more than one answer is possible.

1. Cal used to look forward to going
   fishing with his sons every summer.
   Now, his sons don't have time to go
   anymore. How does Cal feel?

   He feels as if he has lost a

   family tradition.

2. Anna has moved from a small town to a
   big city. It's exciting, and she's meeting
   lots of new people and discovering many
   new activities. How does Anna feel?

   _____

   _____

3. Mia used to spend a lot of time with her
   grandmother. Since Mia moved away,
   she only sees her grandmother twice a
   year. How does Mia feel?

   _____

   _____

4. In his spare time, Chris took an art class
   and discovered he had a real talent.
   Now he's about to have his first show in
   a gallery. How does Chris feel?

   _____

   _____

4 GRAMMAR

Complete these sentences so that they are true for you. Use *as if*, *as though*, *as*,
the way, and *like*.

1. I feel ___*as though social media*___ is changing the way I relate to my friends.

2. I don't feel _____

   _____ when I was younger.

3. These days I think many people act _____

4. I still _____

   _____ my family did years ago.

5. Some people my age talk _____

   _____

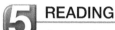

A Read the interview with Malcolm Gladwell about his book *The Tipping Point*.
Find the words in boldface that match the definitions.

1. sudden increases in the occurence of something unpleasant _____*outbreaks*_____

2. the scientific study of epidemics _____

3. a comparison of two similar things _____

4. easily spread _____

THE TIPPING POINT: Q & A with Malcolm Gladwell

1 What is *The Tipping Point* about? It's a book about change. In particular, it's a book that presents a new way of understanding why change so often happens as quickly and as unexpectedly as it does. For example, why did crime drop so dramatically in New York City in the mid-1990s? How does a novel written by an unknown author end up as a national bestseller? Why is word-of-mouth so powerful? I think the answer to all these questions is the same. It's that behavior and messages and products sometimes behave just like **outbreaks** of infectious disease. They are social epidemics. *The Tipping Point* is an examination of the social epidemics that surround us.

2 Do you think the epidemic example is relevant for other kinds of change? I'm convinced that ideas and behaviors and new products move through a population very much like a disease does. This isn't just a metaphor. I'm talking about a very literal **analogy**. Ideas can be **contagious** in exactly the same way that a virus is.

3 How would you classify *The Tipping Point*? Is it a science book? I like to think of it as an intellectual adventure story. It draws from psychology and sociology and **epidemiology**, and uses examples from the worlds of business and education and fashion and media . . . all in aid of explaining a very common but mysterious phenomenon that we deal with every day.

4 What do you hope readers will take away from the book? One of the things I'd like to do is to show people how to start "positive" epidemics of their own. The virtue of an epidemic, after all, is that just a little input is enough to get it started, and it can spread very, very quickly. That makes it something of obvious and enormous interest to everyone, from educators trying to reach students, to businesses trying to spread the word about their product, or for that matter, to anyone who's trying to create a change with limited resources. By the end of the book, I think the reader will have a clear idea of what starting an epidemic actually takes. This is not an abstract, academic book. It's very practical. And it's very hopeful. It's brain software.

B Read the interview again. Choose the statements that are true according to the text.

☐ 1. *The Tipping Point* is a nonfiction book that draws from a number of different fields.

☐ 2. Gladwell believes that ideas, messages, and products spread in similar ways.

☐ 3. Before writing the book, Gladwell started a social epidemic of his own.

☐ 4. According to Gladwell, social epidemics do not occur very often.

☐ 5. Gladwell believes *The Tipping Point* should appeal to a wide range of readers.

☐ 6. *The Tipping Point* is not meant to be a book with practical applications.

8 CONSUMER CULTURE

LESSON A ▶ *What's new on the market?*

 GRAMMAR

Underline the direct objects and circle the indirect objects in each sentence.

1. Some stores offer their (customers) frequent-buyer rewards as incentives to return.
2. Advertising is useful because it gives us information about improved products.
3. The salesperson recommended the latest headphones to me.
4. Someone had to explain the new printer to Daniel.
5. This GPS must have cost you a lot of money.
6. You should return those boots to the store if they're not comfortable.
7. Online auction sites offer collectors a great way to find the things they want.
8. I don't shop online often because I like to ask salespeople questions in person.

 GRAMMAR

Unscramble the words to make sentences describing the woman's shopping experience.

1. the latest tablets / showed / the woman / the salesperson

   The salesperson showed the woman the latest tablets.

2. the woman / to / the GS5 model / recommended / the salesperson

   _____

3. her / the main features / he / described / to

   _____

4. him / the woman / the price / asked

   _____

5. the salesperson / the price / her / told

   _____

6. said / nothing / to / him / she / for a moment

   _____

7. a discount / offered / the salesperson / her

   _____

8. the money / the salesperson / she / to / gave

   _____

Use the words in the box to give advice about what to do in each situation. Include a direct and an indirect object in each sentence.

lend	mention	recommend	return	teach

1. Mai got a book from her brother for her birthday. She already has a copy of the book.
   Mai should return the book to the store and get one she doesn't have.

2. Ray and Pam want to go skiing with Kate, but Pam doesn't have enough money.

   _____

3. Ian speaks fluent Thai. His sister wants to learn Thai but doesn't want to take a class.

   _____

4. Jessica's favorite Italian restaurant is Luigi's. Her father wants to go out for Italian food but doesn't know any restaurants.

   _____

5. Max sold his car to a friend. The car uses a lot of oil, but he forgot to say anything about it.

   _____

VOCABULARY

Write a sentence about each situation using the expressions in the box.

bargain hunter	compulsive shopper	shopping spree
buyer's remorse	credit limit	window-shopping

1. Monica and Emil love to see what's on sale at their favorite stores. They can spend hours doing this without buying anything at all!
   Both Monica and Emil love to go window-shopping.

2. When Jeremy gets paid, he always buys things for himself whether he needs them or not. He often spends all of his money in one day.

   _____

3. Mark never pays full price for anything. He always searches for the best price. He even goes to different parts of town to get a good deal.

   _____

4. Before her wedding, Anne and her mother went shopping for everything they would need for the wedding. They spent a lot of money and had a great time.

   _____

5. Jen bought an expensive pair of earrings today. She loved them at the store, but now that she's home, she feels guilty for spending so much money.

   _____

6. While Eric was on vacation, he used his credit card for everything. At the end of the trip, he tried to buy a present, but his card was denied.

   _____

WRITING

A For each opinion, choose the two examples or details that support it.
Then write another sentence to support the opinion.

1. Using an online supermarket saves you time and money.
   - ☐ a. Groceries purchased online are delivered directly to your home.
   - ☐ b. There is less chance to make an impulse buy because you are not actually in the store.
   - ☐ c. Online supermarkets often offer exotic produce that is not available in local grocery stores.

   _____

   _____

2. There is little reason to buy a camera if you have one on your phone.
   - ☐ a. With the right apps, you can edit your photos on the phone and share them on social media.
   - ☐ b. A good camera will usually produce better images than a phone.
   - ☐ c. It's easy to forget to bring a camera, but you probably always have your phone with you.

   _____

   _____

3. Today's children are too materialistic.
   - ☐ a. Many children have more free time than they have ever had before.
   - ☐ b. They compete to have the coolest gadgets and the most expensive hobbies.
   - ☐ c. Parents complain that children only want money from them.

   _____

   _____

B Write a thesis statement about one of the opinions above or one of your own.

_____

_____

C Write a composition. Include your thesis statement in the first paragraph, and develop your opinion with examples and details in subsequent paragraphs.

GRAMMAR

Read the email from a customer to the manager of a supermarket. Underline the subjunctive verbs.

Dear Manager,

I saw the sales flier for your supermarket, and I felt it was imperative that I <u>write</u> you. All the food on sale this week is snack food or other highly processed foods. Although I buy these foods occasionally, I suggest that local and organic foods be on sale, too. It's crucial that people have the chance to buy affordable local foods, and I recommend that your supermarket start offering these items at better prices. I also propose that you offer a larger selection of fresh fruits and vegetables. Many people don't buy fresh foods because they are not easily available. I think it's essential that your customers get the chance to incorporate these foods into their meals.

Thank you.

Marcella Guzman

 GRAMMAR

Use the words in parentheses to rewrite each sentence using the subjunctive.

1. People should learn how to block offensive ads on their devices. (it is important)
   It is important that people learn how to block offensive ads on their devices.

2. A health-conscious person should eat fast food only once or twice a month. (it is vital)
   _____

3. Parents should read reviews before their children see a movie. (it is essential)
   _____

4. The government must prevent students from dropping out of school. (we insist)
   _____

 GRAMMAR

Complete these sentences with your own ideas.

1. If you are suspicious about an ad for a product, I suggest that *you go online and read some reviews of the product.*

2. If you find an ad offensive, I recommend that _____
   _____

3. If you think a particular product is good, I propose that _____
   _____

4. If you want to pursue a career in advertising, it is important that _____
   _____

VOCABULARY

What marketing strategies would you use for each product or business? Use the phrases in the box to write sentences explaining your decisions.

celebrity endorsements	coupon codes	a loyalty program	search-engine marketing
comparative marketing	free samples	product placement	word-of-mouth marketing

1. ice cream *I would use free samples because everyone would taste the ice cream, and many people might like it so much they'd buy more.*

2. an action movie _____
_____
_____
_____

3. a new restaurant _____
_____
_____
_____

4. sports equipment _____
_____
_____
_____

5. a health club _____
_____
_____
_____

6. electronics _____
_____
_____
_____

A Read the article quickly. Which senses were the focus of the marketing strategies and experiments mentioned? Choose the correct answers.

☐ hearing   ☐ sight   ☐ smell   ☐ taste   ☐ touch

Sensory ploys and the scent of MARKETING

Global brands have become increasingly aware of the power of sight, smell, touch, and sound to influence purchasing behaviors.

A fast-food chain has trialed scents for use in its restaurants with the knowledge that this not only draws in customers but also improves their perception of their overall dining experience. A company that produces a popular deodorant for men has spent considerable sums perfecting the sound of its aerosol can to amplify its brand message of strength and effectiveness. This has led to a spray that is noticeably louder than their "female" deodorants.

A subtle scent or a particular sound can be just enough to awaken positive past associations or simply alter our other sensory perceptions. Charles Spence, professor of experimental psychology and a sensory consultant to brands, points to research conducted by a company about 15 years ago. The company discovered that by adding a fragrance to clothes, they were perceived by users as whiter even when they weren't.

Other tricks, such as using high-pitched music, can drive people toward the top of a website, Professor Spence says. Meanwhile, by simply changing the background color on their website, companies can increase trustworthiness. This is of particular value, for example, when asking customers to enter their credit card details.

But brands do not always get it right. Back in 2008, one food company knew that consumers responded positively not only to crunchier chips but also to noisier packaging. So it introduced new noisy packaging for one of its chips. It was so loud that it reached as high as 105 decibels, louder than a lawnmower or food processor. Two years later, the company withdrew the packaging following widespread consumer complaints. There can be advantages in tapping into consumers' senses, but brands can clearly go too far.

B Read the article again. Choose the correct answer for each question.

1. What is this article mostly about?
   ☐ a. How marketing improves consumers' sensory experience.
   ☐ b. How to avoid being tricked by sensory marketing strategies.
   ☐ c. How marketing makes use of the senses to influence consumers.

2. Which of these statements is true according to the article?
   ☐ a. Sensory information doesn't have to be obvious to affect our perception of a product.
   ☐ b. Sensory information only triggers positive associations.
   ☐ c. One sense has no influence on how the other senses perceive a product.

3. Which of the following is **not** mentioned in the article?
   ☐ a. Particular scents can drive consumers into a restaurant.
   ☐ b. A white product is considered more reliable by customers.
   ☐ c. Packages that produce the wrong sound can drive customers away.

NATURE

LESSON A ▶ *Animals in our lives*

 GRAMMAR

Complete these sentences using *whenever* or *wherever*.
If the time or place is specified, use *when* or *where*.

1. For some reason, _____*wherever*_____ I go with my pet snake, people get upset.

2. Many cats will rub against their owners' legs _____ they want to show affection.

3. Research indicates that _____ a person strokes an animal, his or her blood pressure goes down. Also, it's been argued that trained dogs should be present _____ there are people recovering from illnesses.

4. _____ I grew up, it wasn't common for people to have pets in their homes.

5. _____ I got my pet, I took on a serious responsibility. Being able to keep an animal healthy and fit depends on constant care and attention.

② GRAMMAR

Rewrite the last sentence of each conversation with a sentence including a clause starting with *whenever* or *wherever*.

1. A: I'm going over to Chelsea's apartment. Would you like to come with me?
   B: No, I can't. She has a cat, and I'm allergic to them. Any time I'm around a cat, I start sneezing.
   Whenever I'm around a cat, I start sneezing.

2. A: Did you enjoy your visit to the rain forest preserve?
   B: I did. Everywhere I looked, there were amazing plants and animals.
   _____

3. A: What's wrong with your cat? She looks upset.
   B: She's just excited. She looks like that any time she sees a bird outside.
   _____

4. A: What kind of pet would you like to have?
   B: I'd love to get some fish. Any time I see fish swimming, I feel calm.
   _____

③ VOCABULARY

Write the correct word under each picture.

beak	fangs	fin	hooves	paws	tusks
claws	feather	gills	horns	tail	wing

1. _____feather_____

2. _____

3. _____

4. _____

5. _____

6. _____

7. _____

8. _____

9. _____

10. _____

11. _____

12. _____

④ GRAMMAR

Complete these sentences so that they are true for you.

1. Whenever I spend time with animals, _____

   _____

2. When animals are kept in zoos, _____

   _____

3. Wherever there are performances by animals, _____

   _____

4. Wild animals should be kept where _____

   _____

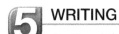

5 WRITING

A Read the thesis statements. Do the topic sentences belong in the composition? Choose yes or no.

	Yes	No

1. Thesis statement: Owning a pet has many health benefits.

   a. People who own pets often have better physical health than people who do not own pets. ☐ ☐

   b. People who own pets handle daily stresses better. ☐ ☐

   c. Pet owners often spend a lot of money on medicine for their pets. ☐ ☐

   d. People who have pets may be happier than other people. ☐ ☐

2. Thesis statement: There are several effective ways to promote the survival of endangered animal species.

   a. Animals held in small enclosures often feel high levels of stress. ☐ ☐

   b. Conservation groups work to restore the natural habitats of endangered animals before reintroducing them to the wild. ☐ ☐

   c. Zoos are often successful at breeding endangered animals. ☐ ☐

   d. Hikers rarely spot endangered animals in the wild. ☐ ☐

3. Thesis statement: Animal studies may lead to advances in technology.

   a. Spider web research could result in stronger buildings being built. ☐ ☐

   b. Learning more about how bats "see" in the dark may lead to new medical technologies. ☐ ☐

   c. Insects such as bees and ants live in highly structured societies. ☐ ☐

   d. Understanding how butterfly wings reflect light is inspiring engineers to create new types of computer screens. ☐ ☐

B How are animals viewed in your culture? Write a thesis statement and topic sentences for three paragraphs.

Thesis statement: _____

_____

1. _____

2. _____

3. _____

C Now write a classification essay that includes your thesis statement in the introduction, three paragraphs corresponding to your topic sentences, and a conclusion.

GRAMMAR

Choose the words that best complete the sentences.

1. *Whatever / Whoever* has some free time this weekend should volunteer for the yearly beach cleanup.

2. Helen went to the woods to photograph *whatever / whoever* she could find for a project on medicinal plants.

3. The members of our surfing club are doing *whatever / whoever* they can to save enough for a trip to Hawaii.

4. I would never swim with sharks, but *whatever / whoever* does is very brave, in my opinion.

5. Can you tell me *whatever / whoever* you know about Professor Blake's research in the Arctic?

6. *Whatever / Whoever* has been dumping trash in the wildlife preserve should definitely be punished.

VOCABULARY

Complete the conversations with the correct idioms from the box.

a breath of fresh air	a walk in the park	the tip of the iceberg	set in stone
a drop in the ocean	as clear as mud	under the weather	up in the air

1. A: Do you understand these instructions?

   B: Not at all. They're _____ to me.

2. A: Are you feeling all right?

   B: Not really. I'm afraid I'm a little bit _____.

3. A: The new park director is full of great ideas!

   B: I know. She's _____ after working with the same people for so long.

4. A: I hear that the city spent way too much on the new waterfront park.

   B: Yes, but that's just _____. They overspent on many other projects, too.

5. A: Is it going to be difficult to raise money for the Save the Pandas campaign?

   B: I don't think so. They're such popular animals, it should be _____.

6. A: How closely do we have to follow the guidelines?

   B: They're not _____ yet, but let's keep them in mind while they're being finalized.

7. A: Have they decided who is going to speak at the biology convention in June?

   B: Not yet. It's still _____.

8. A: It's great that you're helping to save endangered owls.

   B: Unfortunately, it's just _____. There are many other animals that need help.

3 GRAMMAR

Do you agree or disagree with these statements? Respond to what the first speaker says.
Write sentences with *whoever* or *whatever*.

1. A: It's acceptable to build resorts in protected natural areas.

   B: *I disagree. We should do whatever we can to protect natural areas.*

2. A: People who drop litter in parks should pay very large fines.

   B: _____

   _____

3. A: Everything governments usually do to protect endangered species is enough.

   B: _____

   _____

4. A: We should do everything we can to keep wild animals in their natural habitats.

   B: _____

   _____

5. A: People should never hike alone in unfamiliar forests.

   B: _____

   _____

4 GRAMMAR

Complete these sentences with ideas of your own. Use *whoever* or *whatever.*

1. *Whoever wants to have a real wilderness experience* should think about *trekking in the Australian outback.*

2. Whatever you need for your trip _____

   _____

3. _____

   must watch this nature documentary about _____

4. I do whatever I can _____

   _____

5. _____

   _____ will be amazed by the beautiful views.

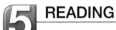

READING

A Read the title and first paragraph of this story, and answer the questions. Then read the rest of the story.

1. How well known is the fairy tale mentioned in the first paragraph? _____

2. What sentences indicate that the story will be true? _____

_____

A Fairy Tale Comes True

Every Bosnian child knows the story of a poor woman who caught a golden fish, released it, and in return gained wealth and happiness. It's a Balkan fairy tale, but it turned into reality for one poor family. "Whatever happened here is beyond good luck — it really is a fable," said Admir Malkoc.

In 1990, Smajo Malkoc returned from working in Austria to Jezero, a village surrounding a lake, in the former Yugoslavia. He had an unusual gift for his teenaged sons Dzevad and Catib: an aquarium with two goldfish.

Two years passed. War broke out, and Smajo Malkoc was killed.

When his wife, Fehima, sneaked back into the destroyed village to bury her husband, she spotted the fish in the aquarium. She let them out into the nearby lake. "This way they might be more fortunate than us," she recalls thinking.

Fast-forward to 1995. Fehima returned with her sons to Jezero to find ruins. Eyes misting over, she turned toward the lake and glimpsed something strange. She came closer — and caught her breath.

"The whole lake was shining from the golden fish in it," she said. During the years of war and killing all around the lake, life underwater had flourished.

After their return, Fehima and her sons started feeding the fish and then selling them. Now, homes, bars, and coffee shops in the region have aquariums containing fish from Jezero.

The Malkoc house, rebuilt from ruins, is one of the biggest in the village. The family says it has enough money not to have to worry about the future.

Other residents are welcome to catch and sell the fish. But most leave that to the Malkocs. "They threw the fish into the lake," said a villager. "It's their miracle."

B Put the events in order. Write an *X* for events not mentioned or indicated in the story.

_____ a. Mrs. Malkoc put the fish in a lake.

_____ b. The war broke out and Mr. Malkoc was killed.

_____ c. The Malkoc family started taking care of the fish in the lake.

_____ d. The Malkocs opened an aquarium in the village.

_____ e. Mrs. Malkoc and her children returned to their home.

_*1*_ f. Mr. Malkoc worked in another country.

_____ g. People from the region started buying fish from the Malkocs.

_____ h. The Malkocs provided money for other villagers to rebuild their homes.

_____ i. Mr. Malkoc presented two goldfish to his children when he came home.

10 LANGUAGE
LESSON A ▶ *Communication skills*

1 GRAMMAR

Choose the words or phrases that best complete the sentences.

1. Kyle (was giving) / *was being given* a presentation in front of the whole company for the first time in his life.

2. When he *introduced* / *was introduced* by the vice president of the company, she got his name wrong.

3. When Kyle turned on the projector, everyone saw a family photo instead of the presentation that *should have displayed* / *should have been displayed* on the screen.

4. He was so flustered that he *dropped* / *was dropped* his tablet on the floor.

5. When he picked up the tablet, it *wasn't working* / *wasn't being worked*.

6. Kyle knew a copy of the presentation *might have saved* / *might have been saved* on his manager's tablet, so he borrowed it.

7. In spite of the initial problems, the presentation went well, and Kyle's manager *has praised* / *has been praised* him for a job well done.

2 GRAMMAR

Rewrite each sentence using the passive voice. Do not include the agent.

1. After the soccer team won the championship, the coach thanked the players.
   The players were thanked after the soccer team won the championship.

2. People have told me that I have good presentation skills.

   _____

3. Schools should teach foreign languages beginning in elementary school.

   _____

4. My college is awarding a new prize to the best debate team.

   _____

5. Someone is going to interview the best-selling author on TV tonight.

   _____

3 VOCABULARY

Rewrite the sentences by replacing the underlined words with a word or phrase from the box. If there are two possible answers, write both of them.

first of all	in addition	likewise	next	to begin	yet
furthermore	in conclusion	nevertheless	similarly	to sum up	

1. <u>To start with</u>, welcome to our seminar, "Giving Your Best Presentation."

   To begin / First of all, welcome to our seminar, "Giving Your Best Presentation."

2. When faced with giving a presentation, many people don't know where to start. <u>Also</u>, many of us get very nervous just thinking about presenting our ideas in public.

   _____

3. So, here are a few tips. <u>Before anything else</u>, outline your ideas carefully.

   _____

4. Make sure you have all the visuals you need for your presentation. <u>However</u>, don't depend too much on pictures and charts – what you say is just as important.

   _____

5. Don't rush the preparation of your materials. <u>In the same manner</u>, give yourself plenty of time to become familiar with the information you want to communicate.

   _____

6. <u>Then</u> practice the presentation a couple of times to build your confidence.

   _____

7. <u>To conclude</u>, preparation, practice, and confidence are the keys to a successful presentation.

   _____

4 GRAMMAR

Complete the sentences with your own ideas. Use the passive.

1. *My best friend's team was awarded* first prize in the university debate competition.

2. _____

   _____ when he / she turned the radio up too loud in the car.

3. _____

   _____ he / she talks too much while watching movies.

4. _____

   _____ a speech at our school's graduation ceremony.

5. _____

   _____ for being one of the most generous people in our country.

WRITING

A Read the two positions about whether or not schools should focus on teaching students how to do research online. Then find the supporting reasons for each position, and write them on the lines below.

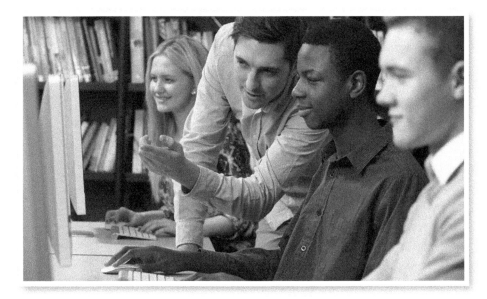

Positions

1. Since knowing how to do research online is essential for twenty-first century learners, it should be focused on in schools.

   _____

   _____

   _____

2. While knowing how to do research online is important for twenty-first century learners, it should not be a focus in schools.

   _____

   _____

   _____

Reasons

- Most students in the twenty-first century already have the necessary skills to do research online or can learn these skills on their own.
- The Internet is changing rapidly, and the skills students learn today may no longer be relevant in the near future.
- Most students would benefit from training on how and where to find reliable information online.
- Learning how to successfully do research online is as important to future studies and careers as learning subjects such as math and history is.
- Class time should be used for teaching more complex content and skills.
- Many students need guidance to learn how to distinguish trustworthy sources from unreliable ones.

B Which position is closer to your own? Write a persuasive composition to explain your point of view. Be sure to argue against the opposing view.

GRAMMAR

Choose the correct form of the verbs. Sometimes more than one answer is possible.

At first, most social media sites **(1)** *was /* (were) seen as a fun way to keep in touch with friends, share photos, and play games. But anyone who **(2)** *uses / use* one of these websites today can see that many more important things **(3)** *is / are* going on, and no one using these sites regularly **(4)** *is / are* able to ignore the fact that their uses are changing. A lot of people **(5)** *shares / share* political news and information, and new ideas can start and grow on these sites. Also, if someone **(6)** *needs / need* help after an accident or disaster, social media can be used to spread the word. In some instances, a majority of the money raised for emergency situations **(7)** *comes / come* through social media, and many volunteers can be brought together in a matter of hours. Of course, none of us **(8)** *puts / put* our social media account to such serious uses all of the time, but it is great to know that the possibility is there if we need it.

GRAMMAR

Read these results from a student survey. Then use the words in the box to make statements. If the verb can take both singular and plural forms, write them both.

Why do you study a **foreign language**?	Percentage of students
1. I need to know the language to get a better job. ———————→	**85%**
2. I want to be able to speak the language when I travel. ———————→	**100%**
3. I have to study the language because it's a required subject. ———————→	**30%**
4. I need to be able to read literature in the language. ———————→	**0%**
5. I study the language because I enjoy it. ———————→	**50%**

all	half	majority	minority	none

1. need to know the language to get a better job
    A majority of the students needs/need to know the language to get a better job.

2. want to be able to speak the language when they travel
    _____

3. have to study the language because it's a required subject
    _____

4. need to be able to read literature in the language
    _____

5. study the language because they enjoy it
    _____

3 VOCABULARY

Complete the conversations by using the correct form of the expressions in the box.
Make any necessary changes to the expressions.

have a sharp tongue
have a way with words
love to hear oneself talk
stick to the point
talk behind someone's back
talk someone into something
talk someone's ear off

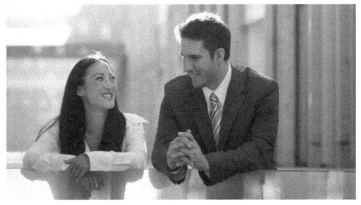

1. A: I really liked what Justin said about working together as a team.

   B: I agree. It was very inspiring. He really ___*has a way with words*___.

2. A: Did Peter say anything about me after I left?

   B: No. He'd never _____. He'd tell you directly.

3. A: Did you tell Lisa about our plans for her birthday?

   B: I tried to, but she just kept _____ about her problems
   with her car.

4. A: Ms. Jones read my report and said awful things about it.

   B: Well, she _____, but she's also very perceptive.
   Just try to focus on what she's saying about your work.

5. A: I know you want to continue discussing the report, but I'd like to talk about
   my new customer.

   B: Let's _____. We can talk about that later.

6. A: That meeting was so long! I thought Bob would never stop talking!

   B: He sure _____, doesn't he?

7. A: Are you going to the company picnic this weekend?

   B: Well, I wasn't planning to, but Kelly convinced me to go. She knows how to
   _____ I don't want to do!

4 GRAMMAR

Complete these sentences with your own ideas. Use verbs in the present.

1. Each language in the world ___*is unique.*___

2. All bilingual people _____

3. Every one of my classmates _____

4. The majority of celebrities _____

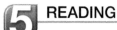

5 READING

A Read the article. Find the words in boldface that match these definitions.

1. form an idea of ___conceptualize___   4. only _____

2. researches _____   5. indicate _____

3. incredible _____   6. native _____

Does the language you speak change the way you think?

Do people who speak different languages actually think differently, or are the 7,000 languages in the world just different means for expressing a universal human way of thinking? To answer that question, linguist Lera Boroditsky **surveys** differences between languages across a number of fundamental categories, including how speakers of different languages **conceptualize** space and time, and how they think about gender.

Regarding spatial orientation, she says, "There are some languages that don't use words like 'left' and 'right.' Instead, everything in the language is laid out in absolute space. That means you have to say things like, 'There is an ant on your northwest leg.'"

The language of the Kuuk Thaayore, an **aboriginal** group in Australia, works like that. Boroditsky's research has shown that the unique way they think about space also affects the way they think about time. Whereas English speakers tend to conceptualize time as running from left to right, the Kuuk Thaayore visualize it from east to west.

Then there is gender. Some languages, like Hebrew, **mark** gender for both people and objects, while Finnish has almost no gender information at all. "English," says Boroditsky, "is somewhere in the middle."

Boroditsky explains the degree to which a language emphasizes gender in its grammatical structure actually affects the way speakers think. She cites a study by Alexander Guiora, who looked at kids learning Hebrew, Finnish, and English as their first language. He asked them, "Are you a boy or a girl?" and had all kinds of clever ways of figuring out how aware they were of their gender. What he found was that kids in these three groups figure it out at different rates. The Hebrew-speaking kids got it first, then the English-speaking kids, and the Finnish-speaking kids last.

These are just a few examples of the **mind-bending** differences Boroditsky has found. She also talks about how the language you speak affects the way you look at colors and changes the way you think about the relationship between cause and effect.

As to the main question – does language affect the way people think – Boroditsky's answer is a clear "yes." At the same time, she allows that language is not the **sole** determinant of thought. "Language shapes thought, and also the way that we think importantly shapes the way we talk," she says, "and aspects of culture importantly shape aspects of language. It's a bi-directional cycle."

B Are the statements true (*T*), false (*F*), or is the information not given (*NG*) in the article? Write the correct letters.

_____ 1. Boroditsky believes that language does affect thinking.

_____ 2. All languages indicate gender in the same way.

_____ 3. Most of the aboriginal languages in Australia conceptualize space and time in similar ways.

_____ 4. Boroditsky believes that language is not the only thing that influences thought.

11 EXCEPTIONAL PEOPLE

LESSON A ▶ *High achievers*

1 VOCABULARY

Choose the words that best complete the sentences.

1. The *coolheaded* / *soft-hearted* athlete was able to score despite the noisy crowd.

2. I'm so *absent-minded* / *hardheaded* that, after staying up late to finish my paper on time, I forgot to bring it to class!

3. Sam is the kindest and most *cold-blooded* / *warm-hearted* guy I know.

4. Although Emily appears to be silly and *narrow-minded* / *empty-headed,* she's actually quite intelligent.

5. Ethan is *hardheaded* / *hot-blooded.* Once he makes up his mind, he doesn't change.

6. I hope Zach is *cold-hearted* / *open-minded* about our idea. He isn't always willing to consider new approaches to solving problems.

7. My cousins are so *narrow-minded* / *soft-hearted* when it comes to music. They won't listen to anything except jazz.

8. The *cold-hearted* / *absent-minded* killer was sentenced to life in prison.

2 GRAMMAR

Rewrite these sentences using compound adjectives to replace the words in boldface. Sometimes more than one answer is possible.

1. The famous conductor is **recognized by many people**.
   The famous conductor is widely recognized.

2. In my opinion, the politician's speech was **too long**.
   _____

3. Nicole is a model **with curly hair and brown eyes**.
   _____

4. Alyssa is a **very relaxed** boss. She lets employees choose their hours.
   _____

5. Maxwell's is not a restaurant **that many people know about**.
   _____

6. Dr. Kendall's lectures really **make us think about things**.
   _____

7. Katy made a good impression at the interview because she was **dressed so well**.
   _____

3 GRAMMAR

What qualities should these people have? Write a sentence using two compound adjectives.

elementary school teacher

1. An elementary school teacher should be kind-hearted and well educated.

mountain climber

2. _____
_____
_____

surgeon

3. _____
_____
_____

judge

4. _____
_____
_____

salesperson

5. _____
_____
_____

soccer player

6. _____
_____
_____

4 WRITING

A Read this biographical profile of composer and conductor Leonard Bernstein. Answer the questions below.

LEONARD BERNSTEIN

LEONARD BERNSTEIN was perhaps the single greatest figure in American classical music in the twentieth century. Born in 1918 in Lawrence, Massachusetts, he studied piano as a child in Boston. ❶ Upon his graduation from Harvard University in 1939, he moved to Philadelphia to study at the Curtis Institute. ❷ By the time Bernstein finished his training, he was widely respected as a major talent in the music world. ❸

In 1943, Bernstein became the assistant conductor of the New York Philharmonic. One night, he was asked to substitute for a conductor who was sick. This was a particularly difficult concert, but Bernstein performed brilliantly and was a great success. ❹ Over the next 15 years, he held conducting positions in several of the great orchestras of the world, and he performed as a guest conductor with many others. His work included both live concerts and recordings. ❺

In 1958, Bernstein became the music director of the New York Philharmonic. That same year, he started a series of televised programs called *Young People's Concerts*, designed to teach children an appreciation for great music. At the Philharmonic, Bernstein was a very popular conductor. He brought new music to the orchestra and revitalized older music that hadn't been played for some time.

❻ Bernstein died in New York City in 1990. He conducted and composed music up until the time of his death. Through his lifetime of conducting, composing, teaching, and helping people understand music, he left a great gift to the world.

1. In what year did Leonard Bernstein leave Harvard University? _____

2. How long did Bernstein conduct orchestras all over the world before he became the music director of the New York Philharmonic? _____

3. In what year did Bernstein start *Young People's Concerts*? _____

B There are six numbered circles in the biographical profile. Find where each of the following sentences should go, and write the number of the circle next to the sentence.

_____ a. In 1969, Bernstein left the New York Philharmonic and spent the remaining years of his life composing a wide variety of music, conducting all over the world, and teaching young musicians.

_____ b. At 17, he entered Harvard University, where he studied composition.

_____ c. During his years there, he spent his summers at the Boston Symphony Orchestra's institute at Tanglewood, where he studied with the conductor Serge Koussevitzky.

C Choose someone you admire who has made a difference in people's lives. Research the key facts of the person's life, and write a biographical profile with an introduction and at least two other paragraphs.

GRAMMAR

Read the text and underline the superlative compound adjectives.

Without a doubt, <u>my most fondly remembered</u> teacher is Mr. Hill, my college French professor. He was the most kind-hearted man, and he always showed concern for his students. He went out of his way to make us feel comfortable in class, so we never felt too nervous or anxious to participate. He was the hardest-working teacher I've ever had, and he would always come up with creative ways to help us understand the most difficult lessons. Mr. Hill truly loved French culture, so the cultural lessons were the most thought-provoking of all my classes. He made me feel that I was looking through a window into another world, and he made me want to be a part of that world. I'm afraid I don't remember much French now – it's not the most easily retained language, especially if you don't use it often – but I did learn how great a teacher can be and how rewarding it can be to learn about another culture.

GRAMMAR

Read these conversations and fill in the blank with the superlative form of the adjectives in parentheses.

1. Kay: What did you think about the president's speech?

   Mindy: I thought it was **the most thought-provoking** (thought-provoking) speech she's ever given.

2. Sung: Don't you think Tom is a good cook?

   Nate: Definitely. His paella was _____ (great-tasting) dish I've had in a long time!

3. Oscar: What did you think of the lead actor's performance in the movie we saw last night?

   Valerie: I thought he was terrific. He gave one of _____ (heartbreakingly convincing) performances in the movie.

4. Rich: Have you seen the video of the singing dog?

   Linda: No, I haven't. But I've heard that it's _____ (widely downloaded) clip of the week.

5. Tai: Cory is always so kind to people!

   Sarah: I agree. He's probably _____ (warm-hearted) person I've ever met.

6. Brad: How was your trip to Morocco? Were you able to visit the desert?

   Nora: Oh, I was. It was one of _____ (breathtakingly beautiful) things I saw on my entire trip!

3 VOCABULARY

Correct the underlined mistake in each sentence with one of the words in the box.
Some words will be used more than once.

after	on	to	through	with

1. I always look <u>through</u> my older sister for fashion advice. _____ *to* _____

2. I know coping with a broken arm is difficult, but just be patient and you'll get <u>after</u> it. _____

3. I'm not sure who to side <u>to</u> in this argument! You both have valid points. _____

4. Many middle-aged people not only look <u>with</u> their children, but they take care of their elderly parents at the same time. _____

5. Who do you take <u>through</u> more, your mother or your father? _____

6. I have very high expectations for myself, and I get frustrated when I don't live up <u>on</u> them. _____

7. Excuse me while I check <u>after</u> the baby. I think I just heard her cry. _____

8. If you don't face up <u>with</u> your problems soon, they'll only get worse. _____

4 GRAMMAR

Use the cues to write sentences that are true for you.
Use superlative compound adjectives in your sentences.

1. incredibly talented actress I can think of

   The most incredibly talented actress I can think
   of is Scarlett Johansson.

2. action-packed movie I've ever seen

   _____

   _____

3. time-saving invention I use

   _____

   _____

4. easily learned subject I've studied

   _____

   _____

5. well-intentioned person I've met

   _____

   _____

6. physically demanding sport I know

   _____

   _____

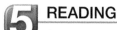

A Read this article about the Awesome Foundation. Choose the adjectives that best describe the organization.

☐ 1. old-fashioned   ☐ 3. highly structured   ☐ 5. nontraditional

☐ 2. loosely organized   ☐ 4. crowdsourced   ☐ 6. widespread

TINY GRANTS KEEP "awesome" IDEAS COMING

It was down to two finalists: a woman who wanted to buy a couple of goats to rent out as urban lawnmowers, and a sculptor who wanted to buy a portable welder so he could go around and fix his city. They were both awesome ideas, the trustees agreed, but only one of them could win money that month. And so they had to ask the ultimate question: Which idea was more awesome?

This is the basic premise behind the Awesome Foundation, which is not an actual foundation. It is more like a support group for good ideas. It began in Cambridge, Massachusetts, in 2009, when a group of tech-savvy twenty-somethings, frustrated by the bureaucracy of traditional funding, got together and, in essence, said, "You know what would be awesome? If there were an organization that gave you money if you had an awesome idea." Then they became that organization, loosely.

It works like this: Ten trustees each kick in $100 a month, and together they review the submissions. The winner is given $1,000 for the project, with no strings attached.

The idea is so simple that it has multiplied organically and become a new nonprofit model for the crowdsourcing generation. Today there are more than 20 chapters around the world. Anyone can start one, and the only real rule is that there is no definition for "awesome." That's for each trustee to decide.

The concept of a small grant, handed out by individuals, means the idea has a built-in lightness, according to Tim Hwang, who conceived of the Awesome Foundation shortly after he graduated from college. But there is a recurring bent toward socially conscious public projects. Christina Xu, one of the original trustees who had become frustrated with the failings of traditional nonprofits, says that she "realized maybe the Awesome Foundation was an answer" to that problem.

That may be a reach, but it's indicative of what attracts people to the Awesome Foundation – the belief that ordinary people can create positive change outside of the establishment.

In the end, the trustees unanimously chose the sculptor. They had questions about the goats, but there was no question that the sculptor's idea was awesome.

B Choose the statements that can be confirmed in the article.

☐ 1. Trustees generally fund Awesome awards with their own money.

☐ 2. Traditional nonprofit organizations admire the foundation's work.

☐ 3. There are no rules on who can set up a branch of the Awesome Foundation in a new city.

☐ 4. The foundation has funded thousands of projects around the world.

☐ 5. The foundation consciously avoids strictly defining what should be considered "awesome."

BUSINESS MATTERS

LESSON A ▶ *Entrepreneurs*

VOCABULARY

Choose the words that best complete the sentences.

1. I would rather work *around* / *for* a boss who is organized and strict than a boss who is disorganized and nice.

2. Janelle worked *off* / *on* some of her debt to her cousin by designing and managing the website for his business.

3. Showing up late for appointments can work *against* / *toward* you if you are trying to start a new business.

4. If we don't find a way to work *toward* / *around* this problem, we'll never make our deadline.

5. The more people we have working *for* / *on* the report, the faster we'll get it done.

6. Jesse is working *off* / *toward* a degree in marketing and finance.

GRAMMAR

Read each sentence and then answer the questions with *yes* or *no*.

Had Natalie not lost her job at a bakery, she would never have considered starting her own business.

1. Did Natalie lose her job at the bakery? _____*Yes*_____

2. Did she consider starting her own business? _____

Should Natalie's business continue to grow, she might hire another baker.

3. Is Natalie's business growing? _____

4. Has she hired another baker yet? _____

Had Natalie raised a large family, she might not have been able to spend a lot of time developing her business.

5. Was she able to spend a lot of time developing the business? _____

6. Did she raise a large family? _____

Natalie's Cookies might not have become the best-selling cookies in the city had she not worked so hard.

7. Did Natalie's Cookies become the best-selling cookies in the city? _____

8. Did Natalie work hard? _____

Complete the sentence for each situation using a conditional clause with *Had . . . not . . . .*

1. ___*Had*___ the woman ___*not answered the ad*___, she'd never have become a veterinary assistant.

2. _____ the couple _____, they wouldn't have had so many kittens at home.

3. _____ the man _____, he wouldn't have won first prize.

4. _____ the woman _____, she wouldn't have started her own business.

5. _____ the man _____, he would never have been served.

6. _____ the woman _____, she wouldn't have bought her new laptop.

WRITING

A Read this formal letter. Three sentences do not belong because they are too personal or irrelevant. One has already been crossed out. Cross out the other two.

JD 85 SUN ROAD
PHOENIX, AZ 85051

June 7, 2014

Ms. Rosa Marquez
4226 E. 22nd St.
Phoenix, AZ 85016

Dear Ms. Marquez:

I am writing in response to the advertisement for a social media marketer in last week's edition of *Career Focus E-News Digest*. I am very interested in the position and am enclosing my résumé for your consideration. ~~It is very kind of you to read this letter.~~

I believe you will find that I meet all of the qualifications that you specify. In fact, you have probably never had a candidate as qualified as I am! I have had two years of experience as a social media marketing intern at a major nonprofit. Although this was an unpaid position, it gave me valuable experience in managing social media accounts, creating content, and working with analytics.

Additionally, I enjoy working as part of a team and am very good with people. None of my current colleagues wants me to leave.

I would appreciate the opportunity to discuss this position with you in person. I look forward to hearing from you at your convenience.

Sincerely,

James Ditzler

James Ditzler

B Imagine a job that you would be interested in having. Make notes on the following.

Why you want the position:

_____

_____

Your experience:

_____

_____

Why you should be considered:

_____

_____

C Use your notes to write a formal letter applying for the job you are interested in.

GRAMMAR

Choose the expressions that best complete the sentences.

1. (*Assuming that*)/ *Provided that* I were required to travel for a job, I would turn it down because I don't like to fly.

2. *On the condition that* / *Whether or not* we continued to get more business, we would have to move to bigger offices anyway.

3. *Whether or not* / *Provided that* an applicant had the right job skills, I'd definitely hire him or her.

4. *Supposing that* / *Provided that* your boss wanted to transfer you to another department, how would you feel about it?

5. *Assuming that* / *Whether or not* you have a good reason to change jobs, I'd strongly recommend staying at your present company.

 GRAMMAR

Respond to what the first speaker says in the conversations. Write sentences using the adverb clauses of condition provided.

1. A: If I were offered an interesting job that paid well, I would accept it. (provided that)

   B: *I would probably accept it, too, provided that the benefits were also good.*

2. A: If I had to commute to work on a daily basis, I would definitely do it. It can't be that much of an inconvenience. (on the condition that)

   B: _____

   _____

3. A: If I didn't receive a raise within the first year I worked at a job, I'd leave it and find a new job. (assuming that)

   B: _____

   _____

4. A: Under no circumstances would I ever accept a demotion. No one should move down in a company. (supposing that)

   B: _____

   _____

5. A: If my boss said something in a meeting that I strongly disagreed with, I would definitely speak up. (whether or not)

   B: _____

   _____

6. A: I think that it's OK to lend a family member a large amount of money in order to help them start a business. (provided that)

   B: _____

   _____

3 GRAMMAR

Under what conditions would you do or not do these things? Write sentences using the expressions in the box.

assuming (that)	on the condition (that)	provided (that)	supposing (that)	whether or not

1. take a pay cut

   I'd take a pay cut on the condition I were given more interesting projects at work.

2. work every weekend

   _____

   _____

3. agree to be transferred to a different country

   _____

   _____

4. work two jobs at the same time

   _____

   _____

5. quit your job and go back to school

   _____

   _____

4 VOCABULARY

Choose the quality that you consider to be the most important for each job.
Then write a sentence explaining why.

1. doctor (leadership ability / training)

   Training is most important for doctors because people's lives are in their hands.

2. artist (self-discipline / initiative)

   _____

3. politician (charisma / influence)

   _____

4. teacher (communication skills / leadership ability)

   _____

5. writer (initiative / training)

   _____

6. business executive (influence / leadership ability)

   _____

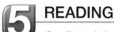

5 **READING**

A Read the article quickly and answer the questions.

1. What percentage of employees report being truly engaged in their work? _____

2. How many companies does the author say completely meet his criteria? _____

The Twelve Attributes of a
TRULY GREAT PLACE TO WORK

More than 100 studies have found that the most engaged employees – those who report they're fully invested in their jobs and committed to their employers – are significantly more productive, drive higher customer satisfaction, and outperform those who are less engaged. But only 20 percent of employees around the world report that they're fully engaged at work. So, what's the solution? The answer is that great employers must shift the focus from trying to get more out of people to investing more in them by addressing their four core needs – physical, emotional, mental, and spiritual – so they're freed, fueled, and inspired to bring the best of themselves to work every day.

Think for a moment about what would make you feel most excited to get to work in the morning and most loyal to your employer. The sort of company I have in mind would:

1 Commit to paying every employee a living wage. No employee working full time should receive a sum that falls below the poverty line.

2 Give all employees a stake in the company's success. If the company does well, all employees should share in the success in meaningful ways.

3 Design working environments that are safe, comfortable, and appealing to work in. In offices, include a range of physical spaces that allow for privacy, collaboration, and simply hanging out.

4 Provide healthy, high-quality food at the lowest possible prices.

5 Create places for employees to rest and renew during the course of the working day and encourage them to take intermittent breaks.

6 Offer a well-equipped gym and other facilities that encourage employees to move and stay fit.

7 Define clear and specific expectations for what success looks like in any given job. Then treat employees as adults by giving them as much autonomy as possible.

8 Institute two-way performance reviews so that employees not only receive regular feedback about how they're doing but also have the chance to provide feedback to their supervisors.

9 Hold leaders and managers accountable for treating all employees with respect and care.

10 Create policies that encourage employees to set aside time to focus without interruption on their most important priorities.

11 Provide employees with ongoing opportunities and incentives to learn, develop, and grow.

12 Stand for something. Create products, provide services, or serve causes that add value in the world, making it possible for employees to feel good about the companies for which they work.

I've yet to come across a company that meets the full range of their people's needs in all the ways I've described. How about you?

B Answer the following questions with information from the article.

1. What are some of the benefits of having engaged employees?

_____

2. According to the author, what are the four core needs of employees?

_____

3. How does the author think office environments can be made more appealing?

_____

4. According to the article, how does a two-way performance review work?

_____